Waves of Resistance

Waves of Resistance

Surfing and History in Twentieth-Century Hawai'i

Isaiah Helekunihi Walker

University of Hawai'i Press

Honolulu

Library of Congress Cataloging-in-Publication Data
Walker, Isaiah Helekunihi.
Waves of resistance : surfing and history in twentieth-century Hawai'i /
Isaiah Helekunihi Walker.
p. cm.
Includes bibliographical references and index.
ISBN 978-0-8248-3462-3 (hard cover : alk. paper)—
ISBN 978-0-8248-3547-7 (pbk. : alk. paper)
1. Surfing—Hawaii—Oahu. 2. Surfers—Hawaii—Oahu. 3. Hawaiians—
Politics and government. 4. Hawaiians—Ethnic identity. I. Title.
GV839.65.H3W35 2011
797.3'2099693—dc22
2010035181

University of Hawai'i Press books are printed on acid-free
paper and meet the guidelines for permanence and durability
of the Council on Library Resources.

Designed by Janette Thompson (Jansom)

Printed by Sheridan Books, Inc.

For my dad, Murray, who taught me
to care about people and their stories

Kū mai e nā kama o Hawaiʻi nei
Paʻa pono i ka papa e
Hoʻolono i ka poʻi ʻana o ke kai
Pā mai ke ahe Kamoaʻe
Hui pū i ka malu o ke Koʻolau
E hoʻomau (i) ka hana (a) ke kupuna
Aloha e, aloha mai e, aloha mau loa

Arise children/people of Hawaiʻi
Hold fast to your board/your foundation [where you are from, your
    ʻohana, your beliefs, the things that make you who you are]
Listen to the waves forming in the ocean
And the gentle blowing of the tradewinds
We gather in the shelter/protection of the Koʻolau mountains
To continue the work/the traditions of our kupuna or ancestors
Our love is shared and is without end.

"Ka Oli Hālau Nalu," composed by Ahulani Wright, 2007

Contents

Acknowledgments

Many people helped make this book possible. First, I would like to acknowledge my wife Rebekah, who has not only been a supportive and understanding spouse while I wrote this book, but also an inspiring colleague who provided honest and succinct feedback on my writing and analysis. Our four children have been a source of motivation and example to me. I have also enjoyed their company in the surf, a place of inspiration for me. As with every author, many of my central arguments are also reflections of my own ideals, values, and perspectives. Much of my worldview has been shaped by my parents, Murray Walker, Carol Helekunihi, and Judy Walker, who, in their own ways, have taught me to value individual voices and alternate perspectives. However, I am also a product of my kūpuna (ancestors), whose stories of faith, perseverance, and aloha have contributed to this work. I am especially grateful to my Hawaiian grandparents, Mal Helekunihi Duke and Abigail Kaheokalani Cutter, and great-grandparents, Elia Helekunihi, Minerva Fernandez, and Abraham Kaleimahoe Fernandez, who survived the dramatic changes in the late nineteenth and early twentieth centuries and passed down to me a deep love for the moana (ocean) and the poʻina nalu (surf zone).

Mahalo to all the individuals who shared their manaʻo with me in our oral history interviews. It was an honor to meet and talk story with so many legendary surfers, founders, and members of the Hui O Heʻe Nalu and others. Among them, I want to thank Moot Ah Quin, Terry Ahue, Bryan Amona, Chuck Andrus, Billy Blankenfeld, Kealoha Kaio Jr., and Tom Pohaku Stone in particular for their extra time and support. While all the interviews were memorable, two other individuals, who have since passed away, have made a significant impression on my work. Imbert Soren was the first person I interviewed for this project. Imbert gave me rich stories, a new perspective, and lots of aloha. After he passed away, I was motivated to talk to other Hawaiian surfers of his generation and convey their version of this story. While Imbert gave aloha, Kealoha Kaio Sr. embodied the very meaning of the word. Our interview together was more of an experience for me than a conversation. His kind and gentle tone and spirit contrasted with the intensity of his experiences in the surf—where he rode enormous waves on outer North Shore reefs in the early 1960s, did big turns in sizable Waimea surf, and explained how he wished the Jet Ski had been invented earlier so he could have been towed into even bigger waves. Although the surfing world knows little of this Hawaiian surfing legend, Kaio has made an indelible mark on it.

I would also like to thank various colleagues for providing feedback and support to this work. My mentor and PhD advisor Paul Spickard not only helped shape my research, but also my confidence. His unwavering support has made its mark on a surfer boy from Keaukaha. I want to express my appreciation to the anonymous reviewers of this book; their specific suggestions helped make it better organized and theorized. Mahalo to former professors like David Stannard and James Brooks, who helped me in the early stages of this project.

Large portions of the research conducted for this book were accomplished through the assistance of key people and resources. Thanks to the Kelly family, who donated copies of many flyers, photographs, and articles to the University of Hawai'i's Hamilton Library; a digital collection of Save Our Surf is available on line. The materials from this Web site served as the primary source for my section on this anti-development environmental surfing group formed in the 1960s. In the mid-1980s a small team of historians interviewed many old-timers of Waikīkī. The result was volumes of valuable oral history records that became foundational to my section on the Hui Nalu and the Waikīkī Beachboys. The Historical Committee of the Outrigger Canoe Club did a similar, though less extensive, project in 1986. I appreciate their giving me access to these transcribed interviews and other materials from their private archive. I also want to thank Ulukau.org for digitizing volumes of Hawaiian-language newspapers and making them easily accessible on line. Mahalo to student researchers like U'i Wallace, Kaumana Barton, Kalei Johnson, and Beth Kimokeo, who either helped search and translate Hawaiian newspaper articles or proofread my Hawaiian grammar and spelling. The Joseph F. Smith Library at Brigham Young University–Hawai'i houses a fantastic collection of Hawaiian, Pacific Islands, and surfing materials in their Pacific Islands room and university archives. How grateful I am that such collections exist on the North Shore of O'ahu. Over the last couple of years I have taught a course on the cultural history of surfing at BYU–Hawai'i. In this class students read and commented on an earlier draft of this book. Their undergraduate feedback offered a fresh, unique, and useful perspective. There are many other individuals whom I have not mentioned by name, but who have nonetheless helped me in various capacities to complete this project. I want to mahalo them for their support. Finally, I would like to thank Ke Akua for guiding and directing me in this endeavor. Mahalo nui loa, aloha kākou.

Introduction

Ku mai! Ku mai! Ka nalu nui mai Kahiki mai,
Alo poʻi pu!
Ku mai ka pōhuehue
Hu! Kai koʻo loa.

Arise! Arise, you great surfs from Kahiki
The powerful curling waves!
Arise with the pōhuehue
Well up! Long raging surf.[1]

Shortly after the dramatic 1976 Hawaiian winter surfing season, thirty to thirty-five Native Hawaiian men and a handful of non-Hawaiian locals from the north and east sides of the island of Oʻahu gathered in a home under the green, jagged hills behind Sunset Beach to form an organization centered on a Hawaiian cause.[2] After naming themselves the Hui O Heʻe Nalu (or Club of Wave Sliders), they outlined their chief objectives. Their primary goal was to preserve Native Hawaiian control over the waves of the North Shore. At meetings held in succeeding months, they voiced their concerns about an endangered Hawaiian space, ka poʻina nalu (the surf zone), and developed tactics to offset what they saw as exploitation—in fact, virtual colonialism—by the surfing industry. As their agenda grew, club membership also expanded.

Months prior, International Professional Surfing (IPS) had made Hawai'i's North Shore an essential leg of a world surfing series in 1976 and asserted exclusive rights to North Shore waves. So the Hui began protesting IPS competitions through surfing sit-ins in which members would paddle into the competition zone, sit on their surfboards, and then ride the forbidden waves. In extreme cases, such resistance devolved into fistfights, where haole[3] (foreign to Hawai'i, or white) surfers were usually overpowered by large and strong Native Hawaiians. After a difficult initial phase, tensions began to settle, and the promoters and surfers made some concessions. Through such compromises, the Hui helped reduce the number of professional competitions on the North Shore and found employment for Hui members in the surfing industry. But they simultaneously shaped resistant identities and maintained a Native ranking atop a social hierarchy in the Hawai'i surf—a ranking that Hawaiian surfers had enjoyed from ancient times, and one contested over with elite haole shortly after the illegal overthrow of the Hawaiian kingdom.

Hawaiian cultural and political activism was rejuvenated in the 1970s. However, the Hui O He'e Nalu's resistance seems unique in comparison to other Hawaiian projects of cultural rediscovery and restoration. In an era when Hawaiians rekindled the idea of political restoration on land, the Hui's work to preserve Hawaiian control over a Native space (the surf zone) distinguishes them. However, preserving Native space in the surf was not a new concept, as Hawaiian surfers have successfully resisted colonial encroachment in the po'ina nalu (surf zone) since the early 1900s. To better understand this, we must look further into the surf.

Ka po'ina nalu, the surf zone, constitutes a Native Hawaiian realm, an overlooked space extremely significant to Kānaka Maoli (Native Hawaiians). While surfing was a thriving aspect of Hawaiian culture in ancient days, in the twentieth century it served as both a refuge and a contested borderland for many Native Hawaiians. In other words, it was a place where Hawaiians felt free, developed Native identities, and thwarted foreign domination. As Hawaiian surfers secured control over ka po'ina nalu, haole colonial authority was less influential there. On land, many Hawaiians were marginalized from political, social, and economic spheres during much of the twentieth century. Yet in the ocean Native surfers secured a position atop a social hierarchy. In this book I provide a history of this contested Hawaiian surf zone by analyzing particular Hawaiian surfers, including ancient Hawaiians, Waikīkī surfers of the early 1900s, a radical environmentalist group called Save Our

Surf, iconic professionals like Eddie Aikau, and finally the North Shore club Hui O Heʻe Nalu. These surfers are unique to Hawaiian history in that they provide examples of ardent and successful Hawaiian cultural-based resistance that thrived throughout the twentieth century.

While recording stories about surfers and waves of resistance, this book explores history from a different direction. By observing history from the vantage point of the ocean, issues of colonialism, politics, and resistance appear strikingly different. Doing so also engages with an underrepresented period of study in Hawaiian history, the twentieth century. While analyzing peculiar relationships in the Hawaiian waves, I suggest that several uncharted pockets of Native resistance existed in Hawaiʻi's past. Although specific to Hawaiʻi, the lessons of perspective, resistance, and issues of masculinity analyzed in this book also apply to locales distant from Hawaiian beaches. And, the cultural encounters discussed in this book implicate characters from Australia, the United States, and Brazil, to name a few.

Unlike histories that emphasize only Native displacement, this story stresses Hawaiian agency. It also determines that identities are complex, as Hawaiian surfers defined themselves in both opposition and relation to colonialism. This book not only highlights encounters between Hawaiians and haole, but also analyzes certain media portrayals. In an effort to market the islands to tourists, American media have often feminized, sexualized, and emasculated Hawaiian men. Whereas the history of Hawaiian masculinity has only more recently been studied, this book also addresses issues of Hawaiian manhood.[4] Through the surfers discussed in this book I argue that Hawaiians did not always subscribe to stereotypes about Hawaiian men, but instead contested, rewrote, or creatively negotiated within them. Because Hawaiian surfers preserved ka poʻina nalu from foreign domination in the twentieth century, they were empowered to defy haole definitions of how Hawaiian men should behave. As they transgressed these expectations and categories in the waves, Hawaiian surfers simultaneously defined themselves as active and resistant Natives in a history that regularly wrote about them as otherwise. Ka poʻina nalu is a place where resistance proved historically meaningful and Hawaiian men regularly flipped colonial hierarchies and categories upside down.

Heʻe Nalu: History and Identity

As Natives of Oceania, Hawaiians have viewed the moana (ocean) as essential to their existence. Since their first encounter with them, Westerners have acknowledged Hawaiians as masters over their aquatic domain and have revered them as ocean experts—in swimming, fishing, wave riding, canoe racing, sailing, and long-distance ocean navigation.[5] Throughout the nineteenth century many haole, Calvinist missionaries in particular, deemed many Hawaiian practices barbaric. Despite their efforts to vilify Hawaiian cultural practices, Native ocean traditions like heʻe nalu (surfing) still continued. Thus it remains a source of pride for Hawaiians today. As one surfer explained, "Surfing has been a part of our history for thousands of years, and when you surf you have that connection, you connect spiritually and physically to all the elements around you; this is a part of you, it's a Hawaiian thing."[6]

We all make sense of our present through our understanding of the past, and our articulations of the past are "the medium of our present relationships."[7] Thus Hawaiian surfers approached their present and future while looking back toward their past. According to both Lilikalā Kameʻeleihiwa and Jonathan Kamakawiwoʻole Osorio, Hawaiian tradition taught Hawaiians to look toward the future (ka wā mahope) while facing their past (ka wā mamua).[8] Although people often romanticize, idealize, and even invent tradition when remembering the past,[9] Kanaka Maoli surfers found strength in a living Hawaiian art and tradition that was celebrated by Hawaiians from ancient times, through the annexation of Hawaiʻi, and down to the present.

David Malo, a nineteenth-century Hawaiian historian, described heʻe nalu as a "national sport for the Hawaiians."[10] In chapter 1 I discuss the importance of surfing in ancient Hawaiian society by drawing from Hawaiian moʻolelo (histories, legends) about surfers—including accounts found in Hawaiian-language newspapers. Hawaiian moʻolelo about Native surfers express the significance of surfing in Hawaiian society. This is conveyed in moʻolelo about surfers like Kaʻiliokalauokekoa, Lāʻieikawai, Kelea, Moʻikeha, Kahikilani, ʻUmi, Paʻao, Naihe,[11] and many others. Through many surfing moʻolelo we learn that mutual respect in the waves is an important cultural concept for Hawaiians. Ancient surfers conveyed such respect by maintaining healthy relationships of social exchange, even in the surf. In ancient times tension often arose when surfers violated protocols of respect—as seen specifically with stories about Palani, Hiʻiaka, and Kapoʻulakinaʻu. Whereas wāhine (women) surfers are popular characters in ancient moʻolelo, we are reminded of the important role women played in Hawaiian history through these stories. Although women are often portrayed as empowered in several moʻolelo, such representation stands in stark contrast to twentieth-century

tourist-driven images that sexualize and objectify women. In these surfing
moʻolelo we also learn lessons of Hawaiian values regarding honesty, fidelity,
parenting, and so on. Ultimately, these stories reveal that heʻe nalu has been
an integral part of Hawaiian society.

He'e nalu is significant to Hawaiians today because it is a tradition that
continuously survived the destructive power of colonialism.[12] It has been,
and remains, a living Hawaiian sport significant to the ʻŌiwi (Natives). Using
this perspective in chapter 1, I write a narrative contrary to most surf history
accounts by challenging, rather than emphasizing, the idea that heʻe nalu dis-
integrated and became extinct in the nineteenth century. Although diseases
took the lives of hundreds of thousands of Native Hawaiians[13] and many
missionaries frowned on "idle and sensuous" practices such as the hula and
surfing,[14] Hawaiians continued surfing in the nineteenth century, and several
Hawaiians, even members of the royal family, still made time to surf in the
late nineteenth century. Among those who frequented the waves at that time
was Princess Victoria Kaʻiulani, Queen Liliʻuokalani's niece and the designated heir to the throne.[15] According to William A. Cottrell, a Hui Nalu
surfer of Waikīkī, the princess was an expert surfer in the late 1890s.[16] Her
cousin, Prince Jonah Kūhiō Kalanianaʻole, was also known for regularly riding the Waikīkī surf. He, along with his two brothers, was also the first to surf
waves in California in 1885.[17]

Although some Hawaiian aliʻi (chiefs, rulers) enjoyed serenity in the surf,
they struggled to maintain their political sovereignty in the late 1800s. Their
troubles with haole business elite culminated on January 17, 1893, when a company of U.S. Marines stormed the Hawaiian kingdom's ʻIolani Palace. Without
clearance from Washington, U.S. minister John L. Stevens used these troops to
help a cohort of haole businessmen overthrow Hawaiʻi's Native government.
With their Gatling guns and cannons pointed at the palace, Queen Liliʻuokalani
temporarily surrendered. Although U.S. president Grover Cleveland admonished the provisional government to return Hawaiʻi's administration to the
queen, the monarchy was never restored, and Hawaiʻi was declared a republic
on July 4, 1894.[18] In 1897 a coalition of three Hawaiian political organizations
(Hui Aloha ʻĀina for Women, Hui Aloha ʻĀina for Men, and Hui Kālaiʻāina)
initiated petitions to oppose (kūʻē) annexation. These petitions, once delivered
to Congress in 1898, helped kill the annexation bill.[19] However, Hawaiian
celebrations were cut short that year. With the election of a new president and
the outbreak of war against Spain and the Philippines, the United States seized
Hawaiʻi's government with an illegal joint resolution bill in 1898.[20] This story

of political conquest and turmoil is essential to understanding twentieth-century Hawaiian surfers and is the main topic of chapter 2. Hawaiian motives, identities, and frustrations, even in the surf, are directly related to the political violence inflicted at the time of overthrow and annexation.

While haole business elites settled into stolen seats of government, disillusioned Hawaiians flocked to the Waikīkī surf. In the decades just following the overthrow of the Hawaiian kingdom, the popularity of surfing surged in Honolulu. For many Hawaiians, heʻe nalu provided solace and escape from injustice and political conquest on land. Native Hawaiian surfers like George Freeth,[21] the Kahanamoku brothers, the Kaupikos, the Keaweamahis, and many others popularized surfing and took the sport to new heights.[22] The resurgence of heʻe nalu was most noticeable in Hawaiian ocean-based communities like Waikīkī. However, this Hawaiian realm was challenged when an elite haole surf club called the Outrigger attempted to wrest the surf from Native Hawaiians. Thereafter, it became a zone of contestation and rivalry, a Native respite that Hawaiians now had to defend from the same individuals who had overthrown their kingdom a few years prior. A group of Hawaiian surfers called Hui Nalu united to protect ka poʻina nalu and ensure Hawaiian control over their ocean domain.

In the 1930s many Hui Nalu surfers began moonlighting as Waikīkī Beachboys—essentially Hui Nalu surfers turned popular surf instructors. Through their interactions with visiting celebrities and other tourists, the Beachboys became fashionable playboys who often shared intimate relationships with white women and made a decent living in the process. Although racist discourses and American laws discouraged much of this type of behavior on land, ka poʻina nalu was a unique place where Hawaiians, Beachboys in particular, regularly and visibly broke through colonial social categories. After charting the historic contestations between Hui Nalu and Outrigger surfers in chapter 3, I then analyze the ways Beachboys flipped images of Hawaiian men in the surf. In the end, Hui Nalu surfers, like the chiefs of old, remained atop the social hierarchy in the waves.

In chapter 4 I chart a history of gender-based stereotypes defined by colonial categories in Hawaiʻi—the same kinds of categories that surfers in Waikīkī and the North Shore ignored, combated, or redefined. Such stereotypes were generated and proliferated through tourism, American popular culture, Hollywood films, and history books. In the first half of the twentieth century Hawaiʻi's tourist industry worked to convince prospective visitors that Hawaiʻi's Natives were safe and accommodating hosts. Since a strong male presence potentially jeopardized that impression, images of sexualized Hawaiian women eclipsed the Hawaiian man in tourist advertisements. Haunani-Kay Trask has criticized this tourist agenda. In *From a Native Daughter,* Trask condemns Hawai'i's government-supported tourism industry, calling it the pimp that prostitutes Hawai'i, its culture, and its people. She also contends that such marketing not only sexualized and commodified the islands as a female prostitute, but was "invented to lure visitors and disparage Native resistance to the tourist industry."[23] Although Hawaiian men were rendered nearly invisible next to the attractive female in tourist advertisements, Hollywood repeatedly found a place for them in South Seas films. Popular since the 1920s, movies set in the Pacific Islands blossomed in the mid-1900s.[24] In films like *Wake of the Red Witch, Bird of Paradise,* and many others, Hawaiian men are depicted as submissive and incapable next to American heroes. One example of the American hero is John Wayne, typically depicted as strong, cunning, and attractive—essentially the polar opposite of Native men. With the help of historical narratives, tourist-driven media venues painted Hawaiian men as insignificant players in their own society. Such depictions emasculated Native Hawaiian men and rendered them nearly invisible.

Issues of masculinity are also central to this study. Colonial definitions of successful manhood, modeled after Western criteria, may have instilled feelings of ineptitude in some Hawaiian men. However, many Hawaiian surfers redefined their manhood in the waves. As Ty Tegan theorized in *Native Men Remade,* late twentieth-century Hawaiian notions of masculinity were often constructed in contrast to emasculating tourist images and in light of contemporary definitions of what it meant to be na koa (warriors).[25] Although competing definitions of manhood often clashed in the waves, for many Hawaiian surfers expertise in the surf helped strengthen their identities as both men and Native Hawaiians. Often, identities forged in ka po'ina nalu bolstered self-confidence in Hawaiian men and helped them combat Western definitions of manhood. While Western culture defined successful manhood through the accumulation of Western notions of wealth, education, and social standing, these new definitions often belittled Hawaiian men. However, Hawaiian surfers expressed confidence as men through their skills in the waves—as seen in the jib debate between Buffalo Keaulana and Ben Finney on board *Hōkūle'a* (see chapter 5). While gendered identities were forged in the waves and elsewhere, ethnic identities were fueled in the cultural movements of the Hawaiian renaissance.

A climate of resistance and cultural revitalization grew among Native Hawaiians in the mid-1970s. Hawaiian activists were influenced by other indigenous groups of the United States and the Pacific during this time. Most notably, Hawaiian activists drew inspiration from the Native American occupation of Alcatraz when they defiantly landed on the U.S. military–controlled island of Kahoʻolawe. Renewed Hawaiian activism and revitalization in the 1970s is often referred to as the Hawaiian renaissance. Although the Hui O Heʻe Nalu was a product of this period of heightened cultural awareness and resistance, another group of Hawaiian and local surfers helped instill the spirit of pride in the 1960s. Save Our Surf (SOS) was a grassroots organization that comprised surfers determined to protect Hawaiian waves and coastlines from overdevelopment in the 1960s and 1970s. Leaders of this organization, such as John Kelly, combined Marxism and Hawaiian cultural pride to create a highly influential, politically active group of surfers. Over the course of several years, their protests stopped numerous large-scale development projects in Hawaiʻi—projects that threatened many local beaches and surfing breaks. They regularly hosted rallies and protests at Hawaiʻi's state capitol, lobbied for change in legislation, and pursued developers in courtrooms. In chapter 5 I contextualize the Hui's resistance by elaborating on the history of cultural and political movements of the 1960s and 1970s.

In 1975 the Polynesian Voyaging Society built *Hōkūleʻa,* a sixty-two-foot waʻa kaulua, or twin-hulled voyaging canoe—a replica of what Hawaiians used to travel long distances in ancient times. In 1976 the *Hōkūleʻa* sailed from Hawaiʻi to Tahiti with traditional navigational methods. Several *Hōkūleʻa* crew members were also famous Hawaiian surfers, many of whom had helped form the Hui O Heʻe Nalu on the North Shore.[26] In 1978 Eddie Aikau, a Hawaiian civic ambassador, lifeguard, and member of the Hui, became a crew member of *Hōkūleʻa* when it embarked on its second trip to Tahiti. Aikau was selected as a crew member because he had an in-depth knowledge of the ocean and was known as one of the world's best lifeguards. While sailing from Hawaiʻi to Tahiti, the ship hit rough seas a few miles off the island of Lanaʻi and capsized. Hoping to find help for the troubled crew, Aikau paddled his surfboard toward Lanaʻi. Although help eventually arrived, Eddie Aikau was lost to the Hawaiian seas. Because the canoe was a symbol of the Hawaiian renaissance, Aikau was immortalized by the Hawaiian community for his efforts and courage. Aikau was not only revered as a Hawaiian who sacrificed his life for his crew, but his sacrifice was also seen as an offering on behalf of his people. The Hui O He'e Nalu inherited the spirit of these voyages through some of its members, Eddie Aikau in particular.

In chapter 6 I analyze the history of the Hui O He'e Nalu. Drawing primarily from oral history interviews, I discuss how history, culture, and resistance shaped their identities. In these interviews many Hui members linked their 1970s North Shore experience to the late 1800s and the overthrow of Hawai'i's Native government. For example, Billy Ho'ola'e Blankenfeld characterized International Professional Surfing (IPS) as a group of business-minded exploiters interested only in personal economic gain. He explained, "It was inconceivable in their mind to give anything back to the community. They were taking!" Later in the same interview he described those who overthrew Hawai'i's kingdom in 1893 with similar language: "Missionaries turned businessmen . . . saw the profit, and they misled the Hawaiian people."[27] Bryan Amona recognized Queen Lili'uokalani's call for peaceful nonretaliation as honorable (since many Hawaiian lives were saved) and regrettable (because passive resistance did not succeed in the end). When describing his participation with the Hui in the 1970s, Amona stated that he defied his "laid-back nature," "ran out of aloha," and actively fought for what belonged to the Hawaiians.[28] Amona, like other Hawaiian surfers, participated in an unfinished colonial history that he metaphorically revisited, reenacted, and rewrote. In waging protest in the waves, they staged resistance against late nineteenth-century Hawaiian colonialism. As the colonialists of the past became fused with colonizers in their present, these Hawaiian surfers invited the possibility of restoring the deposed self and resurrecting a marginalized people.

Despite their amiable self-characterizations as freedom fighters, Hui surfers gained their greatest fame in the mid-1980s with *Honolulu Advertiser* and *Honolulu Star-Bulletin* stories that followed the court trial of two Hui members arrested on cocaine charges. The Honolulu papers popularized the prosecution's allegations that the Hui O He'e Nalu was a gang of "strong-arm collectors and dealers."[29] These articles were often published alongside stories about terrorism in the Middle East and the Iran-Contra affair. Several newspaper articles in 1987 described the Hui members as "terrorists," as seen in stories like "'Reign of Terror' on the North Shore told" and "Threats forced him to hire terrorists, Hemmings says."[30] Although reporting on the proceedings of the trial, the articles frequently repeated characterizations of Hui members as extortionists and narrated their history as Native troublemakers. As the newspapers labeled Hui members terrorists, several American movies and television shows introduced many non–North Shore residents to a group of Hawaiian surfers who harassed whites. Through such media venues, American viewers learned that some unruly Hawaiians could be very uncivil to foreigners on the North Shore. I discuss the implications of this in chapter 7.

As Hui members were defined as aggressive terrorists, these stories reduced their disillusionment to hatred and their resistance to barbarism. The terrorist label served a particular function—to undermine Hawaiian resistance and preserve the status quo where haole dominated and Hawaiians were marginalized.[31] Although these labels placed limitations on the Hui's success, the Hui often manipulated such stereotyping to its advantage. In chapter 7 I also explain how the terrorist label both helped and hindered the Hui. Throughout each of these chapters I draw from various theoretical perspectives to analyze this research; I particularly adapt the concept of borderlands to Hawaiian surf zones.

Borderlands and Boarder-Lands

Ka poʻina nalu has attributes similar to the theoretical concept of a borderland, which is a place where differences converge and social norms are often fluid. Because state-sanctioned authority is often absent from the borderlands, unique social and cultural identities are formed there. In such a place accepted hierarchies are often undermined. Susan Lee Johnson found this in the southern mines during California's Gold Rush. Before U.S. control existed in the region, Chinese, French, Navajo women, Mexicans, Blacks, and Anglo-Americans living in the region violated American social expectations of how each race and gender should behave. It was essentially a world "turned upside down."[32]

Like the regions Johnson studied, ka poʻina nalu was a place where American control was uncertain, Natives inverted dominant social categories of how they should behave, and surfers accomplished all that they were expected not to. For example, in the early twentieth century Hawaiian surfers in Waikīkī successfully combated elite haole annexationists, had sex with elite white women, ran lucrative beach concession businesses, beat up American and European soldiers, and dictated what haole could and could not do in their surf. All this was done in plain sight of public spectators. But unlike the frontiers described by others, where gender and ethnic fluidity confounded authority, the Hawaiian boarder-land was a place where Hawaiians subverted white hegemony by enacting their Hawaiian identity. Although several

Hawaiian surfers were of multiracial origin, it was their Hawaiian-ness, rather than their mixed heritage, that united and fueled their objectives.

What made this boarder-land community more intriguing was that it flowed like powerful waves against haole hegemony on land. The beach was not just a physical buffer between the land and the ocean, but a cultural and metaphysical border, as Greg Dening has theorized about the significance of the beach in the Marquesas Islands. For Dening, the beach was a place where the apparently "unbridgeable" worlds of Te Aoe (haole) and Te Enata (indigenous Pacific Islanders) collided.[33] Beaches divided their worlds; they were "beginnings and endings" and "the frontiers and boundaries of islands."[34] According to Dening, the beach was also the place where both peoples struggled to make sense of the other, and, as each considered the other's world incomprehensible, violence became the language of reason, and many Marquesans were slaughtered.[35] In the end, Te Aoe crossed Marquesas beaches and brought with them baggage of all sorts. Hoping to make the island intelligible by giving it new names and civilizing its Natives, Te Aoe remade the islands in their own image with each beach crossing.

This is a useful, though incomplete, model for understanding Hawaiian beaches and surfers. The beach was historically a place where haole and Hawaiian worlds collided, and violence was sometimes a substitute for mutual understanding. But the beach has a particular historical burden in Hawai'i—why else would Australian surfer "Rabbit" Bartholomew (see chapter 6) compare himself to Captain James Cook and the Kealakekua beach where he was killed while he himself bled on Sunset Beach in 1976 after a struggle with Hawaiian surfers there?[36] Waikīkī Beach was also a place where both Hawaiian and haole worlds were redefined and reconstituted. And the ocean was not simply a place from which haole, on the decks of their ships, transposed their image of the islands onto Hawaiians, as Dening has suggested. It has been and remains more significant than that. The ocean has been a place of autonomy, resistance, and survival for many Pacific Islanders. Although some have more recently analyzed the significance of the moana (vast ocean) as a place of resistance and survival—especially in regard to seafaring and navigation—thus far scholars have overlooked the surf.[37] Ka po'ina nalu constitutes another zone. Beyond Dening's islands and beaches, we must immerse ourselves in the waves.

While Europeans obsessed over exploring and later colonizing the Pacific, they defined the islands as specks of land in a faraway sea. According to Tongan scholar Epeli Hau'ofa, this limited perspective overlooked the importance of the ocean, which was far more significant to indigenous peoples of Oceania.[38] He argued that as Westerners defined the islands as small and limited in resources, they undervalued historic interactions between Pacific Islanders and depicted the ocean as merely a space to be crossed. According to Hauʻofa, rather than a border—generating isolation and restriction—the Pacific Ocean is (and always has been) a highway linking the myriad islands and their peoples to each other and to the bordering continents of the Pacific.[39]

Although the perspective in this book may resonate with academic concepts of borderlands and cultural studies, Hawaiian and Pacific Islander scholarship has also made a permanent mark on this book. For example, Noenoe Silva's *Aloha Betrayed* inspired me to search for better examples of Native agency and resistance in history. While using neglected Hawaiian-language newspapers and newly found petitions to U.S. annexation by the majority of Hawaiians living in 1895, Silva uncovered an indisputably rich history of Hawaiian resistance—a history that was previously determined nonexistent. In many ways this book hopes to accomplish a similar objective: to analyze an overlooked place in Hawaiian history where stories of agency and resistance billowed.

While I draw from magazine articles, books, newspapers, and other written sources (in both English and Hawaiian) to create a narrative about Hawaiian surfers, much of the information used to write this book was gathered from oral interviews. A decisive criticism of mine is that Native Hawaiian voices, male voices in particular, have frequently been quieted by colonial discourses—like the media. Thus this book regularly draws from oral interviews, often directly quoting Hawaiian surfers, to ensure that their words resonate in this narrative. Though it is virtually impossible to create an unbiased, objective history, this book nonetheless constructs a comprehensive historical narrative that resonates from a Hawaiian surfer's perspective.[40] And the voices in this story convey more than perspective; they highlight personalities, motives, identity, and soul. Although stereotypes depersonalize and marginalize peoples, this book aims to personalize and humanize individuals.

Historically, heʻe nalu has been an integral part of being Native Hawaiian; it has also been a cultural identity marker for Kanaka Maoli surfers. For many Native Hawaiians, the ocean surf has been a window for looking into their precolonial Hawaiian past, and a place where contemporary identities have developed in relation to both the past and present. The identities fostered in ka poʻina nalu often imbued confidence in Native men because of the surf. Such identities were often defined in contrast to haole definitions and expectations of Hawaiian men. These unique identities were forged because the surf became a puʻuhonua—a historic Hawaiian place of refuge from strict colonial laws. And in such a place identities could be constructed in opposition to colonialism. This is not to say that colonialism had no influence on the shaping of such identities; rather, Native Hawaiian identities fostered in the surf zone were developed in opposition to haole conquests on the shore. Ka poʻina nalu has been a space where Hawaiian men redefined themselves as active agents, embodying resistant masculinities.[41]

CHAPTER 1

He'e Nalu

A Hawaiian History of Surfing

In 2004, Sony Pictures Classic released Stacy Peralta's *Riding Giants*, a historical documentary of surfing and big-wave riding in particular. It was one of only a few surf films to play in mainstream theaters across the United States. The film starts with surfers from ancient Hawai'i, where chiefs and kings developed the sport over centuries. Then, after quoting eighteenth-century voyagers who confirmed Hawaiian expertise on the waves, the film explains that Calvinist missionaries banned the sport, thus causing its extinction. "Fortunately," the script continues, "the extinct Polynesian pastime was then re-introduced in the early twentieth century by Alexander Hume Ford, a globe-trotting promoter who set about reviving island tourism by romanticizing surfing at Waikīkī."[1] The film then spotlights modern surfing icons. First is Duke Kahanamoku, an expert swimmer and surfing champion who took he'e nalu to Australia, California, and New York. As the "father of modern surfing," Duke's ceremonial passing of the he'e nalu torch to white Americans and Australians is a critical juncture in the surf history narrative. According to the film, Tom Blake, the first to run with it, became "one of the twentieth century's most influential surfers."[2]

As if they stopped surfing or existing altogether, Native Hawaiians have little place in the story from this point on—in common surf history narratives generally and in this film particularly. Instead, the film focuses on the evolution of surfing at the hands of converted Californians, from Greg Noll and Gidget to northern California surfers in the 1980s. Despite the fact that Hawaiians continued to surf, the film explains that California surfers brought big-wave surfing to the Hawaiian Islands in the late 1950s. Ironically, the Hawaiian surf is first portrayed as Mecca and later as a site of discovery. The story of Noll stumbling onto an unoccupied North Shore surfing paradise is confounded by the fact that Native Hawaiians are still living in the backdrop. The film then accentuates the heroism and primitive manliness of Californians risking their lives at places like Pau Malū (called Sunset Beach) and Waimea Bay. Such surfing history narratives erroneously suggest that surfing was extinct until resurrected by haole surfers in the early twentieth century.

This chapter also chronicles a history of surfing, but from a Hawaiian perspective. First, I chart centuries-old histories of Hawaiian surfers from ka wā kahiko (times of old, prior to 1778) to show that Hawaiian pride in he'e nalu has deep historical roots. Here I draw from several mo'olelo (history, legend) not previously recorded in popular surf histories and found in Hawaiian-language sources. Although much of this book emphasizes male identity construction in the waves, this chapter spotlights several stories about Hawaiian women. While surfing was arguably a male-dominated sport in the twentieth century, in ka wā kahiko women had a strong presence in the po'ina nalu and were the primary characters in most of surfing mo'olelo. Through these histories we not only learn about human relationships in the waves, but can also contextualize the sentiments of Hawaiians in the twentieth century to better understand their feelings of ownership of and identification with he'e nalu—even with Hui Nalu and Hui O He'e Nalu surfers in the 1900s.

While twentieth-century Hawaiian surfers battled colonialism in the waves, they often found cultural continuity in the surf. Although surfboard technology and wave-riding maneuvers had evolved by the close of the twentieth century, Hawaiian surfers still saw it as inherently Hawaiian.[3] Through these convictions, we better understand Hawaiian reactions to Californian, Australian, and other visiting surfers. For Kanaka Maoli surfers, it was presumptuous and disrespectful for haole to claim birthright to a Hawaiian cultural practice still in full swing. My second objective, then, is to refute key myths generated by popular versions of surfing history. By showing that Hawaiians continued surfing in the nineteenth and twentieth centuries, I argue that he'e nalu's "extinction" at the turn of the twentieth century was indeed a fallacy. Thus Alexander Hume Ford did not resurrect surfing, as is often purported, but rather learned to surf from Native Hawaiians like George Freeth, who had been surfing and continued to do so in Hawai'i during this so-called restoration period. Furthermore, throughout the 1900s and despite construed historical memory, Hawaiian surfers still ranked as top performers and competitors in the world surfing arena—even on the North Shore in the 1960s, 1970s, and today. Thus Hawaiians took offense at a continual lack of recognition by haole surfers who assumed dominance in a surf zone already run by Hawaiians. In this chapter I often draw from previously ignored accounts of he'e nalu found in nineteenth- and early twentieth-century Hawaiian-language newspapers, as well as oral history research, to support my arguments.

Ka Wā Kahiko

Although Pacific Islanders throughout Oceania have most likely been riding waves on wooden boards for over the last couple thousand years, the more developed form of he'e nalu, standing while riding, is estimated to have begun in Hawai'i and perhaps Tahiti about fifteen hundred years ago.[4] Hawaiian mo'olelo passed down from ka wā kahiko are filled with epic tales of heroic surfers, daring competitions, romantic surfing encounters, and lessons of betrayal in the waves. David Malo, a nineteenth-century Hawaiian historian, described he'e nalu as a Hawaiian national sport, one that Hawaiians often competed in and gambled over.[5]

But surfing was more than competitive sport; it was a cultural practice embedded within the social, political, and religious fabric of Hawaiian society. For example, Hawaiian prayers were believed to summon and control ocean swells,[6] ho'okupu (offerings) were presented on altars at heiau or temples on behalf of the surf,[7] and chiefs were commonly valorized and validated in stories of great surfing feats. Although some great men have been highlighted in Hawai'i's past, many have erroneously classified he'e nalu as the sport of kings. In truth, contemporary class and gender boundaries had no place in the waves. Though a few waves were designated for ali'i (chiefs), all Hawaiians could enjoy wave riding regardless of status, age, or gender.[8] Malo explains, "Surf riding was one of the most exciting and noble sports known to the Hawaiians, practiced equally by king, chief, and commoner. . . . It was not uncommon for a whole community, including both sexes and all ages, to sport and frolic in the ocean the livelong day."[9]

Although surfing was an egalitarian sport, in Hawaiian mo'olelo gods and ali'i were also celebrated as great surfers. Under the ancient Hawaiian religious system there are four primary gods: Kū, Kanaloa, Kāne, and Lono. God of fertility and sport, Lono was also an expert surfer. When Lono looked down upon the earth, he marveled at its beauty and wished to marry a woman from such a beautiful place. Searching mountains, forests, and valleys from Kaua'i to Hawai'i, he finally found Kaikilani, a beautiful woman who lived by the great waterfall Hi'ilawe in Waipi'o Valley. Riding from the heavens down to Waipi'o on a rainbow, Lono disguised himself as a chief. Shortly after their marriage, the couple relocated to Kealakekua, Kona, to enjoy surfing when the west winds blew and fishing by torch at night. Of the many things that Lono was venerated for, his surfing prowess was top among them.[10]

Although several men, gods, and chiefs surfed, female surfers were far more popular in Hawaiian histories. One example is Hi'iakaikapoliopele (Hi'iaka in the Bosom of Pele), the youngest sister of the fire goddess Pele. While traveling around the island of O'ahu, Hi'iaka had an unfriendly encounter in the surf in the Ko'olauloa district on the east side of the island. When Hi'iaka and her traveling party approached Kahana Valley, she appropriately called out to the chiefs of that area with an oli kāhea (a greeting/protocol chant asking permission to enter). Palani and his wife Iewale, known as the surfing chiefs of Kahana, were in the ocean surfing at the time. Perhaps annoyed by the oli, Palani answered Hi'iaka with contempt, shouting,

Ae, o Palani au o ke'lii hee nalu o keia aina o Kahana nei. Owai hoi oe e na wahine hookano o kau hele ana mai nei a kahea mai ia'u? Ua ike mai no paha oe ia'u e heenalu ana me ka 'u wahine, he wahine ike ole no ka oe ia'u, o ka'u puni no nei, owai hoi oe?[11]

Yes, I am Palani the surfing chief of this land, Kahana. Who are you, conceited women who have come and called out to me? Perhaps you have seen me surfing here with my wife; you are an unfamiliar woman to me; I rule this place; who are you?

Angered by Palani's disrespectful response, Hi'iaka caused the waves to quickly rise. As both Palani and his wife tried to catch the fast-growing surf, the giant waves overcame them, eventually consuming and killing them both.[12]

Kapo'ulakina'u, a surfer and sorceress of Kaua'i, was another Hawaiian woman who demanded respect in the Hawaiian surf. Determined to find suitable husbands for her nine companions, she escorted them to a famous surfing break in Wailua, Kaua'i. Upon their arrival they were greeted by a handsome surfer called Kaumaka'amano. After describing the bending wave conditions at the esteemed Makaīwa, he lent his eight-foot koa board to

Kapoʻulakinaʻu. With impressive form, she quickly paddled the heavy board into the surf zone and began conversing with a group of surfers. Causing the waves to become small, Kapoʻulakinaʻu drew their attention to the beautiful women on land. Enchanted, eight of the men rode to shore to meet them. Kapoʻulakinaʻu then paired each man with one woman and sent them all back into the surf so the men could court their new spouses-to-be. Meanwhile, Kaumakaʻamano had already fallen in love with the ninth woman, Kahalaiʻa. Assured that her female companions would be cared for, Kapoʻulakinaʻu anticipated the prospect of her own future and began thinking of pursuing a lover. But shortly thereafter, all the women (except Kahalaiʻa) returned to shore without their surfing partners. After they explained each man's excuse for not marrying them, Kapoʻulakinaʻu's relief quickly turned to rage. She charged out into the surf and challenged the eight men to a surf competition. "What are the stakes?" the men asked. "Our bones," she replied.[13] Intimidated but still interested, the men tried to keep up with the surfing sorceress. She then called the great waves of the deep ocean with her pōhuehue vine and chanting. As the waves grew, only she was able to ride the monstrous surf. The waves eventually consumed the men and buried them in the Makaīwa surf forever. Today eight submerged rocks symbolize these surfers and stand as a reminder to men to be both respectful of and committed to women.

As seen in both ancient and modern times, Hawaiian surfers have placed a high value on the notion of respect in the waves. Like Hiʻiaka and Kapoʻulakinaʻu, Hawaiians in the twentieth century took offense at surfers who failed to create and reciprocate relationships of respect and exchange. Although many assume that most tension in Hawaiian waves is attributed simply to brute territorialism, I disagree. Disrespect and a lack of recognition are the core issues that ignite most conflicts in the Hawaiian surf.[14] In the story of Iewale and Palani, for example, it was Palani's failure to recognize and respect Hiʻiaka as an individual (and goddess) that got him into trouble—not necessarily his claim over the territory of Kahana. In both ancient and contemporary Hawaiʻi, recognition is still critical in social settings. Recognition of one's family, community, and origins are essential to social relationships, even in the surf.[15] Thus Hiʻiaka, as a visitor to Kahana, followed proper protocol by recognizing Palani's family and status before she asked to enter. She was angered when Palani failed to reciprocate in the social exchange.

Throughout most of Oceania, Native peoples have historically relied on relationships of exchange in their various social systems. In such systems exchanges of love, respect, mutual assistance, and nurturing sociospacial ties are core principles in maintaining healthy social relationships.[16] Focusing on the vā, "the social or relational space connecting people," Tevita Ka'ili explains that most Pacific Island societies value the maintenance of such social spaces with their "commitment to sustain harmonious social relations with kin and kin-like members." He continues, "Such nurturing ties between individuals and kāinga [family] generally involves reciprocal exchanges of economic and social goods."[17] Thus when those sociospacial ties were ignored and undermined in the Hawaiian surf, people like Hi'iaka, Kapo'ula, and others felt disrespected, offended, and angry. The concept of honoring others, respecting individuals, and reciprocating benevolent relations resonated in several mo'olelo. They also uncover specific values and rules within a Hawaiian surfing hierarchy. For example, Hi'iaka and Kapo'ula expected recognition and respect because of specific status markers they both held. Genealogy (who your family is and where you are from), social/political rank, and surfing skill were all criteria for ranking a person in a surfing lineup. Although it evolved, some of these criteria for defining hierarchy still existed in twentieth-century Hawaiian waves.[18]

Mo'ikeha was a surfer remembered for maintaining healthy sociospacial ties on Kaua'i. After traveling to Kaua'i from Raiatea, Mo'ikeha fell in love with Makaīwa's bending waves and two surfing sisters, Ho'oipoikamalanai and Hinau'u. Unlike the eight Makaīwa surfers, Mo'ikeha committed himself to both surfing and family life—he eventually married the sisters.[19] These new commitments anchored Mo'ikeha to his new community, and instead of returning to Raiatea, he moved his Tahitian sons to Kaua'i as well. Finding favor with his father-in-law, Mo'ikeha inherited the chiefly title to the island.

Through Ho'oipoikamalanai, Mo'ikeha had a daughter (or granddaughter) named Ka'iliokalauokekoa (The Skin of the Leaf of the Koa Tree).[20] Growing up in the surf, Ka'ili became an accomplished surfer. However, as a youth she lived a sheltered life. After her birth, a seer prophesied that she would one day leave, fall in love with a godly man, and stop listening to her parents. In that relationship, the prophecy continued, she would find misery and finally death. Because of this prophecy, her parents kept a close eye on Ka'ili, but not close enough. One day she left home to find the man who had persistently appeared to her in her dreams. While she and her attendant searched, Ka'ili heard someone chanting with a flute, calling to her, "O Kaili, O Kaili-e, you have slept and you have heard."[21] Following the sound of the flute and chant, they went to the uplands of Pihanakalani, where the godly man Kauakahiali'i lived. When they arrived at his impressive home of lehua flowers, he called to Kaʻili to come to him, and the two were married shortly thereafter. But just as foretold, their relationship was filled with drama, mainly because they were both unfaithful to one another.

Since living far from the ocean was difficult for a surfer like Kaʻili, she began hiking down to Makaīwa while her husband performed his daily task of catching birds in the mountains. He approved of her surfing exploits as long as she returned home in the evenings. Over time, and particularly when Kaʻili began sleeping on a separate bed, Kauakahialiʻi became suspicious of his wife's surfing excursions. So one day he followed and spied on her. Watching from a distance, he learned that Kaʻili was both a skilled surfer and a popular wahine at Makaīwa.

Kaʻili was a better surfer than any of the other women in Wailua, and because of this all the chiefs admired and desired her. As time passed, Kaʻili grew increasingly fond of two young brothers named Kalehuakuikawaokele and Kalehuakuikawao. One day Kaʻili rewarded the persistent brothers with kisses while they were in the water on their surfboards. But it did not end there; Kaʻili then returned to their home, where they proceeded to make love.

On the day that her husband was spying on her, Kaʻili was again in the brothers' home. Kauakahialiʻi's heart sank as he watched all three exit the home and enter the surf together. As Kauakahialiʻi watched in disillusionment, a woman named Makaweli approached him on the trail, recognized who he was, and confirmed that his wife was indeed sleeping with the brothers. Although he was troubled by his wife's infidelity, Kauakahialiʻi himself was no innocent victim.

Shortly after this experience, Kauakahialiʻi became fond of Makaweli, the woman on the trail, and devised a plan to be with her. One day he told Kaʻili that he would be hunting birds in a special place, where he could go only at night. He then explained that if he was unsuccessful, his god would become angry and kill him. "So do not worry if I do not return," he explained. "I will need a day, a night, and another day to catch these birds." But of course this was just a ploy—instead of hunting for birds at night, he was sleeping with Makaweli. This continued for six months, until Kaʻili learned of his deeds from a bird in one of her dreams. After she confronted Kauakahialiʻi, he confessed.

He oiaio no kau moe, noʻu nae ka olelo a ka hihio i ka po, a no hai ka olelo o ke ao, mai manao oe i ka ka po olelo he oiaio, e hele no au i kau hana, ua ike no oe i kau kane iloko o ko kaua mau la, aole au i haalele ia oe ua noho no au me ka maluhia a hiki i kou haalele ana iaʻu, o oe no o kaua kai lalau,

a o wau no ko kaua i hoaa aku ia oe, a loaa oe ia'u iloko o ka papai kilu me
na kane elua, nolaila, mai aua oe ia'u.[22]

Your dream is true. But I was the one who spoke in the dream; someone
else spoke during the day. Don't think what was said at night is true. I went
to your work, you saw your husband in our days; I didn't leave you. I was
just residing with peace until you left me; you are the one that strayed and I
am the disconcerted one. I caught you inside of the small kilu hut with the
other two guys, so don't you hold a grudge against me.

After the argument, Ka'ili decided she would watch Kauakahiali'i more
closely, instead of divorcing him. So she did not allow him to leave home
unless she accompanied him. Over the next three days he brooded, wishing
he was with Makaweli. After Kauakahiali'i pleaded to go to work, Ka'ili
released him to go bird hunting, but she followed him and watched as he
sneaked to the surfing area to meet Makaweli. Ka'ili's heart sank as her
husband lingered in Makaweli's home. When the door finally opened, the
secret lovers sat together, and with Kauakahiali'i's head on her lap, Makaweli
stroked his hair and nibbled on his shoulder. Ka'ili fell into a depression,
ran home, and hanged herself with Kauakahiali'i's malo (loin cloth) from
their front door. Later, Kauakahiali'i found his wife's body and mourned
deeply, consumed with regret. Seeking to escape the grief, Kauakahiali'i
searched the islands for a woman as exceptional as Ka'ili. He eventually
found a beautiful surfing chiefess on the southeast side of Hawai'i island.
Her name was Lā'ieikawai.

The legend of Lā'ieikawai explains that Lā'ieikawai (Lā'ie of the Water)
was born in Lā'ie, in the moku (district) of Ko'olauloa (the North Shore of
O'ahu). Moments before she was born, her mother, Mālaekahana, told her
husband that she craved 'ōhua fish—a tall order for any fisherman. However,
this was merely a ploy; in truth, she wanted to conceal her newborn daughter,
since her husband had wanted a son and would not accept another girl. While
he was away, Mālaekahana gave birth to twin girls. Lā'ielohelohe (Obedient
Lā'ie), the first born, was raised far away in Wahiawā, while Lā'ieikawai was
hidden from her father in a nearby underwater cave called Wai'āpuka. After
persistent rainbows exposed her secret location,[23] she escaped with her guard-
ian, Waka, to Kea'au, on Hawai'i island, to live at Paliuli—a house made of
yellow bird feathers in the middle of a beautiful 'ōhi'a forest. While living in
Kea'au, Lā'ieikawai would often surf the waves of Hā'ena, and she became

fond of heʻe nalu. Although she was regularly pursued by various men, most were unsuccessful at winning her interest.[24]

Shortly after Kaʻili died, Kauakahialiʻi learned of Lāʻieikawaiʻs whereabouts from one of his servants, and he desired to marry her. He first heard of her beauty after his servant stumbled upon Lāʻieʻs bright-yellow feather house and met with her. Hurriedly, the boy asked if she would marry his master, Kauakahialiʻi. Lāʻie flatly refused, but she agreed to meet his chief later that night behind her house. She instructed the servant to first listen for the voice of the ʻElepaio bird, then the ʻApapane, and finally the yellow ʻIʻiwi, and then she would come to see Kauakahialiʻi. But Lāʻie was toying with the chief and his servant, and left them waiting in vain.

While Kauakahialiʻi was struggling to meet Lāʻieikawai, Kaʻili was resurrected by Kauakahialiʻiʻs cousin and her magical bamboo flute. Upon recovering, Kaʻili traveled to Hawaiʻi island and restored her relationship with Kauakahialiʻi, thus leading him to abandon his pursuit of Lāʻie. Kaʻili and Kauakahialiʻi then returned to Kauaʻi. Although they lived out their lives as rulers of Kauaʻi, the chief did not forget Lāʻieikawai. Later, he told stories about the beautiful surfing chiefess to other Kauai chiefs.[25]

ʻAiwohikupua and Kekalukaluokēwā listened intently to Kauakahialiʻiʻs stories. ʻAiwohi was enchanted by the story of Lāʻie and hastily embarked on a quest to win her heart. After painstaking attempts to impress her—with boxing matches, a feather cloak, his five sisters, gentle and sweet like Maile vines—he ultimately failed. Kekalukaluokēwā, on the other hand, was more successful, and was even engaged to Lāʻie for a short while.

Before he died, Kauakahialiʻi told Kekalukaluokēwā to marry Lāʻie after he and Kaʻili were gone. Then, he said, Kekalukaluokēwā and Lāʻie could rule together in his stead. Later, after the passing of Kauakahialiʻi and Kaʻili, the new chief traveled to Hawaiʻi to meet Lāʻie. Shortly after his arrival, Waka encouraged Lāʻie to see the handsome Kauaʻi chief and decide for herself. After four days she went to the shoreline with her attendant and watched a group of Kauaʻi surfers ride the waves in Keaʻau. But Lāʻie could not determine which surfer was Kekalukaluokēwā. Wisely, her attendant suggested that they wait for the men to return to shore. The one who did not carry his own board, she explained, would be the chief. After discovering his identity in this manner, Lāʻie returned home and told Waka she had agreed to marry him. The ceremony was planned by Waka and would take place in the surf, on their boards. Wakaʻs instructions were very specific, and she was adamant that protocol be meticulously observed. On the day of the ceremony,

Kekalukaluokēwā first entered the surf, and Waka caused a great mist to cover the Puna area. Then Lāʻie was carried out to the surf break on the wings of birds, where her husband-to-be awaited her. Lāʻie was instructed not to speak to anyone until after they had surfed their first wave together and then kissed. After the kiss, and after having ridden four consecutive waves together, the couple planned one last ride before returning to Paliuli (Lāʻie's sacred home of feathers) to consummate their marriage. But on their fifth and final wave, a young Hawaiʻi island local surfer interfered with the ceremony.[26]

Halaʻaniani, with the help of his sister, Maliʻo (Dawn Light), devised a scheme to snatch Lāʻie from Kekalukaluokēwā. Aware of Waka's plan and with her own cunning sorcery, Maliʻo blinded Waka and sent her brother into the surf during the wedding ceremony. Knowing that the fifth wave would be their final one, Halaʻaniani remained behind and grabbed Lāʻie's feet just as she and Kekalukaluokēwā began to catch it. As the Kauaʻi chief rode the wave to shore alone, Halaʻaniani convinced Lāʻie (who, perhaps because of the heavy mist, believed him to be Kekalukaluokēwā) to ride the longer waves farther out in the ocean. After he impressed her by riding high on the crest of the largest wave (perhaps doing a long floater), the two were married and returned together to Paliuli.[27] When Waka discovered the two sleeping in

Lāʻieikawai. (Drawing by Halam Ah Quin)

their home, she removed her magical powers from Lāʻie and publicly scorned her for her mistake. It took Halaʻaniani only a couple of months to betray Lāʻieikawai, when he inappropriately propositioned his wife's twin sister, Lāʻielohelohe, to have sex with him. Many years later Lāʻie's second husband, Kaʻōnohiokalā, restored Lāʻieikawai's honor and punished her offenders.

Like the stories of Kapoʻulakinaʻu, Kaʻili, and Lāʻie, the moʻolelo of Kelea highlight the mana (power) and agency of Hawaiian women. Keleanuinohoʻanaʻapiʻapi was a high-ranking woman of Maui whose long, ʻehu- (reddish) tinted hair fluttered, birdlike, while she masterfully rode waves.[28] In her youth Kelea enjoyed the large waves of Wailuku, Kekaha, and Hamakuapoko, on Maui. But while surfing one day, she was lured onto a waʻa kaulua (double-hulled canoe) piloted by a group of Oʻahu chiefs who impressed her by surfing with their canoe. Shortly after she boarded the canoe, they were blown out to sea by a fast-approaching squall. Several hours later, one of the chiefs, Kalamakua, explained to her his quest to find a wife (as great as she) for his high-ranking cousin, Lo Lale. Kelea consented to marry Lo Lale, but secretly Kalamakua wished to marry her himself. Lo Lale was a good man, but ever since his childhood sweetheart had drowned, he suffered severe grief and depression. Kelea left him to his grief after ten years of marriage and searched for a happier life near the surf—Wahiawā (in central Oʻahu) was not an ideal place for a surfer. On the day she left, Kelea asked her attendants to take her surfing in Waikīkī. Once she arrived at Kawehewehe, she asked for a papa heʻe nalu (surfboard) and skillfully made her way out to where the largest waves were breaking. She then proceeded to out-surf the Waikīkī locals. As the community cheered, Chief Kalamakua rushed to the shoreline—he assumed they were cheering the surfing chiefess from Maui. Wondering why it had taken her so long to leave Lo Lale, the Waikīkī chief (an accomplished surfer himself) asked Kelea to marry him and be a mōʻī wahine (chiefess/queen) in Waikīkī.[29] She agreed.

The central characters in most surfing moʻolelo are empowered women. Such stories not only reflect the human agency of women in old Hawaiʻi, but also contrast sharply with contemporary surfing narratives on women and gender roles. In contemporary media, "surfer girls" and islander women are often portrayed as lifeless images that wear bikinis and sell products as sexualized bodies. While I confront these representations in chapter 5, I draw attention to such imagery here to highlight how they contrast with ancient Hawaiian histories. For example, Kalamakua's attraction to Kelea was kindled while he surfed and sailed with an impressive ocean expert. Although

Kelea is remembered as beautiful, at no point in the story does her physical image overshadow her human character. Likewise, women like Kapoʻula are portrayed as powerful. While men were often defeated and overpowered by women in these surf stories, these moʻolelo remind readers that many contemporary gender-based stereotypes had little place in surfing moʻolelo.

In the story of Kahikilani we find another example of empowered women of old Hawaiʻi. Although most of the moʻolelo abridged in this chapter are about surfers on Hawaiʻi, Kauaʻi, Maui, and at Waikīkī, Hawaiians of ka wā kahiko also surfed the giant waves of Oʻahu's North Shore. Among the many breaks to surf, Kahikilani favored the large, fast waves of Pau Malū, or Sunset Beach.[30] Traveling from his home island of Kauaʻi, Kahikilani worked to master these challenging waves. While surfing one day, a maid with supernatural bird powers watched him from a nearby cave. She sent her bird messengers to give Kahikilani her lehua lei and lure him to her dwelling place. Kahikilani remained with her during the summer months, but could not resist Pau Malū when the large winter waves swelled again. Vowing never to kiss another woman, Kahikilani returned to the thundering surf. But he broke his vow by accepting a lei and a kiss from another wahine at Pau Malū. Although he thought little of the kiss, the heartbroken maid confronted him, tore off the lei, and ran for the hills. He chased after her, but halfway up the hill, Kahikilani turned to stone.[31]

Hawaiian surfers regularly caught the attention of admirers from shore, and those who had never before witnessed heʻe nalu were especially intrigued. European voyagers to Hawaiʻi marveled at Hawaiian surfers in the late 1700s. From early January to the middle of February 1779, the British ships HMS *Resolution* and *Discovery* anchored in Kealakekua Bay on the southwest coast of Hawaiʻi. Captain James Cook's crew, while living among the Hawaiians, were astonished at locals who rode large winter waves on wooden planks. Perhaps even more perplexing were the "young boys and girls of nine or ten years of age playing amid such tempestuous waves that the hardiest of our seamen would have trembled to face."[32] In other accounts, like this one from Cook's first lieutenant, James King, Hawaiian surfers are described as both fearless and coordinated.

> As soon as they have gained, by these repeated efforts, the smooth water beyond the surf, they lay themselves at length upon their boards, and prepare for their return. As the surf consists of a number of waves, of which every third is remarked to be always larger than the others, and to flow higher on the shore, the rest breaking in the immediate space, their first

object is to place themselves on the summit of the largest surge, by which they are driven along with amazing rapidity toward the shore. The boldness and address, with which we saw them perform these difficult and dangerous maneuvers, was altogether astonishing.[33]

In addition to their amazement with surfing, voyagers also remarked on the strong character of Hawaiian women in Hawaiian society, who often performed seemingly masculine exploits like surfing. Analyzing the perspective of Cook's men toward Hawaiian women, Karina Kahananui Green explains that they characterized Hawaiian women as masculine because wahine blatantly contradicted European imaginations of Native women as sexually and socially submissive to men. Unlike later portrayals of Hawaiian women through tourism, Hawaiian women's "strength and power were not limited to her sexuality."[34] Furthermore, Green argues, "The power of the Hawaiian woman extended to more direct action."[35] Thus many voyagers viewed Hawaiian women as powerful and active in society as they participated in politics, fought in wars, boxed in matches, and surfed large, intimidating waves—similar to the way oral Hawaiian histories, or mo'olelo, remembered them.

Myth of a Dead Sport and Nā Nūpepa

Although fewer Hawaiians were surfing in the decades after the first Europeans arrived in Hawai'i, neither Hawaiians nor he'e nalu were extinct. While others have pointed to cultural colonialism as the cause for this decline, there were fewer wave riders in the nineteenth century because diseases introduced by foreigners ravaged Hawaiian society. According to David Stannard, the population in Hawai'i just before Captain Cook arrived was 800,000.[36] While some critics say Stannard's numbers are too high, more conservative estimates still place the population near 500,000. Although these calculations have been disputed, the 1823 census, which determined the Native Hawaiian population to be at 134,925, has not. Whether the Native Hawaiian population was reduced by 365,000 or 665,000 between 1778 and 1823, these deaths were nonetheless catastrophic. The first wave of diseases swept through Hawai'i after initial encounters with Cook's men in 1778. Illness continued to bombard the islands as more human carriers disembarked onto Hawaiian shores. Diseases like syphilis, tuberculosis, measles, Hansen's disease, and many others unleashed what some scholars called a holocaust in Hawai'i.[37] Naturally, such rapid depopulation inevitably thinned crowds at even the more popular surf breaks. However, of the many Hawaiians who survived the ailments of the 1800s, many continued to surf.

Additionally, some missionaries disregarded he'e nalu and discouraged Native Hawaiians from surfing. The first American Calvinist missionaries, who arrived in Hawai'i in 1820, were an especially conservative brand of American who considered Hawaiian cultural practices savage and immoral.[38] While early mission leaders like Hiram Bingham believed surfing promoted idle and sexual behavior, this idea was not expressed in all publications, but mostly in particularly conservative missionary-run newspapers. For example, in 1838 the Honolulu-based, missionary-supported newspaper *Ke Kumu Hawaii* ran an article in which a teacher castigated Hawaiian surfers as lazy "pigs" who were careless and negligent by surfing instead of doing their schoolwork.

> Eia kekahi, o ka lilo loa o na kanaka i ka heenalu a me na wahine a me na keiki i ka lelekawa i ka mio. Eia ka hewa o ka lelekawa a me ka heenalu a me ka mio, o ka huipu ana o na kane a me na wahine me na keiki i kahi hookahi, e like me na holoholona; haluku pu lakou i ke kiolepo hookahi.[39]

> Furthermore, the men, women, and children are engaged (or lost) in he'e nalu and lelekawa [cliff diving] and mio [another diving game]. The problem (or sin) of lelekawa, he'enalu, and mio is that men, women, and children do this together in a single location like animals; they are like pigs that wallow together in the mire.

However, while some missionaries and teachers rebuked he'e nalu, many Hawaiians ignored their admonitions. The fact that teachers in the mid-1800s wrote letters and newspaper articles in an effort to dissuade people from surfing suggests that it was popular among many Hawaiians—enough, at least, to disturb mission schoolteachers. Despite what their teachers called them, Hawaiians continued to enjoy their aquatic haven during a so-called period of surfing extinction.

In contrast to most mission publications, journal entries from other missionaries and visitors described surfing as a pastime commonly practiced by Hawaiians in the nineteenth century. While some missionaries and converts continued to scorn he'e nalu in the 1840s and 1850s, others celebrated the Hawaiian sport and recognized its livelihood. Even some haole Christians deemed surfing healthy. For example, in 1851 Reverend Henry T. Cheever, on Maui, admiringly described the sport as "so attractive and full of wild excitement to the Hawaiians, and withal so healthy, that I cannot but hope it will be many years before civilization shall look it out of countenance, or make it disreputable to indulge in this manly, though it be dangerous, pastime."[40] In 1866 Samuel Clemens (Mark Twain) came to Hawai'i as a reporter for the *Sacramento Union.* Reporting mostly on Hawaiian trade, industry, and labor, Clemens also spent time at the beach. Mesmerized by Hawaiian men and women who surfed with skill, Clemens himself was determined to learn the Hawaiian art of wave riding. After several attempts, however, he explained, "None but the natives can master this sport."[41] More than just funny commentary on his surfing bloopers, Twain's letters also convey the livelihood of he'e nalu in the 1860s. At the very least, this account demonstrates that surfing was visible enough for visitors like Twain to notice from shore. Perhaps because of visitors like him (too uncoordinated to participate in surfing but fascinated by it nevertheless), Hawaiian author J. Waiamau explained in an 1865 Hawaiian-language newspaper article how surfing is properly performed.

> O ka heenalu, oia kekahi paani nui loa o Hawaii nei, mai na'lii a na makaainanana. Penei nae hoi ka hana ana o keia hana: Ua hoomakaukau e ia ka papa mamua, oia hoi ke koa, ke kukui, ke ohe, ka wiliwili, a me kekahi mau laau e ae no i kupono no ka hana ana i papa. I ka hana mua ana nae hoi, oia no hoi ke kalai ana i ka wa hou o ka. laau, a pau hoi ia, waiho hou aku a maloo, alaila, hana hou a maikai loa, me ka paele ana i ka mea eleele, a wahi hoi i ke kapa a paa, a kauia ma kahi kupono; a hiki mai hoi ka wa e, lealea ai i ka heenalu, o ka hele no ia i ka heenalu. Penei nae hoi ka hana, i ka wa e au a hiki i kahi o ka uahi e hai mai ana, alaila, nana no hoi a ka nalu kupono i ka pae, alaila no hooino iho, a o ka pae no ia. He ekolu no hoi wahi e hee ai; hee iloko o ka hua, a o kekahi hoi, hee i ka muku, a o ke kolu, hee iluna o ka opuu; a o ka papa kupono iluna oia nalu, oia hoi ka olo, he elua anana a oi aku ka loa oia papa; ina e hee iluna oia nalu, aole no e poi mai ke kai maluna o ke kanaka.[42]

Surfing is one of the most popular games in Hawai'i for both royalty and commoners. Here is how it is done: A board must first be prepared; koa, kukui, ohe, wiliwili, and some other woods are used for making boards. The first thing that needs to be done is carving the board; when the wood is fresh it is left to dry, then it is worked on again until it is ready, [then] it is blackened and wrapped in tapa and left to settle in a suitable place. After some time has passed it is ready to have fun by surfing; let's go surfing.

Here is how it is done: swim out to the place where the mist is coming in, then watch for where the waves break; this is the dangerous part, the break. There are three places to surf: surf in the whitewash, another place is to surf on the crest, and thirdly, surf on the swell; there is a specific board for this type of riding, the olo board; it was two fathoms [about twelve feet] long; if this was ridden on the wave, the wave would not break over the person.

Hawaiian-language newspapers highlight a clear picture of he'e nalu; it remained important to Hawaiians in the 1800s, and it was a hot topic in those newspapers of the 1860s. In addition to articles—like J. Waiamau's— that gave detailed descriptions of surfing, the newspapers are filled with exhaustive accounts of Hawaiian surfers, both contemporary and ancient. In fact, most of the stories highlighted earlier in this chapter were first printed in these Hawaiian-language papers. While Hawaiian mo'olelo were passed down orally for centuries prior to the 1800s, in the middle of the nineteenth century Hawaiian authors laboriously transcribed these traditions onto paper. Noenoe Silva explained that 1861 marked a shift in Hawaiian newspapers, and newly established papers were often deemed opposition or resistance literature.[43] Hawaiians who wrote for these opposition papers labored to meticulously preserve culture and history, wrote in very nationalistic tones, and spoke out against haole influence in the Hawaiian kingdom.[44]

Ka Hoku o ka Pakipika (Star of the Pacific) was a quintessential Hawaiian opposition newspaper, run by Native Hawaiians who used print media not only to preserve Hawaiian history, but to advocate Hawaiian pride and resistance. As Hawaiians were one of the most literate people in the world in the 1860s, the majority read the papers. Between the years 1861 and 1863, *Ka Hoku o ka Pakipika* painstakingly gathered and published extensive Hawaiian oral histories, many written in series, published in the newspapers over several weeks or sometimes months. For example, the mo'olelo of Ka'iliokalauokekoa is nine chapters long, published in *Ka Hoku o ka Pakipika* over a period of four months. Mo'olelo presented in this chapter from these papers are mere abridgments of lengthy stories and can only scratch the surface of a vast collection published in the papers. Stories of other surfers like Kawelo, Pueo, 'Umi, Pamano, Kihapi'ilani, and more abound in *Ka Hoku o Ka Pakipika* (and other Hawaiian papers). The popularity of surfing mo'olelo in the 1860s, printed in Hawaiian national opposition papers, not only reveals that surfing still held value in the 1860s, but also suggests that he'e nalu was heavily associated with both Hawaiian cultural pride and resistance.

Although fewer newspaper articles were written on surfing in the 1870s and 1880s, many Hawaiians still frequented the waves during those decades. Even busy traveling members of the royal family found time to surf in the 1880s. While attending St. Matthew's Military School in San Mateo, California, three Hawaiian brothers—Prince Jonah Kūhiō Kalaniana'ole, Prince David Pi'ikoi Kupio Kawananakoa, and Prince Edward Kawananakoa—surfed at a beach outside the mouth of the San Lorenzo River on redwood surfboards. A Santa Cruz newspaper reported, "The young Hawaiian princes were in the water, enjoying it hugely and giving interesting exhibitions of surfboard swimming as practiced in their native islands."[45] Prince Jonah Kūhiō was an avid surfer in the late 1800s and early 1900s, a prominent figure whose influence was felt not only in the surf, but in Hawaiian Territory politics as well. While I analyze Kūhiō's influence in chapter 3, I mention him here to show that Hawaiians were still surfing in the late 1800s, a time when surfing was supposedly extinct (or nearly extinct). Kūhiō had other relatives who surfed during this period, namely his cousin, Princess Ka'iulani. Growing up in her Waikīkī 'Āinahau estate, Ka'iulani enjoyed surfing not far from her pristine garden. Today, one of her surfboards is on display at the Bishop Museum in Honolulu.

The Bishop Museum's extensive collection of historic surfing photographs confirms that Hawaiians were indeed still surfing in the 1890s and early 1900s. In the recently published book *Surfing: Historic Images from Bishop Museum Archives,* archivist Desoto Brown showcases some of his favorites. While there are several photos of Hawaiians riding waves on wooden boards at Waikīkī in the 1890s, there are also pictures of Hawaiians surfing on the outer islands. This is significant for two main reasons. First, these images show that more people were surfing in Waikīkī in the 1890s than previously assumed. Second, they demonstrate that Waikīkī was not the last remaining habitat for the endangered he'e nalu species; rather, surfing was done in the 1890s at various breaks throughout the Hawaiian Islands. In one particular shot taken in Hilo, estimated to be from the 1890s, two Hawaiian men are shown exiting (or perhaps entering) the surf in Hilo Bay with their papa he'e nalu (surfboards).[46] In contrast to some turn-of-the-century postcards that promoted the islands with staged, posed, and de-contemporized Natives[47]—as a way of promoting a nostalgic, primitive past—this picture is a snapshot of real surfers enjoying a real swell in Hilo Bay.

Although fewer people surfed in the late 1800s than in centuries prior and after, he'e nalu was neither extinct, nor even nearly extinct, as often purported.[48] He'e nalu was witnessed by visitors, written about in newspapers, captured in photos, and performed by chiefs and chiefesses (like the Kalaniana'ole brothers and Ka'iulani) and commoners around the island chain during this time.

Twentieth-Century Surfing in Brief

Surfing gained more popularity at the turn of the twentieth century with Native Hawaiian surfers like George Freeth, the Kahanamoku brothers, and many others. The sport found its greatest popularity in densely populated, ocean-based communities. During this time Hawaiian surfers increasingly rode Honolulu waves and gained global attention as a burgeoning tourist industry witnessed their exploits in Waikīkī. As Hawaiian surfing surged, American visitors such as promoter Alexander Hume Ford and author Jack London became increasingly drawn to it. Although Ford and London did seek to promote surfing and tourism to other haole visitors, they have been erroneously credited with restoring surfing in general at the time. In reality,

Hilo Bay surfing in the 1890s. (Courtesy of Bishop Museum)

the two were merely boosters—promoters who saw the economic potential of marketing the sport and Waikīkī to other tourists. Rather than being innovators, Ford and London in fact learned to surf from an already established cohort of Hawaiian surfers in 1907. By that time surfing's resurgence was well under way, led by Hawaiians who had formed the Hui Nalu club in 1905. In London's own writings he extolled at least one of these Hawaiian surfers as "brown mercury." He recognized them as experts who not only excelled in the waves, but who also inspired visitors like Ford and himself to learn.[49] These "brown mercuries," then, kindled the boom in heʻe nalu at the turn of the century. Ironically, or perhaps tellingly, after Hui Nalu surfers taught Ford and London to surf, Ford established an exclusive whites-only surf club called the Outrigger Canoe Club. In reaction, Hawaiian surfers, also great in number and surfing skill, challenged these racist haole in the Waikīkī surf—as I explain in chapter 3. It was from that group of Hawaiians that the first twentieth-century surfing legends and icons—like Duke Kahanamoku and the Waikīkī Beachboys—were born.

Even after Duke and the Beachboys introduced surfing to much of the outside world in the twentieth century, they continued to thrive as surfers in Hawaiian waves. Thus they did not "die off," as some surf films and histories subtly suggest. Whereas the Beachboys made surfing popular with haole visitors throughout the twentieth century, it was Kahanamoku who introduced the sport to the East Coast of the United States and to Australia while en route to the Olympic Games and other global events. On one of his many overseas trips in 1915, Duke gave a swimming exhibition at Manly Beach, Australia. Then, after making his own board from a native Australian sugar pine tree, he amazed spectators with heʻe nalu. Ben Marcus explains that at this particular event Duke "single-handedly put Australia on a path to superpower status in the surfing world."[50] Later, between 1922 and 1929, while pursuing an acting career in Hollywood, Kahanamoku regularly surfed in southern California, inspiring others to take up the sport. In many surf history narratives, Hawaiians disappear shortly after Duke brought surfing to Australia and America—as seen in films like *Riding Giants*. In this story, haole surfers not only inherited the Hawaiian art of kings from an "extinct" culture and people, but go on to dominate it. In truth, Hawaiian surfers thrived in their own right, and surfing remained a common practice for many Kānaka Maoli throughout the twentieth century. Kahanamoku himself lived until 1968 and remained, until his death, a surfer who roused others, including Hawaiians, to move the art further. In Waikīkī the Hawaiian surfing scene remained strong during the prewar years and regained momentum shortly after World War II. In the mid-1900s Mākaha continued to be a hotspot for surfers, a place where Beachboys like Rabbit Kekai and Mākaha residents such as Buffalo Keaulana received accolades in both free and competitive surfing. As Rabbit has explained, several Hawaiian surfers, including many from Waikīkī, often rode North Shore waves at places like Pau Malū, Pipeline, and even Waimea Bay in the 1940s.[51] While Hawaiian surfers have been erroneously and unjustly relegated to third-rate status under Australian and Californian superpowers, in reality they continued to lead twentieth-century surfing into the modern surfing era.

In the late 1950s and early 1960s Hawaiian surfers rode the dangerous North Shore surf alongside legendary Californians like Greg Noll. However, in a key scene in *Riding Giants* Noll and his California cohort are depicted as discovering the North Shore in 1957. In this version, after plowing their way through rugged canefields, Noll and his gang reach a clearing on a bluff and pause. Looking on in amazement, they behold the "seven-mile miracle" (a phrase commonly used by surfers to describe the North Shore), a scene of one perfect surf spot after another. Life on the North Shore for these exploring Americans was reminiscent of eighteenth-century imaginations of Pacific places—where men enjoyed a Rousseau-like, carefree, noble-savage existence of sleeping under the stars and surviving on fish, papayas, and surf. And similar to eighteenth- and nineteenth-century European explorers, these California surfers had "discovered" nothing but a place already occupied by ocean experts. While fewer Hawaiians surfed on the North Shore in the late 1950s and early 1960s than in centuries prior, there were still those who did, most memorably Kealoha Kaio.

Mentioned only briefly—and with his name mispronounced—in *Riding Giants*, Kealoha Kaio charged the same treacherous waves that Noll and his friends did in the early 1960s. A resident of the North Shore community of Lāʻie, Kealoha was an expert surfer and fisherman. Possessing an astounding lack of fear in large waves, he comfortably rode ominous breaks like Third Reef Pipeline without the modern conveniences of ocean rescue crafts or surfing leashes.[52] According to his son, Kealoha Kaio Jr., Kealoha Sr. was known to catch the biggest waves deeper, and in the more critical part of the wave, than anyone else at that time.[53] And among local circles Kealoha is recognized as the first to make a hard bottom-turn at Waimea Bay.[54] Although Kealoha is rarely documented by surfing media, many surfers of his generation hold him in high regard. For example, Greg Noll described him as one of the best

Kealoha Kaio. (Photo
by Parry Medeiros)

Kealoha Kaio surfing at Pau Malū, or Sunset Beach, in the early 1960s. Notice
young Eddie Aikau paddling up the face of the wave. (Courtesy of Kealoha Kaio Jr.)

big-wave surfers from that time, a man with a true Hawaiian heart, and a dear friend.[55] Professional surfers of the 1970s like Ben Aipa, Eddie Aikau, Clyde Aikau, and others were inspired by Kealoha's fearless approach to big waves, particularly the way he drew hard turns in large waves, which was advanced maneuvering for his time. But Kealoha was not the only overlooked Hawaiian standout of the early 1960s; other Hawaiian surfers like Samson Po'omaihealani, Kimo Hollinger, Tiger Espere, and others challenged the "big stuff" in an era dedicated mostly to Noll.

By the mid-1960s some Hawaiian surfers were finally recognized for their prowess through the Duke Kahanamoku Invitational Surfing Championships. In 1966 two young Hawaiian standouts, Eddie Aikau and Ben Aipa, were finally invited to compete in the most esteemed surfing competition of that time. In its formative years, and despite being named after a Hawaiian surfing icon, the Duke Invitational had a reputation for being an event primarily for Californian and local-haole surfers. In the first five events (1965–1969), an

Eddie Aikau surfing at Waimea Bay in 1973. (Photo by Parry Medeiros)

average of only two Native Hawaiian surfers out of twenty-four competitors was invited to compete in the Duke Invitational—and even those limited Hawaiian seats were difficult for locals to procure. For example, Aipa and Aikau were invited to participate in the event only after resorting to some creative solicitation. While the inaugural Duke event was running, they paddled out and surfed alongside the competitors to display their surfing talent and, they hoped, gain an invitation the following year.[56] In addition to this exhibition, Duke Kahanamoku apparently helped their cause by encouraging contest directors to invite the young Hawaiians in 1966.[57] In that event Aikau and Aipa skillfully advanced their way through to the finals. As the single-day competition in large and challenging Pau Malū (Sunset) surf came to a close, Aikau earned sixth place and Aipa seventh. At the awards banquet for that event the two young Hawaiians received accolades from their lifelong hero. As Stuart Coleman explains, when Duke Kahanamoku handed Aikau and Aipa their trophies, the experience was more like a torch-passing ceremony, from one generation of Hawaiians to the next. "Duke shook hands with the young man, looked into his eyes and smiled, and then he put his arm around Eddie's shoulders, embracing him like a son. Two proud Hawaiians, bridging different generations. Duke represented the glory of their past and Eddie the hope of their future."[58]

Both Aikau and Aipa not only inherited mana (spiritual power) from the father of modern-day surfing in 1966, but also opened the door for other local surfers to enter the professional surfing arena on Oʻahu's North Shore. Over the years, more and more Hawaiian surfers were invited to compete in the Duke Invitational. For example, by 1970 Native Hawaiian surfers occupied four out of twenty-four slots, and by 1977 it was up to eight. From the mid-1970s until the final year of competition in 1984, an average of eight Native Hawaiians were invited to compete, but they ranked atop the list of winners, with Hawaiian surfers winning eight of the last twelve events. Furthermore, as Jared Medeiros found, after Hawaiian families like the Aikaus and Medeiroses helped to organize and run the competition, the Duke Invitational seemed to take on a more local flair.[59] For example, opening and closing ceremonies included Hawaiian cultural protocol and prayers. Meanwhile, many Hawaiian surfers gained more popularity through their participation in the event.

Although Eddie Aikau was not classified as a top short-board "ripper," other Hawaiian surfers in the 1970s spearheaded this new method of wave riding—an approach where surfers rip and shred waves with quick, powerful

Larry Bertlemann making a hard backside bottom-turn at Ala Moana bowls. (Courtesy of Merkel/A-frame Photo).

turns on short (five- to seven-foot) fiberglass surfboards. Despite the fact that recent films such as the 2008 *Bustin' Down the Door* erroneously suggest that radical short-board surfing was an Australian innovation, modern surfing often evolved at the hands of Hawaiian surfers like Larry Bertlemann, Michael Ho, Dane Kealoha, Buttons Kaluhiokalani, and others.[60] Commenting on the origins of short-board surfing and the myths promoted in *Bustin' Down the Door,* surfer Bryan Amona explained, "Don't believe all the hype about the Australians and *Bustin' Down the Door* and any of this stuff. He [Larry Bertlemann] was doing this, along with Buttons and Mark Liddell, way before anybody else was."[61] Old video footage of surfing in the mid-1970s corroborates Amona's claim. For example, in the film *Stylemasters* Buttons, Bertlemann, and Kealoha are shown performing the most innovative and before-their-time surfing in the mid-1970s, even in comparison to their non-Hawaiian peers. While the Australians and South Africans surf well in this film, Hawaiian surfers execute more radical and progressive maneuvers—as seen with Buttons' 360-degree frontside and backside turns.

Throughout the history of North Shore surfing competitions, Hawaiian surfers have earned more victories than most other surfers in professional surfing events. For example, in the 1970s Hawaiian surfers won six of ten Duke Invitational events. In the 1970s and 1980s Hawaiians like Clyde Aikau (Eddie's younger brother), Larry Bertlemann, Michael Ho, Barry Kanaiaupuni, Dane Kealoha, and others were among the world's top competitors—especially on the North Shore. As the Duke Invitational faded and the Triple Crown of Surfing (started in 1983) became the leading professional competitive series on the North Shore—and arguably the most prestigious title to win—Hawaiian surfers dominated there as well. For example, Hawaiian surfer Sunny Garcia has earned more Triple Crown titles than any other surfer in its history, holding a total of six (twice the number of any other competitor). Hawaiian surfers have also bested most others in professional long-boarding venues, and in the more recently developed standup paddle-surfing divisions.

While Hawaiian men thrived in the twentieth-century surf, women had a less conspicuous presence in ka po'ina nalu at that time. Women's surfing

Dane Kealoha leading the way in short-board surfing with this late-1970s cutback. (Courtesy of Merkel/A-frame Photo)

has, in more recent years, experienced an explosion in popularity, but in the nineteenth and twentieth centuries ka po'ina nalu was a predominantly male space. The diminishing role of women in the surf at the time began in the nineteenth century, when Hawaiian women's roles were redefined by Western notions of gender. As new gender roles defined "proper" behavior for women, they simultaneously helped alter the gender demographics in the surf zone. According to such rules, initiated by missionaries who helped determine acceptable behavior for "ladies," Hawaiian women should not box, wrestle, or surf.[62] This is not to say that all women complied. Although many defied the new social norms, such categories nonetheless modified the gender balance in ka po'ina nalu, at least prior to the 1970s. While some women belonged to Waikīkī surf clubs like the Hui Nalu, in most of the twentieth century there were far fewer women surfing than men—especially in comparison to surfing mo'olelo. Nevertheless, by the end of the 1900s women's surfing experienced a resurgence of its own.

Especially since the turn of the twenty-first century, the popularity of women's surfing has exploded. While various women helped revive women's surfing in the twentieth century, Rell Sunn's contribution to its current popularity has been particularly noteworthy. Living on the predominantly Hawaiian west side of O'ahu, Rell Sunn grew up surfing Mākaha with famous surfers like Buffalo Keaulana. Sunn has had a profound impact on professional women's surfing since 1975; she also helped establish the Women's Professional Surfing Association in 1979. Furthermore, her love of surfing and of her Hawaiian community is reflected in the Rell Sunn Menehune Surf Contest held annually at Mākaha Beach since 1976. In 1977 Rell Sunn became the first female lifeguard to work for the City and County of Honolulu. Later, as she battled cancer for fifteen years, she became a representative and ambassador of hope, aloha, surfing, and Hawaiian culture to surfers and women throughout the world.

Conflicting Identities

Although surf-history narratives have often ignored the prominent role of Hawaiian surfers in the twentieth century, its authors have ironically looked to Hawaiian culture in establishing a surfer identity. Since the mid-1900s haole surfers have looked to Hawai'i as a surfing Mecca, a cradle for the creation of their new identities as surfers. In the process they incorporated homemade versions of Hawaiian culture in developing a surfing culture and identity of their own. In the 1950s and 1960s this haole surf culture drew from images of Hawai'i not only to distinguish itself from mainstream American society, but also to rebel against it. This is reflected in the 1959 film *Gidget,* in which Gidget's Malibu surfer friends find an escape from postwar American society through surfing. As they experience the primal pleasure of riding waves, these youth are also corrupted by their affiliation with a carefree Hawaiian culture. For example, they play the 'ukulele (although they do not pronounce the word properly), hang out in a grass shack on the beach, wear Hawaiian "tiki" carvings as pendants, and are led by a jobless, carefree surfer called The Kahuna. Though Gidget enjoys her new surfer friends, her family views their lackadaisical "native" lifestyle as lazy rabble rousing. Through films and other images like this, we find that haole surf culture has continued to grow an identity based on invented notions of what it means to be Hawaiian.[63] While much of this American surf-culture identity used Hollywood films like *Gidget* as their Hawaiian cultural informants, it is clear that they were not interested in authenticity. Umbrella drinks, tiki torches, and images of Hawaiian waves seemed "tradition" enough.

This Hawaiian-imagined American surf culture has led to several troubling assumptions. First, it assumes that haole surfers adopted the former Hawaiian pastime of surfing from negligent or dead Natives (negligent in the sense that Hawaiians supposedly abandoned their cultural practice of he'e nalu, and dead in that Natives were relegated to the past and deemed a dying race). Such assumptions helped establish haole surfers as inheritors of the sport at the expense of living Hawaiian surfers. For many haole surfers, especially in the 1960s and 1970s (and even today, as seen in films like *Riding Giants*), contemporary Hawaiian surfers were anachronisms.[64] Living Hawaiian surfers complicated the haole surfer identity because they challenged the assumption that haole inherited he'e nalu from an ancient and extinct people. Whether consciously or subconsciously, haole surfers have often turned a blind eye to contemporary Native surfers. Perhaps this explains why so few Hawaiian surfers were invited to participate in the first Duke Invitational competitions. How confusing it must have been for haole surfers to watch Hawaiians dominate surfing events for decades. In failing to recognize modern Hawaiians, their ideology also encouraged feelings of entitlement to Hawaiian waves, which has led to many confrontations with Hawaiian surfers. This perspective also promotes the myth that haole surfers have solely directed surfing's modern evolutions. While modern Hawaiian surfers in the second half of the twentieth century have been deemphasized to clear the way for heroes of a stolen birthright, Hawaiian innovation has also been relegated to the grave, a place where all Hawaiians are presumed and expected to dwell. However, this formula is frustrated by the fact that living Hawaiian surfers have continued not only to exist, but to thrive in the surf. As "cool" as the haole surf-culture identity may have been in American beach towns, it has not gone over well in Hawaiian waves.

Much of the tension between haole and Hawaiian surfers over the last fifty years has resulted from clashing surfer identities. While haole surfers clung to their own brand of surfing culture, one that borrowed from invented notions of Hawaiian heritage, Hawaiian surfers held tightly to their versions of surfing tradition. From a Hawaiian perspective, surfing's historic roots ran two thousand years deep. Thus feelings of pride in and protection of ka po'ina nalu, especially in the politically tumultuous twentieth century, swelled in Hawaiian surfers. Hence, when haole surfers staked a claim to Hawaiian waves, culture, and he'e nalu, many Hawaiians were insulted and threatened. For haole surfers, Hawaiian reactions were extreme. Though at times they may have been, such reactions, when viewed in the context of history and in light of these conflicting identities, are better understood. Despite what surf-history narratives do to preserve this haole surfer identity in crisis, for many visiting surfers this narrative ultimately works against them—blinding them from seeing Hawaiian perspectives and thus inviting confrontation. The clash of these two surf cultures is critical to understanding tensions and frustrations in Hawaiian waves, especially in the latter half of the twentieth century.

Memory seems to serve surfing filmmakers and historians poorly. The idea that Hawaiian surfers were extinct in the 1800s and then replaced by generations of haole surfers in the absence of Hawaiians is perplexing. Additionally, given the constant and substantial participation (and often domination) of Hawaiian surfers in the waves for the last several centuries, this narrative is an obvious fairytale. And yet it has been regularly and vociferously replayed over the past few decades. Although surf histories have advocated the idea that he'e nalu was nurtured by adopted parents who kindly rescued the sport from negligent Hawaiian cultural practitioners, Hawaiians have remained active caregivers and innovators of the evolving practice called surfing.

CHAPTER 2

Colonial Violence
and Hawaiian Resistance

While an identity crisis has contributed to conflict on the North Shore over the last several decades, contemporary solutions to confrontation are stifled by the historian's inability to connect Hawaiian surfers to their past. The stories of the Hui Nalu, the Hui O He'e Nalu, and other Hawaiian surfers are interwoven with a larger story of conquest and occupation in Hawai'i. In order to understand Hawaiian surfers, we must analyze them in the context of their colonial history. These surf hui were born and shaped from the colonial violence that preceded them. Hawaiian surfers have also drawn from age-old historic colonial encounters to define themselves in the present. Unfortunately, most people today see violence in the surf as one-sided, where dehistoricized haole surfers play the role of random, innocent victims guilty only of the arbitrary crime of disrespect. However, to detach this colonial history from twentieth-century tensions in the surf is simply irresponsible.

In this chapter I contextualize twentieth-century Hawaiian resistance in the surf by chronicling a history of colonial violence in nineteenth-century Hawai'i. The written history of this period has matured over the last few years as more scholars have represented Hawaiians as agents in their own history. While such agency has uncovered stories of resistance and in some cases empowerment, we still cannot disregard the systematic oppression of Hawaiians in this story. Colonial violence and resistance are key themes in nineteenth-century Hawaiian history, and the relationship between the two is still tangible today. Although their identity has evolved, Hawaiian surfers have expressed an inherited version of nineteenth-century colonial resistance in the waves. This genealogy of resistance has survived, in my opinion, because of the unique nature of ka po'ina nalu (the surf zone). By reviewing this history from which many Hawaiian surfers have molded their concepts of resistance, we have a clearer picture of both haole and Hawaiian motives, violence, and protests.

Hawaiian History and the Dispossession of the Kānaka Maoli

The history of Hawaiian marginalization can be traced back to the earliest encounters with European voyagers. Although these late eighteenth-century voyagers did not actively pursue political conquest over the islands, nor directly displace Hawaiian hegemony there, the diseases they brought to Hawai'i killed off a large portion of the population and had a devastating impact on Hawaiian communities. This inevitably altered the political and cultural landscapes of Hawaiian society: because there were fewer chiefs, this contributed to political instability and disrupted social order.

Civil war had plagued the Hawaiian Islands by the close of the eighteenth century. With the aid of Western weapons obtained from explorers like Briton George Vancouver and American Simon Metcalf,[1] the tenacious Kamehameha had conquered the Hawaiian chain and united all of the islands under one mō'ī (or king) by 1810.[2] Such a conquest posed some challenges to Hawaiian leadership at the time. As Jonathan Osorio has pointed out, while Kamehameha created a new leadership that consolidated power around his administration, his "military supremacy suppressed the power of other Ali'i Nui, whose rivalry with one another had contributed so much to the competitiveness and vibrancy of Hawaiian society."[3] Despite such challenges, Kamehameha I ended civil war and introduced long-awaited peace in the islands. He also preserved Native rule for Hawaiians amid looming European colonial window shoppers. He maintained Hawaiian sovereignty by modernizing the Hawaiian military and creating political alliances with competing Western nations such as England, France, and the United States. While Kamehameha I preserved Native Hawaiian control over the islands and maintained rule through traditional Hawaiian religious, legal, and cultural systems, his successors instituted dramatic political and social changes after his death in 1819.

Shortly after his father's death, Kamehameha's heir, twenty-two-year-old ʻIolani Liholiho, was encouraged by his father's favorite wife, Kaʻahumanu, his mother, Keōpūolani, and others who advocated ʻainoa (free eating) to dismantle Hawaiʻi's legal and religious system known as the kapu. Previously, Hawaiʻi's kapu system had prevented the over-exploitation of items such as fish and other wildlife through seasonal hunting restrictions. The kapu system also provided a spiritual balance that was maintained through specific separations between the gods, aliʻi, and makaʻainana in Hawaiian society.[4] Shortly after Liholiho became king, he abandoned the ʻaikapu (sacred eating kapu) by eating with Kaʻahumanu and Keōpūolani at a public gathering. While this event thus rendered the kapu obsolete, Kekuaokalani, a nephew of Kamehameha I and staunch supporter of the old ways of the kapu, led an uprising against Liholiho and those who defiled the kapu. The king's suppression of this revolt marked the end of the kapu system in Hawaiʻi's government. After it was abandoned there was a brief void in Hawaiʻi's political system.[5]

Six months after the kapu had been dismantled, Calvinist missionaries from New England brought a new political ideology to Hawaiʻi. Needless to say, missionaries from the American Board of Commissioners for Foreign Missions (ABCFM) considered the timing of Hawaiʻi's political changes an act of God. Many Hawaiians eventually converted to their ultra-conservative brand of Christianity.[6] However, perhaps because Congregationalists and Presbyterians deemed many Hawaiian cultural traditions barbaric, savage, and sinful, Hawaiians did not initially welcome missionaries with open arms. Upon his first encounter with Native Hawaiians, Hiram Bingham, head of the Hawaiʻi mission, wrote, "The appearance of destitution, degradation, and barbarism, among the chattering, and almost naked savages, whose heads and feet, and much of their sunburnt swarthy skins, were bare, was appalling." He continued, "Some of our number, with gushing tears, turned away from the spectacle. Others, with firmer nerve, continued their gaze, but were ready to exclaim, 'can these be human beings!'"[7] Disgust for things Hawaiian seemed to be an ABCFM missionary trait—but for this particularly stern and somber Calvinist group, dance, leisure, and celebration of any sort were frowned upon. Among several other Hawaiian activities, the missionaries despised hula and heʻe nalu (surfing) because these were considered a waste of time and encouraged too much sexual activity.[8] More than a simple disdain for Hawaiian culture, Bingham also held prejudices against the Hawaiian character. Although Hawaiians developed highly advanced aquaculture and agricultural systems that had sustained hundreds of thousands of Hawaiians for centuries, Bingham still described them as "too stupid and ignorant to farm lands and become self-providing."[9] Augmented by a deep-rooted sense of superiority and blatant racism, such religious conservatives saw Hawaiian social and cultural practices as inferior and heathenish.

However, not all haole in the nineteenth century shared Bingham's hostile view toward Hawaiians. Several whites labored in the Hawaiian kingdom to preserve and protect its grandeur. For example, Kamehameha I adopted John Young, later called 'Olohana, into both his administration and family (through marriage). Young lived most of his years in Hawai'i and eventually became a chief over the island of Hawai'i. Though he gained political prominence, his loyalties were to the kingdom and to Kamehameha in particular. Several other non-Hawaiians assimilated to the islands' culture and environment in nineteenth-century Hawai'i. Unfortunately, many of these have been labeled traitors to their white race—as seen, for example, with Walter Murray Gibson in the 1880s.[10]

Although missionaries were prohibited from assuming political positions in Hawai'i, they nonetheless wielded a great deal of influence in local government throughout the nineteenth century. Their involvement in Hawaiian politics was technically indirect in the 1820s and 1830s—limited to encouraging Hawaiian leaders to pass laws favorable to missionary interests—but their political advice worked to advance their objectives and place a wedge between the Hawaiian people and their leaders.[11] Such missionary influence in politics even led to animosity between the American missionaries and other haole in Hawai'i.[12]

In the 1840s several missionaries traded their religious trappings for political and economic prosperity. In 1842 missionary and physician Gerrit Judd abandoned proselytizing for an esteemed government position in Kauikeaouli's (King Kamehameha III's) administration. After becoming the king's head advisor and being confronted by mission officials for charging a patient for his medical services—while using mission-funded medical equipment—Judd resigned from his missionary duties and quickly stamped his personal agenda on Hawai'i's legislation.[13] Other missionaries climbed the Honolulu political and social ladder after the ABCFM mission was closed down in 1845. After that, several missionary families opted to remain in the islands to pursue political or economic careers. Those who stayed were converted to a new program, one inspired by people like Judd and motivated by a desire to make Hawai'i their home. In the late 1840s apostate and emeriti missionaries worked to remove Hawaiian legal stumbling blocks on their path to success. In the process, they not only achieved monetary and political gain, but also helped remove Native Hawaiians from their 'āina (land).

Land Struggles

According to several historians, Native Hawaiians were most notably marginalized after land became fee-simple and alienable property between the mid- and late 1800s. The Mahele (division of lands between 1848 and 1854) initiated this change in Hawai'i's land tenure system—where communal land ownership was replaced by a foreign system whereby individuals could own land. The Mahele eventually enabled foreigners to purchase land in Hawai'i. Although the Mahele marked the beginning of this shift in land tenure, subsequent laws (in the latter part of the 1900s) enabled and empowered haole speculators, investors, and entrepreneurs to take lands from Hawaiians at alarming rates.[14] Thus historians like Jonathan Osorio have deemed this process of Hawaiian alienation from their land as "the single most critical dismemberment of Hawaiian society."[15]

The Kuleana Act of 1850 allowed Hawaiians, commoners included, to own land. Although chiefs had control over specific territory and people were connected to particular areas or parcels of land, land ownership was essentially a foreign cultural concept. After 1850, the Hawaiian kingdom established a land commission to settle land claims made by Hawaiians. Here, Hawaiians living throughout the islands could secure land if they submitted claims to the government by 1854. Lands claimed by Hawaiians through the land commission are called kuleana lands. There were three types of kuleana land: the pā hale (residential), lo'i (taro-farming land), and kula (dry land parcels). The pā hale were generally 0.25 to 0.5 acre in size, while kula and lo'i varied (0.1 to 5 acres).[16] However, roughly 70 percent of Hawaiians did not submit claims to the commission, either because they were ill informed, they did not support the Mahele, they were discouraged by local chiefs, or they believed they could get land through alternative government tracks. Thus only 8,421 fee-simple land claims were awarded to common Hawaiians by the commission before the 1854 deadline.[17]

The Mahele eventually allowed foreigners who were not naturalized citizens to purchase, own, and sell Hawaiian land. With the population still in decline, a local sugar industry on the rise, and land now used for investment purposes, the newly alienable lands market was just the beginning of what would become a Hawaiian real estate nightmare—one that Hawai'i has yet to awaken from. The ongoing result has been wealth for some and increased homelessness for many Hawaiians.

However, in the initial years after the Mahele, most of the land was owned by the king, the Hawaiian kingdom, the chiefs, and the maka'āinana (common Hawaiians). King Kamehameha III (Kauikeaouli) designated large parcels of land for himself and for the kingdom. Over the years, much of the kingdom's government land (initially totaling over 1.5 million acres) and portions of the king's Crown land have been leased, sold, or stolen (or ceded) by both the federal and state governments, and this continues to be a topic of intense political debate. However, a great deal of the king's family lands was handed down until Kamehameha's last heir, Bernice Pauahi Bishop, placed 378,569 acres into a trust. The trust, governed by the Kamehameha Schools, has used proceeds from these lands to educate many Hawaiian children from preschool through high school and to give scholarships to college students of Hawaiian ancestry, among other things.[18]

Although insatiable investors, foreign advisors, and apostate missionaries may have manipulated the Mahele to their advantage, Kauikeaouli had good reason for endorsing it. On February 25, 1843, just a few years prior to the Mahele and right after Royal Navy commander Lord George Paulet threatened to level Honolulu with cannon fire, the king provisionally ceded Hawai'i to the British government. Great Britain justified its seizure of Hawai'i through a land dispute that ensued between British consul Richard Charlton and a Hawaiian chief. Fortunately for the Hawaiian kingdom, Admiral Richard Thomas of the British Admiralty restored the kingdom five months later, and July 31, 1843, was subsequently observed as Restoration Day in Hawai'i. Meanwhile, Hawaiian advisors and emissaries Timoteo Ha'alilio and William Richards traveled overseas to sign treaties with foreign powers to ensure Hawai'i's independence. Eventually, the Hawaiian kingdom secured treaties in which world powers recognized Hawai'i's independence and its status as a neutral country. In November Great Britain and France also signed treaties with Hawai'i, and consequently November 28 was recognized as Ka Lā Kū'oko'a, or Hawai'i's Independence Day. The king also proclaimed a new motto for Hawai'i: "Ua mau ke ea o ka 'āina i ka pono," or "The sovereignty of the land is perpetuated in righteousness."[19] In the 1840s the kingdom's administration seemed to have a clear objective, which was to preserve the sovereignty of the kingdom and prevent possible conquest by foreign powers. The Mahele was instituted during this period of securing political autonomy. While Hawaiians did not own their land in fee-simple terms in 1843, the Mahele was most likely seen by the king as a way to protect Hawaiian land from future seizure. Since foreigners recognized land ownership with Western-style land deeds, in the event of another foreign takeover Hawaiians would be more likely to maintain their rights to the 'āina as property owners.[20] This also helps to explain why the king deeded large portions of Hawai'i's land to the monarchs and to the kingdom during this time. In hindsight, this strategy had some validity. Although Crown and government lands have been methodically chipped away by state, federal, and business interests for over a century, Hawaiian land deeds often slowed or complicated the process of seizing Hawaiian lands and is still a source of political debate today.

According to some, the Mahele was not the final blow that dislocated Hawaiians from their land. Keanu Sai contends that more Hawaiians received land grants than we currently believe, often through an alternative process where land was gifted to, or purchased by, Hawaiians who appealed to the government after missing the deadline for kuleana grants.[21] These grants or purchases took place through the minister of the interior and have historically flown under the radar of historians.[22] Conducting research on the history of land at Kahana Valley in the Ko'olauloa district of O'ahu, Robert Stauffer uncovered an important finding in the personal files of former Kahana owner Mary E. Foster. He found that subsequent laws, like the 1874 Nonjudicial Mortgage Act and the Bayonet Constitution of 1887, were more likely the culprits in the systematic displacement of Hawaiians from their land than was the Mahele. While the Mahele allowed families to claim and secure property, these subsequent laws enabled foreigners to confiscate and claim kuleana lands from Native Hawaiian families.[23] Stauffer explains that the Nonjudicial Mortgage Act allowed lenders to foreclose on Hawaiian properties without having to involve the judicial system or even the family who owned the property.[24]

Since Hawaiian families had sustained themselves by growing kalo (taro), 'uala (sweet potatoes), mai'a (bananas), and other crops for centuries prior, this land alienation displaced Hawaiians from their place of residence and greatly hindered their ability to survive on subsistence farming. By the 1870s and 1880s several Hawaiian families were marginalized and excluded from their 'āina for the establishment of a real estate market and a haole-run sugar industry. Stauffer also argues that the biggest fault with the Mahele is that it made lands alienable. Alienable lands allowed foreign investors and speculators to buy, take, and sell land, and it also helped fuel the proliferation of haole-owned plantations in the late 1800s. Once the sweet commodity of sugar filled foreign businesses with profits, haole elites (missionary descendants included) became increasingly sour toward the Hawaiian kingdom.

Overthrow

Sugar became a lucrative business for several American plantation owners in Hawai'i after the 1850s and 1860s. There were three key events that fueled this industry. First, the Mahele and subsequent land laws enabled wealthy foreigners to purchase large plantations. Second, the California Gold Rush created a great demand for Hawaiian sugar in the United States. Third, during the American Civil War the North placed an embargo on the South and Hawai'i became a new source of sugar for many Americans.[25] The demand was so great that the United States allowed Hawaiian sugar into their country tariff free. While the sugar business in Hawai'i proved very lucrative for a predominantly American, and predominantly missionary-descended, group, disparities in wealth between the Hawaiian people and the haole population multiplied. As Native Hawaiians continued to die from foreign-introduced diseases, plantation owners turned to China, Japan, Portugal, the Philippines, and elsewhere to recruit laborers. But as the Civil War in America subsided and the United States threatened to revoke its tax-free relationship with island sugar companies, annexation became the touted solution to the haole business community's dilemma.

February 1874 was a politically pivotal month in Hawai'i. In 1873 the sugar planters wanted the king to sign a treaty that would allow Hawaiian sugar to continue entering the United States tax free. Although many Hawaiians were opposed to it, the Reciprocity Treaty reemerged in February 1874 as an important platform for debate.[26] On February 4 King William Lunalilo died of tuberculosis at age thirty-nine. Since he had not designated an heir to the throne, the next monarch was selected by election in the Hawaiian legislature. Two Hawaiian ali'i vied for the throne: Queen Emma Rooke, widow of Alexander Liholiho (King Kamehameha IV), and David Kalākaua, a high-ranking ali'i. Whereas Emma had aligned herself with the British, Kalākaua forged relationships with Americans and the sugar plantation owners in particular. Hoping to win over the pro-business voters, Kalākaua agreed to sign the Reciprocity Treaty if American businessmen would support him in the election. On February 12, 1874, Kalākaua won a majority of the vote and a year later signed the treaty.

Although the United States wanted control over certain parts of the island, namely Puʻuloa, or Pearl Harbor, the 1875 Reciprocity Treaty did not hand Hawaiian property over to it. Instead, the United States waived the 2 percent tax on Hawaiian sugar as long as the king did not "lease or otherwise dispose of or create any lien upon any port, harbor, or any other territory in his dominions, or grant any special privilege or rights of use therein, to any other power."[27] Although Hawaiʻi did not give Pearl Harbor to the United States at this time, the treaty weakened the kingdom as it undermined their relationships with other powerful nations—some historians have argued that up to this time, aligning themselves with various European nations had helped Hawaiians maintain their political sovereignty against U.S. encroachment.

In 1887 reciprocity came up for renewal, but this time the United States wanted more than the Hawaiians were willing to give: Pearl Harbor. Although the U.S. Navy first became interested in Pearl Harbor in 1843, they aggressively sought to possess it after 1874, when American naval commander J. M. Schofield deemed it a superior natural harbor, one that was "suitable for building proper establishments for sheltering the necessary supplies for a naval establishment such as magazines for ammunition, provisions, coal, spars, rigging, etc."[28] As America's Manifest Destiny became reality in the late 1800s, Hawaiʻi and Pearl Harbor became more appealing. So when the 1887 version of the Reciprocity Treaty was drafted, a new clause was added in which the United States would have exclusive rights to Pearl Harbor. To the dismay of his former American business supporters, Kalākaua rejected it. The king had other interests in mind.

Remembered as the Merrie Monarch, King Kalākaua now embarked on ambitious projects to restore Hawaiian culture and Hawaiian leadership. He appointed more Native Hawaiians to his cabinet and promoted the return of Hawaiian cultural practices—ones formerly condemned by Calvinist missionaries. He spearheaded the revival of Hawaiian music, dance (hula), history, and other cultural practices. He also built a new palace called ʻIolani, erected a large statue of King Kamehameha in the heart of Honolulu, and filled his buildings with expensive European furnishings.[29] Although most Hawaiians celebrated this agenda, the foreign community in Hawaiʻi was threatened by his objectives and quickly deemed him corrupt and inept—in no small part because he had refused the U.S. attempt to take over Pearl Harbor.[30]

Shortly after Kalākaua rejected the 1887 Reciprocity Treaty, American missionary descendants turned businessmen and their friends formed a secret organization made up of 405 members. Called the Hawaiian League, this group held confidential meetings in which they debated how best to undermine the Hawaiian monarchy. While some, like Lorrin Thurston and William Kinney, wanted to overthrow the Native monarchy and make Hawaiʻi a territory of the United States, other members wanted new cabinet members and a revised constitution that would favor the haole business community.[31] After they gained the support of the Honolulu Rifles, a haole military unit of the king, they drafted a new and secret constitution—one that they committed to memory rather than paper.[32] Six days later, a group of them forced King Kalākaua to sign their constitution under threat of gunfire. Later coined the Bayonet Constitution, it deprived the king of his executive powers and forced him to surrender much of his authority to them. Article 31 of the new constitution specified that executive power no longer belonged to the king, but jointly to him and his cabinet.[33.] Since cabinet positions were then filled by members of the Hawaiian League, the king essentially became subject to them. While the Bayonet Constitution undermined the king's executive power, "for haole, it meant not only an enhanced representation in the legislature and control of the executive, it also retrieved their ability to define the nation and membership in it."[34] The new constitution not only limited Kalākaua's authority, but also stated that only landowners in Hawaiʻi could vote. With the Nonjudicial Mortgage Act already in place, haole speculators had both political and financial motives for taking Hawaiians' land. Furthermore, while the constitution of 1864 protected Crown lands as "inviolable," the Bayonet Constitution rendered them vulnerable, paving the way for future misuse of Hawaiian land.[35]

Frightened by these aggressive political changes, several Hawaiians organized a political group to combat the 1887 Bayonet Constitution. The Hui Kālaiʻāina was formed at the newspaper offices of Daniel Lyons shortly after the Bayonet Constitution was imposed. Noenoe Silva explains how the Hui Kālaiʻāina worked tirelessly to try and overturn that constitution, restore voting rights to Hawaiians, and preserve the Hawaiian monarchy.[36] Their most effective forms of protest were petitions and mass community meetings. While gaining support throughout the island chain, they petitioned King Kalākaua's sister and successor, Queen Liliʻuokalani, to draft and promulgate a new constitution. The Hui Kālaiʻāina not only represented a majority of the Hawaiian voice, but spoke for Hawaiian desires to return executive authority to the queen. But the new legislature had no intention of resigning their new seats in government. Securing their positions, they denied Hawaiian requests for a constitutional convention. Despite these setbacks, the Hui Kālai'āina teamed up with a local labor union, forming the National Reform Party, and helped elect several candidates in the 1890 elections. Though they were unsuccessful at overturning the Bayonet Constitution, the Hui Kālai'āina secured influence in the legislature and helped pass laws favorable to Hawaiians through their own elected officials.[37]

As the Hui Kālai'āina organized protests, petitions, and political mergers, Robert Kalanihiapo Wilcox took more aggressive action to overturn the Bayonet Constitution. Applying overseas military academy training and while dressed in his Italian officer's uniform, Wilcox launched armed rebellions against the Hawaiian League in 1888 and 1889. Although Wilcox temporarily occupied Hawai'i's government building on July 30, 1889, with his army of 150 Hawaiian, European, and Chinese soldiers, the U.S. military–supported Reform Government eventually suppressed the revolutionaries and the Bayonet Constitution remained intact. The fact that Hawaiian jurors refused to convict Wilcox for his assault on the government reflected a general Hawaiian disdain for the bayonet-run government. Although protests against this constitution continued, Kalākaua did not live to see it revoked. While seeking medical assistance in California, Kalākaua died on January 20, 1891. According to his sister and heir to the throne, Lili'uokalani, the Bayonet Constitution was the ultimate cause of Kalākaua's death.

When Lydia Kamaka'eha Lili'uokalani assumed the throne in 1891, she was determined to restore power and authority to the monarchy. At the top of her agenda was heeding Hui Kālai'āina petitions to write a new constitution. On January 14, 1893, she presented the final draft of her new constitution to her cabinet members. However, two haole ministers refused and quickly leaked her plans to the Hawaiian League. According to Chief Marshal of the Kingdom Charles Wilson, it was obvious that the queen's opponents had begun to plot against her after January 14. Her newly drafted constitution threatened the haole business community as it stated, "The Queen conducts her government for the common good, and not for the profit, honor, or private interests of any one man, family, or class of men among Her subjects."[38] It also designated who was in charge: "The Crown is hereby permanently confirmed to Her Majesty Lili'uokalani and to the heirs of her body lawfully begotten, and to their lawful descendants in a direct line."[39]

Three days after Queen Lili'uokalani attempted to promulgate this constitution, the haole opposition ransacked Hawai'i's government building, stationed armed U.S. Marines outside 'Iolani Palace, and tried to force Queen Lili'uokalani to surrender her kingdom to them—a cabal of haole businessmen and missionary descendants who previously had imposed the Bayonet Constitution and now called themselves the Committee of Safety. While many of the perpetrators were ideologically motivated, they all foresaw the trade benefits of overthrowing the Hawaiian kingdom. To them, the monarchy was a hindrance to their economic prosperity, and annexing Hawai'i to the United States seemed to be a good solution for them. Without clearance from Washington, D.C., U.S. minister John L. Stevens supported their coup by using armed U.S. Marines. Although the queen surrendered, she yielded her authority only temporarily and only to the U.S. government, not to the Committee of Safety. She firmly believed that the legitimate American government would correct the situation and quickly restore her to power. She was confident that the United States would honor Hawai'i's internationally recognized status as a sovereign and neutral nation, as international law stipulated. Shortly after the overthrow, President Grover Cleveland sent Senator James Blount to investigate the situation. After Blount recorded testimony from both Native Hawaiians and pro-annexationists, he condemned the actions undertaken by Stevens and the Committee of Safety and recommended that the queen be restored to her throne.[40] Initially, it seemed that the queen's faith in America was validated, but as time passed and power remained in the opposition's hands, she became increasingly disillusioned. Unfortunately for Lili'uokalani, the perpetrators refused Cleveland's counsel and barricaded themselves in Hawaiian government buildings. Unwilling to use force against other Americans, the president handed the issue over to the U.S. Congress. While politics lay stagnant in Washington, the provisional government daringly declared itself the "Republic of Hawai'i" on July 4, 1894.

The Hui Hawai'i Aloha 'Āina, a political organization established to advance Hawaiian rights in a time of haole conquest (similar to the Hui Kālai'āina), was shocked at the audacity of this self-established Republic. However, unlike the Hui Kālai'āina, this hui, along with its sister organization, the Hui Hawai'i Aloha 'Āina o Nā Wāhine (women's branch of the organization), was formed in direct response to the overthrow of Queen Lili'uokalani. Article 2 of their constitution explained that their objective was "to preserve and maintain, by all legal and peaceful means and measures, the independent autonomy of the islands of Hawai'i nei."[41] Composed of more than 17,000 members combined, the Hui Hawai'i Aloha 'Āina petitioned the United States to rectify the illegal actions of the Committee of Safety. Though they vehemently protested, these hui remained committed to peaceful methods of resistance, and by 1894 they were infuriated by stalled U.S. government efforts. Although the Hawaiians were admonished by Senator Blount not to take up arms but allow the government in Washington to resolve the issue, Native anxieties multiplied after each day passed with no change. By the close of 1894 unsettled Hawaiians plotted to restore the queen to power by force. The attempt began in October 1894, when John Bush and Joseph Nawahi smuggled guns to Hawai'i from San Francisco in hopes of using them for a revolution against the Republic. However, with the help of spies, Republic authorities discovered and imprisoned these Hawaiian royalists. Months later, on January 4, 1895, Sam Nowlein, Robert Wilcox, and Prince Jonah Kūhiō (who later became a popular Hui Nalu surfer) continued the operation by unloading the San Francisco arms near Lē'ahi, or Diamond Head. Though they distributed the guns and exchanged some gunfire with police forces, the operation was thwarted and the kingdom remained out of power and still in limbo.

Ironically, both haole and Hawaiians looked to the U.S. government to champion their respective causes. The haole-run Republic government believed the United States would annex Hawai'i, allow them to remain in power, and secure the future of sugar prosperity. The Hawaiians trusted that the United States would honor treaties signed previously and that President Cleveland would live up to his word and restore the queen. But in November 1896 the Republic's hope for annexation swelled when Republican William McKinley was elected president of the United States. Less than a year later, the pro-annexationists drafted a treaty of annexation and gave it to McKinley. As the treaty sat, waiting for ratification in the U.S. Senate, the Hui Kālai'aina and the Hui Aloha 'Āina (men's and women's) built up their own political arsenal. As Silva has shown, after holding mass meetings on the different islands throughout the Hawaiian chain, the three hui had acquired more than 38,000 signatures protesting annexation—the Hui Aloha 'Āina obtained more than 21,000 signatures on their petition and the Hui Kālai'aina 17,000 on theirs. Between December 1897 and February 1898 four Hawaiian delegates presented these petitions to the U.S. Senate. Upon their arrival, the delegates were informed that the treaty of annexation would most likely be ratified, considering that it needed only sixty votes, and fifty-eight senators already supported it. But after the Hawaiian delegates presented the petitions, accompanied by resistant yet eloquent voices of protest, the treaty was rejected, as only forty-six senators voted in support. To the Hawaiian hui this was a huge victory, one that not only closed the door on annexation but opened another to the possibility of restoring the kingdom.

But Hawaiian celebrations were cut short by the United States' involvement in the Spanish-American War and Congress' Newlands Resolution. Only weeks after the ecstatic delegates returned home, the United States became embroiled in a war against Spain. At the very outset of this war the United States aggressively moved to control Guam and the Philippines, Spanish possessions in the Pacific. Under McKinley's new expansionist administration, Hawai'i was viewed as a port to both launch troops and house recuperating troops during their Pacific exploits. So on July 6, 1898, Congress hastily passed the joint Newlands Resolution to annex Hawai'i with a simple majority, rather than a two-thirds vote. However, as Kēhaulani Kauanui has explained, the joint resolution was for domestic policy making only, and according to U.S. law, a treaty was required for such an act. Thus this joint resolution vote in Congress broke U.S. foreign policy requirements.[42] Once again, the three Hawaiian political hui filed written protests against these illegal actions and boycotted the American flag-raising ceremony in Honolulu on August 12, 1898.[43] When the Hawaiian flag was lowered, Queen Lili'uokalani wrote in her journal, "May heaven look down on these missionaries and punish them for their deeds."[44]

In the decades following annexation, and despite victories in some areas, many Hawaiians were steadily marginalized in their own society. Although a small group of elected Hawaiian leaders advocated Hawaiian rights in the Territorial government (1900–1959), this oligarchy was primarily run by U.S.-appointed politicians and business elites from Hawai'i's "Big 5" companies—many of whom were blatantly racist.[45] While Territory leaders focused their attention on accommodating the U.S. military in Hawai'i, growing sugar profits, and expanding tourism, they continued to exploit land and resources at the expense of Hawaiians.[46] With a history of such unfavorable policies toward Hawaiians, the morale of many Hawaiian communities deteriorated.[47]

In 1993, one hundred years after Queen Lili'uokalani's overthrow, President William J. Clinton signed into law the Apology Resolution. In it, the United States officially apologized for the overthrow of the Hawaiian kingdom. As scholars and activists alike have more closely analyzed the illegal nature of annexation since the 1990s, some have argued that the term "annexation" is a misnomer. In his PhD dissertation, Keanu Sai argues that without a treaty of annexation, annexation never took place. Instead, Hawai'i can be classified as a Military Occupied Territory. And thus, he continues, Hawaiian sovereignty theoretically remains intact. He then outlines the process whereby Hawaiian sovereignty can be transferred back to Hawaiians.[48] However, since the 1990s other Hawaiian activist groups have fought against and within the colonial paradigm, seeking various forms of restitution, autonomy, and sovereignty. While activist groups often differ in their approaches, most emphasize a need for justice and restitution.

CHAPTER 3

Hui Nalu, Outrigger, and Waikīkī Beachboys

In the decade following the annexation, heʻe nalu surged among Hawaiians, especially in the community of Waikīkī. Although some have attributed this rise in participation to a slow but growing tourist industry, I believe the popularity of surfing increased among Hawaiians because the surf offered escape and autonomy for Kānaka Maoli in an unsettling time. While a number of Native Hawaiian surfers flocked to the waves on a regular basis in the early 1900s, there was also a burgeoning community of haole who learned to surf from Hawaiians during this period. Shortly after being taught heʻe nalu, some of them joined Alexander Hume Ford's exclusive beach club to promote surfing among its whites-only members. Several of Honolulu's new political elite joined the Outrigger Canoe Club, many of whom had led the coup against Queen Liliʻuokalani just a few years prior. Like the Hui O Heʻe Nalu in the 1970s, Native Hawaiian Waikīkī surfers earlier in the twentieth century were threatened by haole encroachment in ka poʻina nalu (the surf zone). As the segregated surf club grew, the Hui Nalu directed their attention to preserving Hawaiian control in the surf, keeping it from Outrigger elites in Waikīkī. Pro-annexationist surfers and Native Hawaiians went head-to-head in the water and actively fought over this Hawaiian realm. Through these conflicts Hawaiian surfers maintained control and their social standing in the waves, and helped preserve the ocean as a Hawaiian domain. Although they maintained historical continuity with their past, Hawaiian identities in the surf continued to be shaped and redefined through their conflicts with Outrigger surfers in the waves.

The Hui Nalu had many distinguished Hawaiians in their ranks. While founder Duke Kahanamoku is at the pinnacle of the surfing world, Jonah Kūhiō Kalanianaʻole was a well-known aliʻi and Hui Nalu surfer in the early 1900s. Prince Kūhiō is a critical and underanalyzed character in Hawaiian history. Arrested in 1895 for attempting to restore his aunt, Queen Liliʻuokalani, to the throne, Prince Kūhiō ardently fought to preserve and restore the Hawaiian kingdom, which he was expected to one day rule. Several months after the Hawaiian Organic Act of 1900 was passed—it restored more voting rights and leadership opportunities to Hawaiians—Prince Kūhiō came out of hiding and resurrected his political career. Among his many accomplishments as Hawaiʻi's representative to U.S. Congress and aliʻi to the Hawaiian people, Kūhiō is best known for returning two hundred thousand acres of Hawaiian lands to Native Hawaiians through his Hawaiian Homes Commission bill. His story not only highlights the spirit of Hui Nalu surfers as advocates for the Hawaiian people during this time, but also represents the kinds of resistant identities spawned from the Waikīkī surf zone, or poʻina nalu.

Edward Kaleleihealani "Dudie" Miller, another Hui Nalu surfer, established a profitable concession business on the beach in Waikīkī in 1915. Although he employed other Hui Nalu surfers to give surfing lessons to tourists, the Waikīkī Beachboys were more than surf instructors. They were glorified as tour guides, musicians, and local celebrities. They were ladies' men, especially in the eyes of wealthy American tourists, during a time when American miscegenation laws prohibited men of color from marrying white women. Between 1915 and 1941, Waikīkī Beachboys regularly and publicly disregarded and redefined colonial prescriptions on how Hawaiian men should behave in the Territory. In contrast to other scholarly assessments of the Beachboys, I argue that these men were empowered in the Hawaiian surf zone—enough to defeat and defy colonial notions of what it meant to be a Hawaiian man.

Hui Nalu versus Outrigger

Among those who frequented the Waikīkī waves in the murky wake of the overthrow was Queen Liliʻuokalani's niece and designated heir to the throne, Princess Victoria Kaʻiulani.[1] The princess surfed most frequently between 1895 and 1899, while living in her two-story ʻĀinahau home in a grove of hau and niu trees on the beach at Waikīkī.[2] Kaʻiulani made time to surf during a very busy and stressful period of her life. Although she had attended a boarding school in England in the early 1890s, after her aunt was deposed in the 1893 coup she promptly traveled to Washington, D.C., to plead with Congress to restore the Hawaiian monarchy. She continued to carry out various diplomatic missions over the remaining six years of her life in hopes of restoring the Native Hawaiian monarchy.[3] In spite of all this, and amid all this travel, she still made time to surf in Waikīkī on traditional-style surfboards.[4] According to William A. Cottrell, a Hui Nalu surfer of Waikīkī, the princess was an expert surfer.[5] The fact that she surfed during a time when many Hawaiian women were discouraged from doing so highlights her character. But she wasn't the only Hawaiian to grace the waves of Waikīkī in the wake of the annexation.

According to Cottrell, Hawaiian surfers of the Hui Nalu, such as the Kahanamoku brothers, the Kaupikos, the Keaweamahis, and many others, were responsible for the rising popularity of the sport between 1903 and 1908.[6] Although some Hawaiians like George Freeth and Duke Kahanamoku gained more fame than others, lesser-known Hui Nalu surfers were also active and avid athletes who took great pride and pleasure in their tradition of heʻe nalu.[7] In the early 1900s, as David Stannard has pointed out, sports clubs (like the Hui Nalu), teams, and youth hui were popular throughout Honolulu.[8] Playing a variety of sports, from barefoot football to boxing, club rivalries were intense, competitive, and exciting. But when a whites-only club made up of annexationist families and other racist haole entered the local competitive arena, emotions, stakes, and Hawaiian sentiments ran high. As the Outrigger defined itself along racial lines, and as the traditionally Hawaiian competitive sport was performed on an unconquered Native domain, this rivalry was vastly different from that of local sports leagues. Ka poʻina nalu became an intense zone where Hawaiians, including politically astute and elite ones, clashed with haole on a battleground over more than simply a Hawaiian sport, but their physical and cultural domain.

The Outrigger Canoe Club was formed in 1908 by a former Chicago newscaster, Alexander Hume Ford. Shortly after he arrived in Honolulu in 1907, Ford immediately took an interest in Hawaiian aquatic sports.[9] He was described as an "eccentric promoter" who also had been a successful playwright—according to Joe Stickney, he worked with Mark Twain on a New York production of *Tom Sawyer*. He was also a bachelor, a salesman, a writer, a magazine editor, and a "man of energy and imagination."[10] After he moved into a grass shack that adjoined the old Seaside Hotel in Waikīkī, Ford learned

to surf on canoes and surfboards from accomplished Hawaiian surfers/
watermen. After describing how amusing and out of place Ford looked in
his full-body bathing suit, one local Waikīkī surfer, Judge Steiner, reminisced
about his first encounter with Ford.

> We were out surfing in a canoe and we saw this fellow standing on the
> beach. . . . We asked him if he wanted a ride . . . and he said yes. . . . There
> were very few tourists here then. If one came on the beach he was a spotted
> man. The idea was to take a stranger and put him up in the front seat of the
> canoe, take him right through the surf, and when you go through—when
> the bow went through the wave, and it dropped, why, it's a little discourag-
> ing for the front passenger. We thought that would fix this fellow up. Well,
> he was kind of game.[11]

After learning to stand on a surfboard, Ford then promoted the sport
among other haole residents and visitors. In *Mid-Pacific,* a magazine Ford
created to promote tourism in the islands, he chronicled the Hawaiian
pastime of surfing and proclaimed that "the white man could learn all the
secrets of the Hawaiian [surfer]."[12] While many eventually heeded Ford's
call, famous American author Jack London was one of the first to take up
the challenge. Shortly after he arrived in the islands while on a tour on board
his sailboat the *Snark,* London took notes on Hawaiian surf riding. While he
lay sunburned on his bed after his first try in 1907, London wrote, "I joined
some little Kanaka boys. . . . I watched them, and tried to do everything
that they did, and failed utterly."[13] Calling one particular Native Hawaiian
surfer "brown mercury," London marveled at George Freeth. "I saw him on
the back of it [a wave], standing upright with his board, carelessly poised, a
young god bronzed with sunburn. We went through the back of the wave
which he rode. Ford called to him. He turned an air spring from his wave,
rescued his board from its maw, paddled over to us, and joined Ford in
showing me things."[14]

Months after taking to these lessons, Ford founded the Outrigger Canoe
Club to promote healthy outdoor Hawaiian sports and activities among haole
in Hawai'i. In 1908 Ford leased an acre and a half of Waikīkī Beach (next to
the Moana Hotel) from the Queen Emma Estate trustees. After moving two
grass houses onto the property, from either the Seaside Hotel or the Honolulu
Zoo, he established the club. Ford felt that it was necessary to preserve beach
access for surfers—since the Moana Hotel and other private land owners

limited public beach access. By 1910 the Outrigger had built a new two-story bathhouse and locker room with enough space to accommodate a hundred members. Months later they doubled the size of the facility and built an additional bathhouse for women. In these formative years they purchased canoes, built canoe sheds, and made surfboard racks to hold hundreds of boards. Membership was restricted to whites who could pay an annual membership fee of five dollars. As Ford stated in a 1911 article, it was a club "for the haole (or white person)."[15] Although the Hawaiian Queen Emma Estate trustees agreed to lease this property to Ford for the purpose of "preserving surfing on boards and in Hawaiian outrigger canoes," Ford's club discriminated against actual Hawaiians who engaged in these pastimes.[16]

In the beginning Ford claimed to have organized the Outrigger Canoe Club to preserve surfing for the "small boy of limited means," but as it grew the club quickly became a racially segregated organization for the elite haole in Hawai'i, including those who had ousted Hawai'i's queen only a decade earlier. Membership in this whites-only surf club grew to twelve hundred in 1915, and the names of several Honolulu politicians and businessmen appeared on their roster. In a 1909 article Ford boasted that among the surf riders in his club were "Judges of the Supreme Court in Hawaii with their wives and daughters, ex-Governors and their families, and the greater portion of the prominent business men."[17] In 1910 a former president of the Republic of Hawai'i, Sanford B. Dole, was elected president of the Outrigger.[18] Other leading annexationists became members of and leaders in this club, such as Lorrin A. Thurston and J. P. Cooke.[19] Though several of the Outrigger's members despised the Hawaiian monarchs and had been active participants in the coup that had ousted the queen in 1893, they nevertheless learned the Hawaiian pastime of he'e nalu in the early 1900s as members of Ford's club.[20] Purporting now to be inheritors of traditions they participated in condemning, elite haole were caught in a paradox of negation and appropriation, a paradox that Houston Wood has called the kama'āina anti-conquest.[21]

Wood explains that while the early missionary sentiment toward Hawaiian culture was one of revulsion, haole of the late nineteenth century saw themselves as caretakers of what they believed to be Hawaiian culture. Kama'āina, a word that originally meant "Native-born," became a term by which they (who were either island-born or simply "Hawaiian at heart") referred to themselves. Not only had this name "obscured both their origins and the devastating effects their presence was having on the Native-born," but it supercharged many haole to adopt, adapt, and preserve Hawaiian ways for an "inferior" and "dying Native race."[22] Thus many haole learned the hula and surfing, and wrote Hawaiian history. They also adorned their homes and hotels with Native arts and crafts. Despite such affinity for Native "things," the Hawaiian person was still a marginal and detestable character in their eyes. Wood discusses this disparity. "Kamaʻaina added Hawaiian tools and artifacts to the décor of their now frequently much larger houses. Hawaiian servants were often employed in these houses, to dust and polish Kanaka Maoli creations few Hawaiians themselves now used or owned. These various tools and artifacts served as memorials to the Native traditions the kamaʻaina were industriously displacing."[23] The adoption of Hawaiian customs like surfing was a way in which haole memorialized a living Hawaiian culture and community. On the other hand, it was also a way of "mystifying Euro-American responsibility for the violent changes associated with that past."[24] But for real Hawaiians like Native Waikīkī surfers, these discordant appropriations were simply colonial conquest.

While the Outrigger built beachfront facilities and surfboards and began boasting of their supremacy over Hawaiians in Waikīkī waves, Hawaiian surfers of the Hui Nalu were again feeling challenged by haole colonial jostling and racism.[25] Although loosely organized originally in 1905, the Hui Nalu club was officially formed under a tree in Waikīkī in 1911 for the purpose of preserving heʻe nalu from an exploitative haole constituency. [26] Considered a rival to the Outrigger, Hui Nalu was "one composed almost exclusively of Hawaiians or part-Hawaiians."[27] Speaking of Outrigger and Hui Nalu relations, one Hui Nalu member recalled, "Back in the old days, they were not too friendly. The Moana Gang [Hui Nalu] stuck together by themselves. They would not mix with the old Outrigger gang."[28] Many Hawaiians who gravitated to the Hui Nalu resented the prejudice displayed by Outrigger members. William A. "Knute" Cottrell explained that he, along with Duke Kahanamoku, Kenneth Winter, Edward Kaleleihealani "Dudie" Miller, and other Hawaiians created the Hui Nalu after being "disgusted" by offensive remarks made by Outrigger members.[29]

Unlike the Outrigger, the Hui Nalu did not lease a portion of Waikīkī or have a facility of its own; instead, its members regularly met under the hau tree on the grounds of the Moana Hotel—not far from Kaʻiulani's ʻĀinahau gardens. Club members paid an annual fee of one dollar per year, and because the club needed money, they became exceptional at fundraising. The Hui Nalu used Moana Hotel locker rooms as their bathhouse. Here, black hooks were reserved for Hui Nalu surfers to hang their clothes and towels. They also had uniforms and club colors. Like the Hui O Heʻe Nalu of the 1970s, Hui Nalu surfers wore black swimsuits, but the Hui O Heʻe Nalu printed red and yellow stripes on their black shorts, whereas Hui Nalu surfers wore black shorts and black tank tops with a gold or yellow stripe around the waistline, like a wide belt.[30] The Hui Nalu prided itself in heʻe nalu with its uniforms and club song.

> We love you,
> Hui Nalu,
> Our club
> of the ocean waves.
>
> And we shall
> Never cease to
> Love our royal colors brave.
>
> Firm friendship
> Will entwine you
> ʼRound our hearts
> Where ere we go.
>
> We shanʼt forget
> The fellows
> Who adore
> And love you so.
>
> [Four strokes on the ukulele, "C" chord]
>
> (Chorus)
> Where and when
> Ocean waves
> Are afore you,
> Our fellows are sure to be.
>
> Where the big rollers burst,
> And the surf is the worst,
> Weʼll be there
> To yell with glee.

With our surfboards,
We always are ready
To leap in the deep blue sea.

Our royal black and gold
In victory will unfold.

Always on top,
Hui Nalu.[31]

Although Hui Nalu membership consisted primarily of Hawaiian men, some women surfed in Waikīkī with the Hui Nalu in the early decades of the 1900s. While women surfers dominate the historical accounts of ancient wave riders, their roles in twentieth-century waves were less prominent. Some women, like my grandmother, Abigail Kaheokalani Cutter, surfed in Waikīkī with Hui Nalu surfers, but fewer Hawaiian women surfed than before—perhaps because at that time they were expected to avoid "unladylike" activities, surfing included. This is not to suggest that they all adhered to such social expectations; in fact, women's involvement in the Hui Nalu suggests otherwise. However, early members were mostly men, often brothers from large families, like the Kahanamokus.

As Duke Kahanamoku's surfing and swimming skills became world renowned, the Hui Nalu also increased in popularity, particularly among Native Hawaiians. Born eight years before annexation, in 1890, Duke Paoa Kahanamoku, a descendant of Hawaiian royalty, was an expert surfer and swimmer by his early teens.[32] At the turn of the century Duke had already mastered the waves near his family's home in Kālia, Waikīkī. By 1912 he was the world's greatest surfer and fastest swimmer.[33] Between 1912 and 1922 Duke won a total of six Olympic medals (three gold, two silver, and one bronze) and broke several world swimming records.[34] But his first love was surfing, and he was unparalleled in wave riding. Still known as the father of modern-day surfing, Duke made history by mastering the largest and longest waves in Waikīkī; he also set a new record for the longest ride ever on a massive Waikīkī wave (from outside Castles to the beach in front of the Moana Hotel)—a mile-long ride. He out-surfed all of his opponents in Waikīkī and pushed surfing skills and techniques to new heights. He invented new surfboard designs, created new maneuvers, and introduced surfing to various beaches around the world (including the East Coast of the United States and

Australia). While Duke helped form the Hui Nalu, he was also their brightest competitor in its rivalry with the Outrigger over the ocean and its surf.

In their battles with the Outrigger in ocean-based sporting events, the Native Hawaiian watermen of Hui Nalu proved to be formidable opponents against haole annexationists. Although most people recognized Hawaiian surfers like Freeth and Kahanamoku as the greatest surfers in Waikīkī during this time, in 1911 Ford made bold public claims that Outrigger surfers surpassed the Hawaiians on surfboards and surfing canoes.[35] Many local surfers took offense at Ford's boasting. However, haole surfers did win many Waikīkī surf competitions that were hosted by and for Outrigger club members. In an effort to promote his club, his events, and surfing for tourists and other haole, Ford was able to attract crowds of up to seven hundred tourists to these Outrigger surfing contests. In a 1909 article he bragged that a fourteen-year-old "white boy" won the Christmas surfing championships with a headstand maneuver. After holding surfing fairs and exhibitions for American battleships and cruisers, Ford said that "the white man and boy are doing much in Hawai'i to develop the art of surf-riding. Games and feats never dreamed of

Hui Nalu Club. (Courtesy of Harry Robello and Grady Timmons)

by the Native are being tried."[36] Though the early events were primarily for Outrigger members only, this eventually changed.[37]

As more Hawaiian surfers began competing against Outrigger surfers in Waikīkī ocean events, a rivalry was born, one that Tom Blake called "intense."[38] As Hawaiian surfers pursued victory over haole surfers, Ford taunted them: "Once again the Native Hawaiians are seeking to wrest the laurels from the white men and boys."[39] By 1918 Hui Nalu and Outrigger surfers were directly competing against each other in surfing and canoe-racing events.[40] Native Hawaiian surfers and annexationists went head-to-head in the Waikīkī surf. One observer wrote that the Hui Nalu surfers were the "favorites in the senior events, as their club has among its members most of the oldest and cleverest riders on the beach."[41] Although some called it a friendly rivalry, it was in reality a tense arena where Native Hawaiians and elite haole contended with each other over a Native Hawaiian domain.[42] Ben Finney, a contemporary scholar, explained, "A certain ethnic pride, however, lay at the heart of their competition: haoles vied with Hawaiians in ancient water sports which were considered to be the domain of the latter."[43] In the end, the Hawaiian surfers were victorious. "In this way, the Hawaiians eventually regained their place on the beach."[44]

These Hawaiian surfers claimed their dominance over ka po'ina nalu in more than just surfing contests. During this time it became apparent, as John Lind has recalled, that Hui Nalu surfers like John Kaupiko and Duke

Waikīkī surfing, sometime between 1915 and 1925. (Courtesy of Bishop Museum)

Kahanamoku "controlled Waikiki." Lind continues, "There was a pecking order, like chiefs of old. . . . Everyone did what they said."[45] Hui Nalu surfers were often seen as intimidating to haole, especially as these Hawaiians stood up for their rights in the ocean. Most Hui Nalu surfers are remembered as physically fit and strong, and several had reputations for being extremely tough—like George "Tough Bill" Keaweamahi, who could open a beer bottle with his thumb, and "Ox" and "Steamboat," who were remembered for their size and strength.[46] Although physical battles between Hui Nalu and Outrigger are less frequently discussed today, some historians like Grady Timmons have recorded that fistfights between Hawaiian surfers and haole in Waikīkī during this time were common.[47]

Because of their success, Hui Nalu members remained atop the social ladder in the Hawaiian surf. Allan "Turkey" Love remembered Hui Nalu surfers regulating the lineup in Waikīkī. For the most part the Hui Nalu prohibited young kids (under age nine or ten) from venturing out into the larger surf. Turkey remembered being told to stay near the Waikīkī pier for his own safety. He always followed their instructions. "When I was a kid, they respected the older person. . . . We were afraid we'd get a kick or a slap in the face."[48] Hui Nalu surfers were at the top of a social hierarchy in this aquatic sphere, and members of the Hawaiian chiefly class took notice.

Prince Kūhiō and the Royal Hawaiian Surfers

In the early 1900s, as haole elite poured into the Outrigger Canoe Club, Hawaiian royalists and political elites joined the Hui Nalu. In my opinion, this suggests that the ocean was a significant space of contestation and that embedded in this rivalry was a core tension, a political one that carried over from the overthrow and annexation. While Queen Liliʻuokalani associated with Hui Nalu surfers, the club's most active aliʻi was Prince Jonah Kūhiō Kalanianaʻole.[49] As a nephew of the queen, hanai (adopted) son of King Kalākaua, cousin of Princess Kaʻiulani, and heir to the Hawaiian throne, Prince Kūhiō had been groomed for leadership from a young age. As was often customary for young aliʻi, in his teenage years Kūhiō attended boarding school overseas—in both California and England. While studying in California, he and his brothers David and Edward Kawananakoa took time from their studies to go surfing in Santa Cruz. The first recorded individuals to surf the cold waves of California (and in the United States, for that matter), these Hawaiian surfers found solace even in waves far from home.[50]

After completing his studies, he returned to a kingdom under siege. As the Bayonet Constitution took government control out of the hands of its monarchs, Prince Kūhiō watched his future as king slip away. However, he did not sit idly by. As did the Hui Aloha 'Āina and Hui Kalai'āina, Kūhiō protested the illegal overthrow and worked to topple the Republic established in 1894. Shortly thereafter, Kūhiō, while hunting on the island of Moloka'i, plotted with his long-time friend John Wise to retake the kingdom by force. Their plan was to smuggle two thousand rifles, two Gatling guns, and one hundred mercenaries from the Pacific Northwest to Hawai'i. Once they obtained these provisions, they would commandeer two interisland steamers, recruit a thousand men from the outer islands, and return to O'ahu to storm Honolulu's government buildings. At gunpoint, they would force the restoration of the Hawaiian kingdom.[51] Although the plan was well thought out and they received three hundred thousand dollars in pledges from other royalists, his aunt, Queen Lili'uokalani, rejected this initial plan. She believed that President Grover Cleveland would uphold his promise to restore her as queen. She was also advised by Senator James Blount not to rise up in armed rebellion, fearing that such actions would sway more congressmen to support an annexation treaty. But the queen's faith in the United States slowly faded, and she eventually turned a blind eye to plots to restore her to power. On January 3, 1893, Colonel Samuel Nowlein, the commanding officer of the kingdom's army, smuggled guns into Hawai'i from San Francisco. Although Kūhiō was part of this plan, he, along with his companions Wise and Wilcox, was thoroughly disappointed by the poor execution of it. Somehow, the opposition got wind of the plot and sent police to shut it down. After a brief exchange of gunfire between the police and Nowlein's men at a Kahala home on January 7, the operation was quickly suppressed. For his involvement in the scuffle Kūhiō was arrested and convicted of misprision of treason and served eight months in a Honolulu prison. The queen was also deposed and held in house arrest for five months. Although protests and petitions continued through 1898, after the so-called annexation a disgusted Kūhiō fled Hawai'i to live in Europe and South Africa for the next two years with his new bride, Kahanu. In 1901 the couple returned to Honolulu—perhaps because of changes in Hawaiian Territory laws and politics.

To the disgust of haole elites in Hawai'i, many Native Hawaiians regained their voting rights after the U.S. Congress passed the Hawaiian Organic Act in 1900.[52] With more Hawaiians voting, Hawaiian-run parties and Native candidates won the majority of elections in 1900. The Organic Act split

Hawaiian politics into three main bodies: a single delegate to U.S. Congress voted in by the people; a Territorial legislature made up of two houses, with legislators voted in by the people; and a governor appointed by the president of the United States. In 1900 the Hawaiian-dominated Home Rule Party won nine of thirteen seats in the Territorial Senate and fourteen of twenty-nine seats in the Territorial House of Representatives. The Home Rule Party candidate and Hawaiian political activist Robert Kalanihiapo Wilcox also won the delegate seat to U.S. Congress. While in office, this predominantly Hawaiian-run party promoted bills that benefited Native Hawaiians. For example, they pushed for extended voting rights for Hawaiians and the pardoning of previously imprisoned Hawaiians, and they paved a way for the creation of a Hawaiian Homelands (designated lands for many landless Hawaiians). What infuriated haole elite even more was that Hawaiian legislators often conducted their meetings in Hawaiian instead of English.

In 1902 Prince Kūhiō was elected as Hawaiʻi's delegate to the U.S. Congress and remained for nearly twenty years. Although he was initially a member of the Home Rule Party, he was elected on the Republican Party ticket. Kūhiō's involvement in the Republican Party is, at the surface, perplexing, mainly because the party comprised men who had overthrown his kingdom, imprisoned him for attempting to restore it, and precipitated his two-year exile in Europe. But both Kūhiō and his strange bedfellows consciously used each other. The Republicans wanted representation in Congress, and they knew they needed a prominent Hawaiian to get voted in. And Kūhiō, born and bred to be a king, wanted to lead his people. But even more importantly, Kūhiō knew he could advocate laws that benefited Hawaiians in spite of, and often to the dismay of, his fellow Republicans. As a delegate and a Hawaiian royalist, Kūhiō pushed for Hawaiʻi's right to govern itself, despite its status as a U.S. territory. But among his many accomplishments as a delegate, Kūhiō is best remembered for the 1921 Hawaiian Homes Commissions Act, finally designating homestead land for Hawaiians.

Prince Kūhiō was more than a politician and advocate for Hawaiians in Washington; he was also an avid and lifelong surfer. In the early 1900s, while living in Waikīkī, he often rode a sixteen-foot koa surfboard. The board was so heavy that after surfing, he hoisted it onto his Waikīkī pier with pulleys instead of carrying it home after each use.[53] Although Kūhiō tolerated some of the Republican annexationists in his political work, he drew a hard line against racists in the Hawaiian surf. While details of his surf experiences are limited, judging from his quick and often harsh responses to white racism in Europe and the United States, we can surmise that he did not tolerate the Outrigger's racist policies and attitudes. For example, while sitting at a table in a Geneva café in 1900, three Germans complained because a "colored man" was being served. Kūhiō approached Count von Fursteinheim "and without a word, [he] delivered one of his famous uppercuts that knocked the Count out cold and sent him to the floor."[54] After returning to his seat, Kūhiō was confronted by two of Fursteinheim's friends, who challenged him to a duel. Kūhiō knocked them both out on the spot. On another occasion, a barber in Washington, D.C., refused to serve Congressman Kūhiō and called him a "nigger." Kūhiō grabbed the man by the collar and threw him out onto the street. Lori Kamae explains that Kūhiō never had difficulty getting a shave or haircut in Washington after that.[55]

While Kūhiō had a slippery relationship with haole elite in politics, his participation in the Hui Nalu during its early/tense years of rivalry with the Outrigger perhaps reveals his true allegiances. Kūhiō continued to surf until he died in 1922 at his Waikīkī home called Pualeilani. In the two decades before his death, and in the months when Congress was not in session, the prince regularly returned home to enjoy, among his favorite things, the Waikīkī surf.

Beachboys: Pushing Women and Boundaries

Starting in 1915, Hui Nalu surfers opened lucrative beach concession businesses in Waikīkī. Through them, the surfers found regular and profitable work and became known as Waikīkī Beachboys. The Moana Hotel provided Beachboy founder and captain "Dudie" Miller with a space on the beach and guests from their hotel. The Beachboys were lifeguards, bodyguards, instructors, entertainers, and tour guides for visitors in Waikīkī. For a relatively high price, they took customers out into their Waikīkī surf to ride waves on canoes and surfboards. Fred Paoa recalled making two dollars for a surfing lesson and one dollar per person for a canoe ride in the 1920s. He also remembered giving ʻukulele lessons and selling pineapple-shaped ʻukuleles to tourists for seven dollars and fifty cents.[56] Another Beachboy explained that "[you] could make as much as five dollars a day. Oh, boy, was that big money. . . . We go out and catch three waves. But we fill the boat up with as much as six paying customers. Six dollars."[57] The money went to Dudie Miller, who ran the business and owned the canoes, and each Beachboy got a cut.

By the end of the 1920s and into the early 1930s the Beachboy concession had evolved into a bigger business, one that catered to higher-paying customers. Some Beachboys became constant companions and tour guides for visiting families and made good money for it. As soon as these families stepped off their cruise ships they were assigned, or requested, a particular Beachboy, who not only took them into the ocean for surfing and canoe lessons, but also checked them into their hotels and took them to dancehalls, restaurants, shops, and elsewhere. The Beachboy could stay with this family as a personal guide from two weeks to as long as three months. Sometimes this meant babysitting wealthy children, a job most Beachboys did not enjoy very much. However, the less desirable jobs came with added benefits. For example, one tourist, whom the Beachboys called Honeyman, came every year and brought with him two Cadillacs: one for the family and one for the Beachboy to drive around Honeyman's son. Fred Paoa recalled taking a family "slumming" (bar hopping) in Chinatown in their limousine with a bunch of Beachboys.[58] He also explained how they took wealthy haole tourists to Hawaiian family luaus: "[*Chuckles*] We bring a gang of tourists. And then, they [Hawaiian families] have this big calabash, you know, in the old days, at the head where the birthday child is sitting with its grandmother or whatever. And everybody [tourists] throw a dollar, [or] five dollars. And everybody gets their dance after, hula dancing and singing. The tourists enjoy it."[59] Joe Akana remembered escorting the maharaja of Indore and his party of seventeen through the islands. "I could only take care of [him] and his wife. But I picked certain boys out of the Hui Nalu club to take care of his party."[60] While he made sure they were safe in the water and had plenty of time board surfing and canoe surfing, he also explained, "When the maharaja and maharani went shopping, I went along. When they went in a store, bought things, and went back to the car, I pay. I kept track of everything they spent. I made his interisland itinerary and things like that. They'd go to the different islands. I was the only guy who could ride the same automobile or ride the same elevator with them, the couple. The aide-de-camp and the secretary couldn't even ride the same elevator with them."[61]

Instead of charging these tourists for each event, Beachboys were usually given a lump sum at the end of the family's visit. Sometimes Beachboys would get parting gifts from tourists at the docks when they sent the families home. Louis Kahanamoku recalled, "Us boys would go down the ship. And we'd buy leis for them. . . . We come out of there, twenty, thirty, forty bucks by the time we got out, put [*chuckles*] leis on."[62] On rare occasions, some tourists would try to leave without paying the Beachboys for their services. When that happened, Kahanamoku recalled, "We gotta go down the boat to get our money, you know. Catch 'em before they leave or [*chuckles*] we throw 'em off the ship. You darned right, boy."[63]

Waikīkī Beachboys were revered not only because of their keen knowledge of surfing, canoeing, fishing, and the ocean in general, but because they added flair to their skills. The typical Waikīkī Beachboy was also a comedian who occasionally surfed in outlandish costumes or played practical jokes on visitors. As the tourist spotlight shone on them, they reveled in it. Whether surfing with a dog on a surfboard like Joseph "Scooter Boy" Kaopiki or riding a surfboard while seated on a beach chair and playing an 'ukulele like John "Hawkshaw" Paia, the Beachboy was a performer. Grady Timmons felt that Beachboy antics were more than merely comical, but often therapeutic. "The Beachboy provided the world with much needed comic relief (what characters! everyone said). They took anxious, overachieving executives and taught them how to relax. They took their children and taught them how to surf. They took women who were recently divorced and taught them how to laugh and love again."[64]

As they flaunted their surfing and social skills, they became local superstars who attracted more than just money. White girls and women flocked to the beach to learn to surf from the Hawaiian Beachboys. "In those days," recalled Louis Kahanamoku, "especially the haole wahines [women], they all went for the Beachboys."[65] The Beachboys were known for wooing various types of haole women—divorced, wealthy, showgirls, and daughters of wealthy visitors. Joe Akana said that parents would drop their daughters off with them and say, "Take them around Waikiki."[66] He also remembered showgirls like Carmen Joyce, Hazel Guerrero, and "Peaches" Jackson of the Danny O'Shea Troupe. When they came to Waikīkī in 1924 and 1926 they were not only shown a good time by the Beachboys, but ended up marrying a couple of them—Hiram Anahu married Hazel, Joe Akana's brother married Carmen, and Tony Guerrero married Peaches. Although most women saw the Beachboys as romantic surfers, several haole men considered them "a bunch of lazy male prostitutes who made their living off mainland divorcees."[67]

The Beachboys impressed the ladies in Waikīkī by surfing with them on the same waves. When teaching women to surf, the Beachboys preferred to ride tandem, or share the same surfboard. Often, they would lift women up on their shoulders and glide with them across the glassy, turquoise waves. Louis Kahanamoku explained that the Beachboys especially liked to surf with girls on their shoulders because tandem surfing invited exciting and intimate maneuvers.[68] While paddling back out for another wave, some Beachboys would ride up on haole girls' 'ōkole (behinds) as they lay face down on the front of the surfboard. Another Beachboy recalled teaching a client's daughter to surf. She was a "nice, cute girl, oh God. Nice figure and everything. And she liked me. We got along swell. We joked and we have fun surfing. After I get her on my shoulders and the wave dies off, I push—I grab her legs like that and throw her off in the water like that."[69]

Beachboys were also responsible for protecting their clients from the sun. If a tourist got sunburned under the watch of a Beachboy he got a mark against him.[70] Thus they would lomi (massage) women with oil on a regular basis to prevent sunburn. Joe Akana fondly remembered massaging one of his most memorable clients before taking her out for a tandem surf. "Jinks Falkenberg, she was a model of models. Nationwide. Jinks Falkenberg, oh, my. . . . She came looking for me. . . . I had to see that she didn't get burned. We did all that, you know, lomi, and took care of them as far as protection was concerned."[71]

In the evenings the Beachboys swept haole girls off their feet with music and sharp outfits. Most of them were gifted singers who played an array of instruments and wore tuxedos. Joe Akana said, "You never heard anybody sing until you hear the old Beachboys. They used to habituate the Moana pier on Sunday nights. And people used to wait for 'em, you know, on Sunday nights. The pier used to be so crowded, you'd think it would go down."[72] On other nights they congregated at the beach, the pier, or the stone wall to sing, dance hula, or play 'ukulele. Beachboy songs, like traditional Hawaiian music and dance, were often seen as seductive. The lyrics of one Beachboy song seems to prove this.

Beachboys canoe surfing in Waikīkī. (Courtesy of Bishop Museum)

Won't you
Come teach me
How to swim,
How to swim

I'd like
To swim with you.

I'd like
To have you hold me.

And that's all
You need to do.

Won't you
Come teach me
How to swim,
How to swim.

'Cause I don't want
To swim alone.[73]

For the second verse of this song they would substitute the lines "how to swim" with "how to surf," and in the third verse they sang "how to 'ami" (a hula move where the dancer rotates and sways at the hips), and the fourth verse was perhaps too explicit for Akana to say; instead, during the interview he burst into laughter and said, "Oh, God. Oh, gee."[74] Other songs, like the following, written by Hiram Anahu, were sung to girls at the end of summer vacation.

Hold me, dear
And follow me, dear,
And just let me
Be with you.

In your arms,
The world seems mine,
But I can't believe
It's true.

Don't say I'm wrong
If I go away.
You never gave me
Your heart.

When you say,
"I love you, dear"
And just let me be
With you.

After their musical gatherings on the pier, at the hotels, or on the beach ended, Beachboys were escorted home by seemingly mesmerized females. One Beachboy explained, "When the moon was up and the pier music was going on, oh, God. When the thing broke up at night, when it was all over, one Beachboy he went this way, one went this way with his wahine, and they all go in their different directions. [*Laughs*] Oh, chee. Boy."[75] As seen in the following story, where William "Ox" Keaulani took a girl out for a midnight tandem surf, some Beachboys even returned to the ocean for their moonlight after-parties.

> It was a warm summer night, and as they paddled out into the darkness on his tandem board, Ox surreptitiously slipped off his bathing suit. Out near the reef, they caught a small but well-formed wave. When Ox told the woman to stand up on the board, she stood up. Suddenly, she turned and saw him, framed in the moonlight. "Ox!" she screamed, a look of horror and excitement crossing her face. "It fell off!" he shouted, laughing above the roar of the surf. Then, putting his arms around her waist and pulling her close, they rode the wave toward shore.[76]

Through such interaction, Waikīkī Beachboys violated social rules of an American society governed by anti-miscegenation laws and threatened haole hegemony by conquering engendered, and privileged, property.[77] But this also highlights the fact that Hawaiians battled over property, especially ones that surfers had access to. In many ways sexual encounters with white women in the surf became a mark of identity for these men, because it meant they, too, could participate in engendered conquests. However, such Hawaiian conquests were rare and point to the unique nature of the surf and those Hawaiian men who reigned there. While the tourist industry promoted the islands as a "woman" to conquer, Hawaiian men were not marketed as sex objects in the way female hula dancers were. Thus these Hawaiian men were not playing into or accommodating tourist expectations of sexual conquest; rather, they were defying them.

A similar conflict over engendered properties can be seen through tension between Beachboys and haole military men in their Waikīkī boarder land. Prior to World War II, the Hui Nalu/Beachboys were involved in several brawls with haole soldiers in Waikīkī, many of whom were stationed at nearby Fort DeRussy.[78] One Hui Nalu surfer, Kālia resident, and Kahanamoku relative explained that drunken soldiers would often trample through the yards of Hawaiian families in Kālia, Waikīkī.

> You see in those days, in order for them [soldiers] to catch the rapid transit [short cut], they had to walk up Kālia Road, right? Kālia Road, come up 'Ena, to Kalakaua. . . . So on payday nights, after midnight when they're coming home drunk, you know, the usual thing. Yelling, or they'll come in the yard and go to sleep, things like that. You got to expect it. Got to get the MPs down there. That's the kind of trouble we had. It's the new batch of soldiers who come in to DeRussy that get this way.[79]

When drunken young soldiers caroused, trespassed, and chased Hawaiian girls, Hui Nalu surfers confronted them. According to Akana, fights between Waikīkī Hawaiian surfers and American servicemen were common because the soldiers were "cocky people" who "came down in our neighborhood and sometimes got nasty with our girls." He continued, "So we always protected our girls." [80] By most Hawaiian accounts, the soldiers were opponents quickly vanquished.[81]

In one such account, Hui Nalu surfers beat a group of German sailors from the cruise liner SS *Great Northern* in Waikīkī. Eighteen to twenty of the all-German crew marched down Kalakaua Avenue and provoked a fight with Hui Nalu surfers. Louis Kahanamoku said that once they approached the Hawaiians, "the head guy gave a whistle. He yells, 'Charge!' But we were ready. And we were fast. Bam. Bam. Bam. The whole thing happened so fast. Pretty soon the head guy gave another whistle, retreat!" [82] According to this account, the sailors fled because the Waikīkī surfers had overcome the Germans. Though Hui Nalu surfers were generally characterized as lovable and generous, they fearlessly and fiercely protected themselves and their beaches when necessary.

Tandem surfing at Waikīkī in the early 1900s. (Courtesy of Bishop Museum)

While Hawaiian surfers often justified these fights as acts of protection (over their Hawaiian women), their motives appear paradoxical—since many whites may have had the same motive. While such protective acts, on both sides, were mutual attempts to preserve engendered property, Hawaiian surfers still wanted both: to preserve their property and conquer someone else's—a position usually associated with colonial entities. By defining themselves as both protector and conqueror, Hawaiian men traversed a unique course, one that positioned them as entitled, even over colonial entitlements. Few Hawaiian men defined themselves in this way in the early 1900s. Poʻina nalu was indeed a unique place.

Crashing Boundaries and Academic Models

Hawaiian surfers, and the Beachboys in particular, indeed subverted colonial imaginations of Hawaiian men as passive and submissive, but their story also complicates scholarly arguments about media and tourist representations of Native Hawaiians. Over the last two decades, scholars like Haunani-Kay

Trask, Elizabeth Buck, Houston Wood, and Jane Desmond have rightfully criticized the commodification of Hawaiian culture and the sexualization of Hawaiian women by the tourist industry.[83] Most effectively, Trask has argued that the tourist industry uses sexualized images of Hawaiian women to promote Hawaiians as ideal natives for tourism. She said this was not only a ploy to entice visitors, but to "disparage Native resistance."[84]

In this picture, island women are sexually alluring to white men, and Native Hawaiian men are airbrushed out. Analyzing early twentieth-century images of Hawaiians on postcards and stereoscopes, Jane Desmond states that "Native Hawaiian males were rarely pictured, and when they were, almost never with Hawaiian women."[85] The reason for this, she concludes, was that the Hawaiian male disrupted the tourist industry's ideal native equation: Hawai'i = woman = sexual availability.[86] More recently, Ty Tengan has argued that Hawaiian men have been repeatedly emasculated through Euro-American media. Such representations helped to justify colonial dominance and maintain the idea that Hawai'i was a place of white male consumption—the U.S. military and the tourist industry being the primary utensils for this feast.[87] Although these views have some truth, the Waikīkī Beachboys do not fit this representation. Rather than emasculated and underrepresented, these Hawaiian surfers were popular, sexual, and active agents in a colonial history.

While some, like Desmond, have accurately noted that representations of Waikīkī Beachboys were uncharacteristic, few have explored the relationship between such imagery and the autonomy and empowerment of these Hawaiian surfers. Describing the Beachboys' image as "striking," Desmond rightly notes that unlike representations of other Hawaiian men, the Beachboys were pictured as "strong, competent, completely in control of the situation."[88] However, by simply suggesting that such representations reflected a tone of "celebratory primitivism," and because surfers were "at one with the forces of nature" in these portrayals, they were "akin to the hula girl" and became objects of tourist desires.[89] However, when analyzing the Waikīkī Beachboys from the vantage of ka po'ina nalu, we instead see empowered Hawaiians who broke free from colonial discourse and were actively engaged in pursuing their own interests. Far from being lifeless objects laid out for tourist consumption, Beachboys were pleasure seekers, romancers, athletes, watermen, and Hawaiians. When looking at their history, it is not difficult to see the Beachboys as empowered agents. In ka po'ina nalu, they defied tourist portrayals of Hawaiian men as passive, nearly invisible Natives. Rather than being exploited victims of tourism, the Beachboys defied rather than bolstered common stigmas. Instead of forcing them into a model that insists on the prevalence of colonial discourse over Hawaiians, I argue that there are examples, like the Beachboys, where Native peoples successfully forged their own identities in contrast to colonial categories.

Despite racist American laws and people, the Hawaiian Beachboys broke barriers. Though noted for their kindness and their attractiveness to women of various national and ethnic origins, they were also empowered, successful, and popular. They also worked to preserve their surfing culture, space, and Hawaiian identities. Instead of sexualized primitives of nature, the Beachboys were respected athletes of their aquatic domain. Rather than exploited laborers who commodified their own surfing culture, they operated their own businesses in the 1920s and 1930s as historical agents who made a decent living in Waikīkī, often at the expense of haole.

The Massie Affair and World War II

Although business for the Beachboys was at an all-time high in 1930 and 1931, things took a turn for the worse after 1932. As tourism grew, Hawaiian families were increasingly pushed off their Waikīkī land. As property values increased, taxes went up, and many Hawaiians were unable to keep pace with the rising costs. Hawai'i law at the time allowed speculators to pay the back taxes and confiscate these properties. This is how many haole took Hawaiian land in Waikīkī. Alan "Turkey" Love lamented such losses and explained that many of his friends were victims of this system. One of them was "Tough Bill" Keaweamahi (and family), who lost his home on Hobron Lane to the haole Magoon family, who claimed the property after paying the delinquent tax on it. Love explained, "Plenty Hawaiians lost . . . their land because of that law. . . . My uncle Joe, he lost his land too."[90]

Although land speculation harmed many Beachboy families, the Massie affair of 1931 and 1932 damaged the Beachboy business. In September 1931 Thalia Massie accused five local men (two Hawaiians, one Hawaiian-Chinese, and two Japanese) of raping her. In the trial, defense attorney William Heen proved that given the evidence and time frames of the accused, these men could not have raped Massie (later, the Pinkerton Report determined that she was not raped at all). The case ended in a hung jury. Shortly after the trial, Massie's husband, Tommie, her mother, Grace Fortescue, and two soldiers kidnapped and murdered one of the five men, Joe Kahahawai. Even after being caught red-handed with Kahahawai's body in the back of their car, Fortescue and her associates were found guilty only of manslaughter. Pressured by military and haole business elites, Governor Lawrence Judd reduced their sentences to a mere one-hour lecture in his office. Their white- ness, augmented by American racism, contributed to this unjust verdict. Despite the evidence, in the early 1930s haole spread rumors that Hawaiian men were sexual predators. As American racist discourses of black men as sexual predators were transposed onto Hawaiian men, the Waikīkī Beachboys became a target. While the affair itself exposed the horror of American racism and white insecurities about interracial relationships in Hawai'i, the racist media found a scapegoat in the Beachboys. Writing a commentary on the trial, actress Dorothy Mackaill pointed her finger at relationships between white women and Beachboys in Waikīkī. "The Beachboys . . . have had many romances with rich American women, who have gone to the islands as tour- ists. . . . These affairs have been invited by the white women visitors . . . [who] lie on the beach . . . in abbreviated bathing suits and permit the 'beach boys' to rub them with coconut oil so they will receive a good tan. . . . What can we expect of these people when they see Kanakas openly receiving the attentions of American white women?"[91] The Outrigger Canoe Club then stepped in to control the situation. In 1934 its board of directors, made up of members of Hawai'i's top business and political haole elite (then called the Big Five), were brought together by Outrigger president and annexation- ist Lorrin Thurston to address the Beachboy "problem." They hired William Mullahey—a Hawai'i-raised haole who had previously established a beach patrol and lifeguard service at Jones Beach in New York—to take over the Beachboy concessions and create a beach patrol near the Royal Hawaiian Hotel. Mullahey explained the reasons for this.

> The reason being that the Massie case, which was very much in the news and there were all sorts of rumors about Natives jumping out of the bushes, attacking school teachers, and a lot of rumors that were probably untrue but still were a concern to the beach. So Lorrin suggested that we establish one place to clear all beach activities and buy up all of the equipment that was then being used by a number of individual entrepreneurs on the beach who had canoes, surfboards, umbrellas, chairs and did lomi-lomi and gave swimming instructions and gave surfboard lessons and then took out canoe rides and so on. And in order to consolidate the entire beach front into one organized unit that could be responsible and that could allay any fears that there were about the beach boys' attacks on visitors.[92]

With five thousand dollars they bought all the equipment on the beach (umbrellas, canoes, chairs, etc.) from Kūhiō to the Halekulani (or the larger part of Waikīkī Beach). They even gobbled up Dudie Miller's Hui Nalu concessions. Then, Mullahey tightened his control over the business by micromanaging the operations. He created a central office, made a booklet that outlined guidelines and procedures for all the services offered—from swimming and surfboard lessons to how to massage tourists. Using the racist rhetoric from the Massie case and the members' whiteness to its advantage, the Outrigger colonized a Hawaiian industry and asserted itself over a Hawaiian domain.[93] Desperate and out of work, many Hawaiian Beachboys began working for Mullahey's beach patrol. Alan "Turkey" Love was one of them. He switched over, he said, because business was not good for the Beachboys in 1932 and 1933. Perhaps business was slow because of recent local events like the Massie affair, but the Great Depression was also crippling much of the world's economy. However, not all Hui Nalu members jumped to join Mullahey. While some tried to freelance, others simply left the beach. Perhaps working for the Outrigger was simply too much to bear. Although Hui Nalu and Outrigger members worked together for the first time, divisions between the Hawaiians and haole persisted. The most notable division hinged on pay. Several of the Hawaiian Beachboys complained that the Outrigger paid them very poorly.

During World War II Waikīkī was barricaded with barbed wire and the beaches shut down. Beachboy services were nonexistent during this time, and many Hawaiians left Waikīkī to find other work. Love explained that after the war was over only a small percentage returned. Although Waikīkī Hawaiian surfers were no longer center stage on the Waikīkī tourist scene during the war, some Hawaiians revived the Beachboy business after the war. In 1964 the Outrigger moved near Diamond Head and the Outrigger beach patrol was no more. With many of the old haole elite marginalized politically after the war by local Japanese, and the club increasingly criticized for its racist agendas, Outrigger influence diminished in the Waikīkī surf.[94] Some Hawaiians created new concessions during this time, such as Earl Akana's Hale Auaua Surfboards, among other freelancers. However, as the tourism boom gradually turned Waikīkī into a concrete jungle, the beaches became overcrowded with visitors, and the diverted streams changed the quality of the surf, the ocean seemed less like a sanctuary. While a younger generation of Hawaiian Beachboys still brought in money for surfing lessons, by the 1950s many Hawaiian surfers turned their attention toward other beaches, like Oʻahu's west side—at breaks like Mākaha, where young surfers like Buffalo Keaulana quickly climbed to legendary status. In the 1960s the North Shore became the next proving ground, a place where surfers like Kealoha Kaio dominated the largest surf ridden since ancient times.

Although the spark of the old Beachboy days seemed to fade in the latter part of the twentieth century, the Beachboys are still in Waikīkī today. Their rent to the Department of Land and Natural Resources has gone up a thousandfold, and the spotlight cast on them is not as bright as it used to be, but they are nonetheless very visible, usually busy, and often popular with the ladies. Today, while from the beach the Waikīkī surf zone looks chaotic, filled with myriad tourists and other beginning surfers, surprisingly there are still local and Hawaiian surfers who maintain their positions atop the social hierarchy in Waikīkī waves. While some things change, others remain the same.

The conflict between the Hui Nalu and Outrigger was a continuation of the political battle that had taken place on land a few years prior. But this battle had a different outcome. Because Outrigger annexationists were unable to snatch this Hawaiian space from the firm grip of Hui Nalu surfers in the early 1900s, Hawaiians continued to reign in ka poʻina nalu. Meanwhile, Hawaiian surfers simultaneously redefined colonial boundaries and themselves through their resistance. Because of their successes in the surf, the Hui Nalu-turned-Waikīkī Beachboys defined themselves in direct contrast to films, books, and other Hawaiʻi marketing paraphernalia. By the 1940s haole hegemonic authority in the Territory of Hawaiʻi insisted that Native men be submissive and nonresistant American subjects.[95] Although contemporary researchers like Noenoe Silva have more recently shown that Hawaiian resistance to American colonialism was much more pronounced and active than portrayed by twentieth-century historians, the reach of U.S. colonialism lengthened in the early 1900s. In spite of this, Hawaiian surfers defied colonial categories that insisted on Native passivity. In fact, they directly fought against those who authored such colonial discourse. In resisting haole elites, Hui Nalu surfers disregarded and subverted colonial boundaries placed upon Hawaiian men. But these Hawaiians were not merely fighting colonial discourses; rather, they were fighting for Hawaiian autonomy in the surf. In the next chapter, I explore further the historic implications of these imagined and colonial categories.

CHAPTER 4

Unmanning Hawaiians

Producing "Ideal Natives" via Tourism, Hollywood, and Historical Writings

Throughout most of the twentieth century, Hawai'i's tourism industry has over-promoted Hawai'i as a safe place for visitors to experience paradise. Unfortunately, they accomplished this by emphasizing docile and sexualized Native bodies. Most commonly, Hawai'i's tourism industry used sexualized images of island women to sell the islands. Over time, such tourist and Hollywood images (most commonly Native women as hula girls) became so popular that they still are synonymous with Hawai'i. These images were especially popular in the middle of the twentieth century, when American postwar politics heralded global decolonization and Hawai'i was incorporated as the fiftieth U.S. state.[1] During this time, popular imaginations of Hawai'i and the Pacific Islands were widely circulated by tourism advertisements, postcards, Hollywood movies, and even educational historical narratives. This feminized island image did more than simply denigrate individuals; it also confined the persona of Hawai'i in a gendered metaphoric trap, a fairy tale where the islands became a distressed woman in need of a nation in shining armor to rescue her from her savage past.[2] While Hawai'i's tourist-driven society constantly portrayed the islands with, and as, a sexualized woman in the twentieth century, the Hawaiian man was simultaneously rendered nearly invisible. Thus Hawaiian men rarely took center stage in tourist and

Hollywood productions. When they were portrayed, however, Hawaiian and other Polynesian men were usually shown as submissive, content, non-resistant Natives. Though frequently undetectable next to half-nude Native female bodies, Hawaiian men were nonetheless present in the movies, the pictures, and the books. Regularly held in contrast against the strong, assertive, and heroic haole characters, the Kanaka Maoli male was depicted as the polar opposite of the iconic American: subordinate and passive.

Hollywood films in the early 1950s and academic histories of a similar time helped to emasculate Hawaiian and Polynesian men. Defining the boundaries of Pacific Island men, the stereotypes generated in such representations produced a kind of discourse about Pacific Island men in general and cast them as inconsequential and nonthreatening Natives. Although I focus on specific films and histories as examples, they are representative of a larger discourse about Pacific Islanders in general. In other words, there is a shared language in various representational media that defined and labeled Pacific Islanders. These films and history books are a slice of that larger discourse.

In this chapter I will trace the development of the submissive and compliant Hawaiian male label to show that these emasculating portrayals not only defined the imagined boundaries of Hawaiian and Polynesian manhood prior to the 1970s, but also served to justify and validate colonialism—or more specifically, justify the overthrow of Hawai'i's sovereign kingdom and seize Native land in a so-called decolonizing era. Redefining Hawaiian male identities also undermined the sociopolitical significance and very existence of Native Hawaiian men, as they were rendered insignificant characters in productions about Hawai'i.

Twentieth-century Hawaiian surfers often battled these externally imposed definitions of Native men with direct and visible resistance. They rejected passivity and replaced presumed submission with obvious assertion. The dialectic between imposed notions of Native masculinity and the redefined Hawaiian sense of self shaped the identities of Hui Nalu surfers in profound ways. In this chapter I analyze early twentieth-century Euro-American characterizations of Polynesian men as compliant Natives to show the kinds of labels that Hawaiian surfers often undermined. I use the terms "Hawaiian" and "Polynesian" men interchangeably, because in the Hollywood and tourism imagery I analyze, they lump all Oceanic peoples together. Thus in films and other productions it was common for, say, a Hawaiian-speaking Native to perform a Tahitian dance while wearing a Samoan costume. But since I know the difference, it is difficult to call them only Hawaiian or Tahitian or Samoan. Though in reality each Oceanic society has its own distinctive culture and identity, for both producers and viewers of such films, they are, for the most part, all the same.

Eighteenth- and Nineteenth-Century Representations of Hawaiian Men

Western peoples have created romantic visions of the Pacific Islands for centuries. For the most part, scholars who have studied Euro-American representations of Hawaiians and Pacific Island peoples have been most interested in analyzing and interpreting depictions of Native women, since there is an abundant supply of visual and textual material that clearly supports claims that Hawaiian and Pacific Island women have been unnaturally objectified and eroticized for over two centuries. However, much remains to be said about related representations of Hawaiian and Pacific Island men. While women have been painted as objects of desire in the Euro-American fantasy about Polynesia from the earliest European ventures in the Pacific to the present, perceptions of island men have varied. In the late eighteenth century and throughout the nineteenth, Hawaiian men were seen as either noble or ignoble, but in the greater part of the twentieth century they were cast as insignificant, submissive, and nearly transparent.

From the earliest interactions with the Pacific Islands, Westerners categorized Polynesians with sexualized language. Captain James Cook, the most accomplished European explorer of the Pacific in the eighteenth century, hired artists and authors who objectified Pacific Islanders with sexualized depictions and descriptions. Analyzing the content of these materials, Margaret Jolly concludes that "many of these images are eroticized—beautiful women gazing at the artist and the viewer, the body draped but breasts revealed, or women bathing in the luminous pink light of William Hodges's painting Tahiti Revisited."[3] In such depictions, "Hawaiian and Tahitian women are constantly referred to as alluring: 'a beautifully proportioned shape, an irresistible smile, and eyes full of sweetness and sparkling with fire,' combined with a 'charming frankness.' "[4]

Eighteenth-century European explorers like Cook and Frenchman Louis-Antoine Bougainville depicted Tahitian women as exotic and ideal sexual partners. Analyzing journals from Cook and his sailors on board the *Discovery* and *Resolution,* Karina Kahananui Green concludes that they were in search of Rousseau's natural woman, one who would not "undermine men's potential . . . by refusing to be content with physical love and ensnaring them in the commitments of moral love."[5] In finding the epitome of what Rousseau only fanaticized about, these European men not only reveled in commitment-free, unrestrained sexual encounters with Tahitian girls, but also forever marked the island woman as "a lifeless stereotype, a mere male fantasy."[6] To European readers, Cook's depictions of Tahitian women confirmed that "the West had found an ideal mate" whose "mix of innocence and sin made for a woman-child who was eager, yet safe."[7]

But Pacific Island men were also a part of this Rousseau-envisioned landscape and were heavily represented, if not more so than women, in Cook's voyage accounts and illustrations. For his third and final Pacific voyage, Cook hired John Webber, a well-trained landscape artist and figure draftsman to "embark with me [Cook], for the express purpose of supplying the unavoidable imperfections of written accounts, by enabling us to preserve, and to bring home, such drawings of the most memorable scenes of our transactions."[8] Webber drew everything from landscapes and Native artifacts to historic events and Native portraits. While in Hawai'i, he made engravings and illustrations of both Hawaiian men and women. Although he drew portraits of women (as seen with *A Young Woman of the Sandwich Islands*) whom the voyagers said had "a sweetness and sensibility of look, which rendered them very engaging," he also drew many sketches of Hawaiian men.[9] Whether in canoes (as seen in *Tereoboo or Terreeoboo, King of Owhyhee, Bringing Presents to Captain Cook,* and *A Canoe of the Sandwich Islands, the Rowers Masked*), in group festivities and ceremonies (as seen in *An Offering Before Captain Cook, in the Sandwich Islands*), or singled out in portraits (like *A Man of the Sandwich Islands Dancing, A Man of the Sandwich Islands, with His Helmet,* and *A Man of the Sandwich Islands in a Mask*), images of Hawaiian men were important to both Cook and Webber.[10] They were not only essential to recording Cook's historic ventures in the islands, but also helped promote the islanders as noble yet savage occupants of paradise.

Though Cook's artists were instructed to capture realistic scenes from the voyages, the noble savage image was still purposely sketched into most of the artwork. Using particular drawings from Cook's voyages as examples, Bernard Smith explains this process. "It is important to realize that the so-called 'noble savage' mode of presentation was not a visual stereotype applied indiscriminately, a mis-perception of eighteenth-century European vision. It was, more often than not, the result of a conscious aesthetic decision to elevate where the artist felt that elevation was appropriate."[11] Although island men were later written out of the Euro-American Pacific fantasy, they were critical components of this noble savage aesthetic. While portrayed in their natural and "primitive" form, men, especially chiefs, were regularly sketched in poses, clothing, or styles that borrowed familiar noble imagery. Using the drawing *A Native of Otaheite in the Dress of his Country* by Sydney Parkinson to clarify this point, Smith shows that a Tahitian chief was represented as a Roman magistrate of the *Apollo Belvedere* and *adlocutio* statue types—he wore a toga and stood as if addressing the Roman Senate.[12] Depicting Hawaiian and Pacific Island men as noble leaders in a natural environment placed them in an awkward category, as noble and yet innocently childlike and inferior to Europeans.

Although such characterizations abounded, this imagery shifted after Cook was killed by Hawaiians in Kealakekua Bay in 1779. While sailing home for England after a long and arduous third voyage, the captain-less crew members wrote about and drew Hawaiian men as dangerous and violent. In the scuffle that led to Cook's death, a total of four European men died. However, in this melee, initially over a stolen dinghy, more than seventeen Hawaiians were shot and killed. Also, hours after the incident, Cook's men opened fire with cannons on groups of Hawaiians who stood on the shoreline of Kealakekua, killing many more. In various European accounts written after this event, Hawaiian men were depicted as aggressive savages who killed an innocent hero. Even Hawaiian women were illustrated as masculine—in build, in their preference for sports and other physical activities, and in their desire for self-gratification during sex.[13] In the aftermath of Cook's death, Europeans memorialized Cook as a noble gentleman who was killed protecting Hawaiians. In Webber's 1784 engraving, *The Death of Cook,* Cook is reaching out toward his men, calling upon them not to fire on the Hawaiians looming behind him with daggers. In reality, shortly before he was stabbed by a Hawaiian warrior with a European-purchased blade, Cook fired two shots from his own gun into the crowd of Hawaiians. The second shot killed a chief. The European accounts also under-emphasized how Hawaiians retaliated against Cook because he attempted to kidnap their king, Kalaniʻōpuʻu. Cook had hoped to keep King Kalaniʻōpuʻu as ransom for his stolen dinghy. As Cook dragged Kalaniʻōpuʻu toward his men on the beach, the king's warriors still hesitated before they killed Cook. Some have argued that Cook had sufficient time to escape the crowd, and that had Cook known how to swim he most likely would have survived.[14]

In the wake of Cook's travels, other Euro-American adventurers and missionaries came to Hawai'i and described Hawaiian men as uncivilized, savage, and useless. While early nineteenth-century Hawaiian men were most commonly represented through Euro-American descriptions of the courageous and often fierce Hawaiian monarch, King Kamehameha, ABCFM missionaries, who first arrived in 1820, viewed Hawaiian men as savages who needed to be tamed, civilized, and evangelized.[15] Although much of the missionary perception is similar to those of Cook's descriptions, theirs was essentially more condemnatory and debasing, as these missionaries saw Hawaiians as sinful and barbaric. Often categorizing them as lascivious, immoral, and ignorant, ABCFM missionaries particularly disliked many of Hawai'i's male leaders. This distaste was compounded and evidenced by the fact that every Hawaiian mō'ī (king) was, to varying degrees, leery of missionary influence in Hawaiian politics. Perhaps because of this, missionaries turned to high-ranking Hawaiian women as a way of advancing their objectives in early to mid-nineteenth-century Hawaiian society. Because women like Ka'ahumanu and Kīna'u provided missionaries with power and authority in Hawaiian politics, Hawaiian men seemed merely to stand in the missionaries' way. Hawaiian historian Jonathan Kamakawiwo'ole Osorio has explained that missionaries worked to "dismember" lāhui (the Hawaiian nation) by creating a wedge between the Hawaiian people and their chiefs.[16] By undermining the position and importance of Hawaiian kings, missionaries defined Hawaiian men as not only sinful, but also as incapable rulers. Other haole who wrote about Hawai'i during this time generally followed the missionary template.[17] Through such devaluations, ABCFM missionaries justified their growing influence over Hawaiian governmental affairs and policy making from the mid- to late nineteenth century.

Emasculating depictions of Hawaiian men as insignificant, incapable, and disappearing (because of disease) grew with the sugar industry. While colonial discourses in colonized nations that relied on indigenous populations for labor in the nineteenth century regularly downplayed the intellectual abilities of indigenous men and emphasized them as inherently physical,[18] Hawai'i's sugar barons were less interested in Native labor since they shipped in workers from China, Japan, Korea, Philippines, and elsewhere. As laborers arrived in the late 1800s, and as diseases still ravaged Native communities, Hawaiian men were increasingly viewed as inconsequential, and dying off. Likewise, as haole plantation owners sought control over Hawai'i's government, they saw Hawaiian male leaders as barriers to their progress. Hence, they, too, looked upon them as incompetent and racially inferior.[19] Such characterizations not only helped haole secure economic and political power in the 1880s and 1890s, but also laid a foundation for the tourist industry to build upon.

Tourism's Natives

In the first half of the twentieth century Hawai'i's tourist industry faced the task of convincing prospective visitors that Hawai'i's Natives were safe and accommodating hosts. Since a strong male presence potentially jeopardized that impression, images of sexualized Hawaiian women eclipsed the Hawaiian man in tourist advertisements. Postcards and stereoscopes titled "Hawaiian Hula Dancers," "Hawaiian Beauties, Hawaiian Islands," and "A Hula Girl Dancing" displayed sexualized images as a way of selling the islands as filled with "attractive, warm, welcoming, unthreatening, generous hosts."[20] Desmond has shown that such images were fabricated, and explains that Hawaiian models were dressed in decontemporized traditional clothing.[21] In other words, due to Puritan missionary changes imposed on Hawaiian society since the 1820s, Hawaiian women were rarely, if ever, seen topless in Hawai'i by the late 1890s. The image of the hula girl was most commonly used to sell the islands as a tourist destination.

Using Roland Barthes to make sense of myth making in Hawai'i under colonialism and tourism, Elizabeth Buck argues that "the ideological work of any dominant myth is to make itself look neutral and innocent and in the process, to naturalize human relationships of power and domination."[22] In the process of selling Hawai'i as a paradise, the tourist industry (and supporting venues) appropriated and changed Hawaiian cultural forms, like Hawaiian music and dance. Like other scholars, Buck argues that such changes involved objectifying and sexualizing Hawaiians. "Their symbolic practices," she contends, "were positioned as objects of spectacle and speculation."[23] Like Desmond, Buck also shows that images of decontemporized Native women were essential to selling the islands and that presenting Natives as "happy-go-lucky" was part of the marketing plan of tourism.[24] However, Buck ventures deeper into the history of hula and music to explain the evolution of discourse and myth making in Hawai'i from the late 1700s to the late 1900s. Such Western discourse, Buck concludes, "did violence to Hawaiians and their symbolic practices, transposing Hawaiian religion into myth and superstition, worship into pagan rites, sexuality into sin, and poetry into folklore."[25]

Before both Desmond and Buck, Native Hawaiian scholar Haunani-Kay Trask argued that tourism promoted and sold Hawai'i by objectifying and sexualizing Hawaiian women and culture. She has said that tourist venues marketed the idea that Hawaiians were open, inviting hosts. Taking it a step further, she connects this discourse to the Hawaiian resistance. Describing the allure and erotic Euro-American imagination associated with twentieth-century Hawaiian tourism, Trask states, "Hawai'i is the image of escape from the rawness and violence of daily American life. Hawai'i—the word, the vision, the sound, the mind—is the fragrance and feel of soft kindness. Above all, Hawai'i is 'she,' the western image of the Native 'female' in her magical allure."[26] In a chapter entitled "Lovely Hula Hands," Trask ardently contends that Hawai'i was not only sexualized through erotic images of Native women, but feminized specifically as a prostitute. She says, "The point, of course, is that everything in Hawai'i can be yours. . . . Thus Hawai'i like a lovely woman, is there for the taking."[27] Explaining this metaphor, Trask elaborates that "Hawai'i itself is the female object of degraded and victimized sexual value. Our 'āina, or lands, are not any longer the source of food and shelter, but the source of money."[28] Trask contends that "the Hawaiian values of generosity and love such as aloha were misappropriated to make it seem as if they are particularly suited to the 'visitor industry.'" She continues, "The truth of course is the opposite: the myth of the happy Hawaiians waiting to share their culture with tourists was invented to lure visitors." Unlike Buck or Desmond, Trask concludes that such stereotyping was meant to "disparage Native resistance to the tourist industry."[29]

While tourism made Hawaiian women increasingly accessible to visitors, it simultaneously rendered the Hawaiian man nearly unseen. As the attractive Hawaiian woman became more visible on postcards, magazines, and other advertisements, the Hawaiian man became less visible, less masculine, and ultimately less threatening. Desmond also recognizes the disappearance of Hawaiian men from tourist advertisements and explains that "Caucasian representations of Native Hawaiian men in the early decades of this century were limited to the occasional ethnographic photograph in *National Geographic* or a postcard of men fishing or pounding poi, or even more rarely, of a Hawaiian family together in a domestic scene."[30] While scenes of Hawaiian men became increasingly rare, Hawaiian women seemed to be everywhere. Desmond explains, "It makes the emerging tourist iconography of the hula dancer = beautiful female = Native = Hawai'i stand out in full relief and leaves the pictured women available for visual consumption by white males."[31] In other words, as Native Hawaiian men seemed to be disappearing, Native Hawaiian women were becoming increasingly more available.

Occasionally, Hawaiian men were pictured in tourist advertisements. But, like the military in present-day Hawai'i, as Kathy Ferguson and Phyllis Turnbull explore, Hawaiian men were rendered invisible in plain sight.[32] Two statues in Waikīkī's busiest shopping center illustrate this point. Displayed in the International Marketplace, standing side by side in life-size form, are two statues of a Hawaiian woman and a Hawaiian man. The woman is a hula dancer. Clad in flowers, a grass skirt, and little else, she displays her

Statues in front of the Waikīkī International Marketplace, 2003. (Photo by Sommer Meyer)

grace, beauty, and attractive figure to all who wish to look upon her. Her companion stands in her shadow, strumming his 'ukulele. He is her accompanist, but not her companion. Ironically, as seen with this statue, the tourist industry has shown Hawaiian men and women as incompatible. The male statue here is also her exact opposite: obese, heavily clothed, and a caricature with over-accentuated features. He is not only purposely unattractive; he is also nonthreatening and unbothered by the viewer's infatuation with his Hawaiian sister. Though his relationship to the girl is not explained, it is obvious that she is available for tourists and is not romantically involved with him. Although he is standing in front of tourist onlookers, he is inconsequential next to the stunning hula dancer.

Such narratives not only cast Native men as unseen, but also reaffirm that Native men are safe and insignificant, and that Hawai'i is a white man's sexual fantasyland. Although eighteenth- and early nineteenth-century writings of Hawaiian men alternately characterized them as either "noble" or "ignoble," by the late nineteenth century Hawaiian men were rendered transparent, passive, and nonthreatening. In the process of selling the islands as "she," Hawaiian men were marginalized and emasculated—evidenced not only in the fact that women were more visible, but in that Hawaiian men were characterized as unmanly and weak. Emasculating Hawaiian men and representing them as weak, excessively deferential to White male authority, and inferior was most commonly accomplished when popular media representations juxtaposed Hawaiian men with a manlier, heroic, haole hero, as seen in several mid-twentieth-century Hollywood films.

Representing Pacific Men in Film

Even though Hawaiian men were nearly invisible next to attractive women in tourist advertisements, Hollywood repeatedly found a place for them in South Seas films. Although popular since the 1920s, this film genre truly blossomed in the 1950s and helped perpetuate the stereotype that Hawaiian men were submissive Natives.[33] Several masculine American heroic archetypes—John Wayne, Burt Lancaster, John Hall, and Charlton Heston, to name a few—found success in South Seas productions. Though most such films focused primarily on American characters, they featured cameos of Native men as well. What is said of Pacific Island men in such films can easily go unnoticed, since they played supporting roles at best. Most commonly, Native men were part of the scenery in these films—creatures that climbed trees and picked coconuts, bodies that played drums for sexy hula dancers—or played sub-servient roles of little significance—servants, canoe paddlers, or pearl divers. Occasionally Native men played the roles of chief or king. However, despite the pride normally associated with such a position, these chiefs were regularly eclipsed by the foreign stars.

In contrast, the Caucasian Hollywood male hero in this genre is strong, smart, and powerful. The relationship portrayed between Native men and American heroes in South Seas films emasculates Native men and solidi-fies notions of their inferiority. As the American hero proves to be stronger, smarter, and ultimately superior to even the best of Natives (warriors, chiefs, and priests), the status of these powerful island men is inverted, and they are simultaneously defined as the heroes' opposite—passive, dependent, and weak. Hence, previously powerful Native men are miniscule in these films. With the inversion of their status, these Native men become mere avenues for highlighting the superiority, and in some cases godliness, of the white hero. In fact, the construction and endurance of the American hero func-tions at the expense of Native men. The recurring and insistent emphasis on this relationship is crucial because it situates the haole male hero above Native male chiefs. It is through this relationship that stereotypical mean-ings are generated. Cultural studies critic Stuart Hall has made clear that meaning is regularly established through such difference. For example, "we know what it is to be British . . . because we can mark its difference from its 'others.'—Britishness is not-French, not-American."[34] Hence, as John Wayne, Burt Lancaster, and others become heroic male figures in these films, Native men are simultaneously defined as unheroic and unreliant.

The 1948 film *Wake of the Red Witch* is a good example. Playing the part of Captain Ralls, a ruthless sailor and pearl hunter tamed by his love affair with island-born maiden Angelique Desaix (played by Gail Russell), John Wayne is determined to do what Native chiefs could not do for themselves: rescue a chest of pearls from an oversized, beastly octopus. After unsuccessful attempts by two Native men, Ralls is asked by the high chief, Va Nuku, played by Hawaiian surfing and swimming legend Duke Kahanamoku, to take on the challenge. They are hopeful because they believe Ralls is the son of their god, Tarotato. While a crowd of Natives tries to revive the two Hawaiians who failed, Ralls takes off his shirt and, without hesitation, dives down for the well-guarded chest of pearls, which he retrieves with ease. Nevertheless unsatisfied, he resubmerges and, with spear in hand and accompanied by an inspiring musical score, defeats the angry octopus in hand-to-tentacle combat. As Ralls slowly floats back to the surface, the words are spoken, "Never underestimate a man like Ralls." Later that evening, the chiefs hold a special celebration and ceremony in honor of Ralls, the "son of Tarotato." Here, Va Nuku's advisor presents the islands' greatest treasure, the chest of pearls, to Ralls. The chief proclaims that the "pearls will never return to sacred cave, but will fly over face of earth in the hands of son of Tarotato [Ralls]."[35] As this sort of colonial narrative naturalized itself in the viewers' eyes, colonial conquest appeared honorable, colonial pillage was deemed gracious gift giving, and Native resistance to colonialism seemed nonexistent.

Wake of the Red Witch is a symbolic assault on real Hawaiian men, as one of the eclipsed chiefs in this film was played by Hawaiian icon and surfing legend Duke Kahanamoku. Though Kahanamoku was a symbol of strength for Hawaiians in the twentieth century (especially for Hawaiian surfers), his role in this film rather deemphasizes the strength of actual Hawaiian men. Duke was a global ambassador of Hawaiian culture, an icon of Hawaiian masculinity, and the father of modern-day surfing. As an Olympic gold medalist swimmer, he was, in reality, quite capable of diving to rescue the pearls, but he was unfortunately unable to rewrite his character or the script of this film. Though Duke got this role because of his popularity as an athlete, his performance in it is troubling. How could he play such a role? Perhaps in his quest to star in Hollywood films he overlooked the plot or the outcome of his scenes. Or perhaps he recognized the absurdity of the plot and trusted others would also find it fanciful and thus unrealistic—how often do men wrestle with two-ton octopuses, after all? Either way, his character is quite uncharacteristic of the real Duke Kahanamoku.

South Seas films, including *Wake of the Red Witch,* conclude that Pacific Island men are not political, self-reliant, or resistant to colonization, but are instead naturally passive and dependent. In essence they are not only incapable of governing themselves, but desire the "white man's burden" of colonial dominance.[36] This is seen in several films. In *His Majesty O'Keefe* it becomes apparent that Pacific Island Natives are not savvy or strong enough to govern and protect themselves when Bully Hayes easily infiltrates Yap's society and cages them as slave cargo. He accomplished this by luring the hero, O'Keefe, off the island on a business venture. After O'Keefe returns to the island and becomes aware of Bully's evil doing, he stops Bully in his tracks. After he frees the islanders and forces Bully off the island for good, it becomes apparent, even to the Natives, that O'Keefe is the rightful ruler of their nation, and he is naturally crowned king.

The relationship established between Native men and the American hero in these films presents an effective narrative for justifying and normalizing political conquest or imperialism. Natives want to be colonized in many of these films. Though O'Keefe is at first reluctant to take on such responsibility because he is more interested in exploiting their natural resources for money, he eventually does the noble thing, pleases his island wife, and takes up the "white man's burden" of ruling over them. They want O'Keefe to be their king. They are not resistant; in fact, they beg for his rule. Scenes like this confirm Homi Bhabha's contention that colonial discourse thrives on stereotyping the other. After discussing the nuances of such processes, he states that these stereotypes are used to justify and mask colonial domination.[37] Frantz Fanon also conveys that colonialist discourses generated myths about colonial domination through various representational mediums. Such images depict conquest over Native peoples as a natural occurrence.[38] This is accomplished in many South Seas films.

The discourse elicited from these films also helps normalize the confiscation of Native possessions by foreign nations. This is seen in the aforementioned *Wake of the Red Witch.* For example, after Wayne (as Ralls) defeats the giant octopus, the head chiefs of the island present all of their pearls to him.[39] Outraged, the French governor of the island tries to stop the transaction. While scuffling with Ralls, the governor falls into the fire pit of Tarotato. Ralls then uses the pearls to pay off an old debt. In several of these South Seas films, foreigners are often rewarded with extravagant gifts.[40] This relationship of gift giving or rewarding foreign heroes simultaneously reinforced haole superiority over Native men and normalized colonial securing of Native possessions. We also see an example of this in *His Majesty O'Keefe,* when he begins his road to royalty at an annual island festival. Here, the head warrior, Chief Bugalru, first challenges the lone German resident to a duel, as he does every year. When the German man declines, O'Keefe volunteers to fight the chief in his place. After an unsuccessful round using Native weapons, O'Keefe puts down his club, raises his fists, and shows off his American fist-fighting skills, knocking the warrior senseless with a right hook. Later, when the chief comes to, his interpreter says, "He says you are a great warrior. He asks, what favor can he do for you." O'Keefe replies, "I want a hundred men in the coconut grove tomorrow morning."[41] O'Keefe then uses these men to build his lucrative copra business.

Through such discourses, Native men appear to willingly surrender their possessions to "superior" haole powers. In other words, Natives are not only incapable of defending themselves in these films, but are also portrayed as willing to give their choicest possessions, even their islands, to haole.[42]

Hiding and Validating Colonialism

The act of justifying colonial aggression by portraying indigenous peoples as inferior and incapable has a long and interconnected history with the practice of exhibiting nonwhite people to white audiences. Starting as early as the late fifteenth century, Europeans took people from various parts of Asia, Africa, and the Americas to display as "aboriginal samples" in laboratories, schools, and "freak" shows. Coco Fusco states that these early exhibits became the precursors to succeeding generations of white imaginings of nonwhite people.[43] Pointing out that such human exhibits were referenced in writings by William Shakespeare, Michel Montaigne, and William Wadsworth, Fusco also traces these exhibits to eighteenth-century Europe and says, "In the eighteenth century, these shows, together with theater and popular ballads, served as popular illustrations of the concept of the Noble Savage so central to Enlightenment Philosophy."[44] According to Fusco, these exhibitions successfully lodged evolving notions of the other deeply into the Western imagination. She also states that the practice of exhibiting and displaying Native peoples in a public sphere was a tool for justifying domination and argues that these exhibits labeled Natives as inferior, weak, and dangerous.[45]

Displaying Natives also helped to disguise and divert attention away from colonial violence. An example of this can be found in John Webber's painting, *Poedua*. In this portrait, Tahitian princess Poedua gazes out toward the viewer while comfortably revealing a bare-breasted, partially tattooed body. Webber was inspired to paint Poedua while she was imprisoned below deck in Cook's ship, *Discovery*. Cook had incarcerated Poedua along with her father, Chief Orio of Raiatea, while in the Society Islands in 1777 until two British deserters returned to the *Discovery*. Analyzing this painting and its accompanying narrative, Margaret Jolly contends that the violent and bloody scene surrounding this hostage situation was concealed by Poedua's half-nude female body. The portrait replaced the history by overlaying it with a sexualized island woman.[46] Similarly, Teresia Teaiwa concludes that depoliticized female bodies were used to mask and hide the horrifically destructive nuclear-bomb testing in the Marshall Islands.[47] Juxtaposing the bombing of Bikini Atoll (by the U.S. military) and the advent of the bikini-style bathing suit, Teaiwa argues that the swimsuit became a diversion and mask for the real

Bikini—as both began exploding at the same time.[48] She concludes that the horrifying reality of a nuclear-abundant era was ignored through an over-exposed female body in a bikini bathing suit.

Princess Ka'iulani discovered firsthand how sexualized imaginations on Pacific Island women rendered Native resistance negligible. Shortly after Hawai'i's last queen was deposed and the Hawaiian kingdom seized by American businessmen with the aid of U.S. Marines, Ka'iulani traveled to Washington, D.C., to plead for reconciliation. However, as Kahananui Green explains, American newspapers merely commented on her looks, calling her "the very flower—an exotic" and mentioning nothing about her political grievances.[49]

Colonial Masculinities

Historically, emasculating discourses have helped colonial entities excuse and expedite colonial conquest. Revathi Krishnaswamy found this to be the case in colonial India. After determining that masculinity is the "corner-stone in the ideology of moral imperialism that prevailed in British India from the late nineteenth century onward," she argues that Anglo-India "found its most seductive metaphor for racial, physical, moral and cultural weakness not in the vulnerability of womanhood but in the weakness of colonized manhood."[50] Just as Hollywood films validated colonialism by juxtaposing characters of manly and unmanly status, Krishnaswamy argues, "Colonialism was justified, naturalized, even legitimized through an ideo-logical distinction between English manliness and Indian effeminacy."[51] The binary relationship created through such representations of Indians next to Englishmen also helped substantiate English rule "by equating an aggressive, muscular, chivalric model of manliness with racial, national, cultural, and moral superiority."[52] While defining Indian men as unmanly and devoid of the "chivalric ideal of manhood," the British Empire determined India to be "unfit for self rule."[53] The effects of such discourse on colonized men were unfortunately strong and enduring. Describing the effects of feminiza-tion on colonized Indian men, Ashis Nandy contends that "femininity-in-masculinity was perceived as the final negation of a man's political identity, a pathology more dangerous than femininity itself."[54] However, this is not to say that resistance was nonexistent.

Euro-American representations of Hawaiian men similarly portrayed them as unmanly and unfit for self-rule. Ty Tengan not only recognizes the emasculating effects tourist and Hollywood representations have had on the image of Hawaiian men, but also explains how the unmanly category has played out on the developing identity of indigenous men more recently.[55] Through his experiences with the nā koa (warriors) of the Hale Mua, Tengan has found, as both a Hawaiian and an anthropologist, that many Hawaiian men feel marginal as men and "argue that they need to restore these structures and reclaim their traditional roles and kuleana (rights and responsibilities) as men. . . . Indeed, that was precisely what led to the formation of the Hale Mua in the first place."[56] In the process of discovering an identity that is both contradictory to colonial constructs and traditional in form, Hawaiian men have turned to Tangata Maori, or the indigenous men of Aotearoa (New Zealand), for inspiration—often from their forms of dancing, martial arts, oratory, and other ceremonies.[57] Tengan argues that many Hawaiian men have looked to Tangata Maori because they believe they have been able to retain their image as strong island warriors while Hawaiian men have been relegated to submissiveness and unmanliness.[58]

However, there are limits to the warrior identity. Maori scholar Brendan Hokowhitu also recognizes this. He contends that the image of physically superior Maori men was cultivated by colonial hegemonic forces to keep Maori men in labor, military, and less intellectual professions. Arguing that convoluted notions of Maori masculinity stem from a colonial discourse found in history, education, and contemporary films, Hokowhitu has mapped a genealogy of this discourse. Nineteenth-century Maori men were written about solely as savage warriors who, when displayed against an idealized European masculinity, were seen as inferior. He contends that this encouraged British colonialism and justified conquest as a "taming" mission. Descending from this notion, twentieth-century discourse found a productive place for "physical" and "less intelligent" Maori men as laborers. As colonizers required a labor pool, Maori men were recruited and rewritten as physically refined for manual work. This is evidenced in twentieth-century educational curricula at boys' schools like Te Aute College, which channeled Maori toward manual, and particularly agricultural, kinds of work. For Hokowhitu, this kind of funneling continued throughout that century and into the twenty-first. It also had a profound and personal impact on his life. As a Maori student, Hokowhitu was, like the majority of his Maori peers, dissuaded by teachers from pursuing an intellectual career and encouraged to excel in physical realms like sports. Although he had won accolades as a college and university rugby player, he still disregarded the advice of many Pakeha (haole) and went on to complete a Ph.D. Through his research he found that the success of

Maori men in sport was related to and aided these historic colonial discourses. Among other things, sport promoted the notion that Maori physicality, not intelligence, was their specialty.[59] However, this problem was compounded by the fact that many Maori men "swallowed these constructs" and identified themselves through such definitions.[60]

Both Tengan and Hokowhitu argue that Pacific Island men should seek masculine identities that rely less on hypermasculine, violent, and physical behavior. For Tengan, one way to achieve a decolonized form of masculinity is to structure "gender practices along the lines of pono," or gender relations based on "balance, well-being, and righteousness."[61] Perhaps Tengan sees in the Hale Mua the potential for such balance. However, because such notions of balance often translate into the exclusion of women from men's spaces, this becomes, in my opinion, a concern. In the end, Tengan has determined that the development of new, decolonized masculinities are tricky endeavors—in which Hawaiians need to "reclaim mana [spiritual power] in ways that will help us better negotiate the larger frameworks of gendered, raced and classed power dynamics."[62] For Hokowhitu, the development of a decolonized Maori male identity that Tengan described will require more Maori men to discover "what it truly means to be a Maori man, freed from the dominant construct, and permeated instead with humility, intelligence, creativity, love, and compassion."[63]

Historical Narratives of Hawai'i

There is a correlation between historical narratives and the emasculation of colonized indigenous men, especially in Hawai'i. In the decades following the overthrow of Hawai'i's Native monarchy, several historians have deemed this coup inevitable and buried stories of persistent attempts by Native Hawaiians to restore their monarchy. Throughout the second half of the twentieth century various historians wrote comprehensive narratives of Hawaiian history and attempted to answer a pressing question: how and why was the Native Hawaiian monarchy overthrown? Like tourism and Hollywood movies, many portrayed Native Hawaiians as inferior and ineffectual characters in their own story. By reducing Hawaiian men to submissive characters who were always acted upon in history, rather than actors of it, they helped to justify colonialism—as Natives are again seen as incapable of ruling themselves, subordinate to foreign superiority, and ultimately in need of "help." In contrast, more recent Hawaiian historical narratives such as Noenoe Silva's *Aloha Betrayed,* Jonathan Osorio's *Dismembering Lāhui,* and others have portrayed nineteenth-century

Hawaiians as vigorously and dynamically fighting for Hawaiian political autonomy.[64] While many American versions of Hawaiian history point to inferiority and corruption as reasons for the kingdom's downfall, most non-Native accounts looked to Hawaiian kings for answers. Such works also erroneously claimed that since Hawaiian kings were ineffectual they depended on foreigners for assistance in leadership. Most twentieth-century American accounts of Hawaiian history buttressed the "content Native" myth and emasculated Hawaiian men as tractable and incapable entities in Hawai'i's history.

Ralph Kuykendall wrote a three-volume series, the first published in 1938 and the last in 1968, about the Hawaiian monarchy from 1778 to 1893. *Hawaiian Kingdom volumes I, II, III* is often heralded as a major canon in Hawaiian history. Kuykendall's explicit detail of Hawai'i's people and events during the nineteenth century is exhaustive. His findings, based on English-language as opposed to Hawaiian-language materials, are laid out in a straightforward and chronological manner. As facts seem to build upon more facts, this history appears devoid of interpretation and centered on the truth. However, as with any historical narrative, this is not the reality.

In the opening chapters of *Hawaiian Kingdom volume I,* Kuykendall deems Kamehameha I Hawai'i's greatest king. While he praises Hawai'i's first monarch as strong, courageous, tenacious, and resilient, Kamehameha I's successors never measured up to him. Kuykendall states, "Kamehameha is universally recognized as the most outstanding of all the Hawaiian chiefs of his own and all other epochs."[65] Interestingly, such praise reemerges throughout his narrative as a means to measure up later rulers, including those who were deposed by American businessmen. As Kuykendall compares nineteenth-century monarchs with Kamehameha I, he concludes that none was as capable as the great ruler. Examining Kamehameha's successor kings under a hazy microscope, Kuykendall characterizes Kamehameha II (Liholiho), Kamehameha III (Kauikeaouli), Kamehameha IV (Alexander Liholiho), Kamehameha V (Lot Kapuāiwa), William Lunalilo, and David Kalākaua as less-capable leaders who thus constituted a downward spiral.

As the chapters evolve, Kuykendall judges the effectiveness of these monarchs by juxtaposing them with haole advisors instead of only Kamehameha. Here he depicts successor kings as heavily dependent on foreign advisors and customs. Kuykendall determines that Euro-American men and their culture began eclipsing the strength and ability of the Native kings after Kamehameha I's rule. He highlights this point by plotting the personalities and attributes of the kings against male foreign advisors, traders, missionaries, and sea captains.

Kuykendall not only overemphasizes the importance and prestige of haole male advisors in the early nineteenth century, but in the process also undermines the kings by marking them as less intelligent and less capable than their haole counterparts. For example, shortly after the death of Kamehameha I, the survival of the kingdom was at stake. Because there were tense rivalries among high-ranking chiefs and warriors, rumors of revolution were not unfounded. As tensions evolved into warfare, the fate of Kamehameha's heir, Liholiho, was uncertain. Despite the fact that Liholiho's army of Native Hawaiian warriors defeated his rivals and ensured the kingdom's legitimacy, Kuykendall credits haole male advisors John Young (English) and Captain Louis de Freycinet (French) with Liholiho's victory. According to Kuykendall, Liholiho's rule was preserved and secured because Young persuaded Freycinet's French fleet to stand behind the new young king.[66] However, it was Hawaiian, not French, soldiers who went to battle for the kingdom.

Kuykendall regularly credits haole male advisors with the kingdom's early success, even when Hawaiian kings made aggressive political moves, implemented new policies, or made other advances of merit. For example, despite Liholiho's decision to end the Hawaiian traditional religious legal system called kapu (which at that time was under criticism from other ali'i, like his mother, Keōpūolani, and stepmother, Ka'ahumanu), Kuykendall gives due to haole residents in Hawai'i for this revolutionary change. He states, "The example of the foreigners, their disregard of kapu, and their occasional efforts to convince the Hawaiians by argument that their system was wrong, were the most potent forces undermining the beliefs of the people."[67]

Other historians have also criticized Hawaiian monarchs as dependent on haole. For many, dependence and inferiority meshed with discussions of acculturation in unique ways. As Hawaiian leaders adopted haole laws, education, and religion, acculturation was seen as weakness and a key reason for the kingdom's demise. This perspective is most apparent when historians discuss the reign of Hawai'i's last king, David Kalākaua. Kalākaua was a central character during a pivotal period in Hawai'i, a time when haole political influence escalated and the Hawaiian kingdom lost much of its authority. Although Kalākaua replaced haole cabinet members with Native Hawaiians and royalists, resurrected Hawaiian traditions like the hula, and recorded Hawaiian oral histories and chants, Richard Wisniewski calls him dependent on foreigners, incompetent, irrational, and vain. Wisniewski states that Kalākaua was easily swayed by con artists who gave him ill-conceived advice. Drawing from the story of Walter Murray Gibson, an advisor to Kalākaua who supported Hawaiian sovereignty and limiting the power of haole business elites and planters, Wisniewski concludes, "Schemers and adventurers, by playing on Kalākaua's vanity or his naïve nature, could push the king into actions which invited political trouble."[68] When speaking of Celso Moreno, another influential character on Kalākaua's leadership, he states that despite advice to Kalākaua by haole to stay away from him, he unwisely "remained under Moreno's influence."[69] Wisniewski goes on to argue that were it not for the help of honest white American influences, Kalākaua would have been a failure. After stating that annexationist haole were better educated than Hawaiian kings, and referring to Hawaiians as "remnants of the Hawaiian race," Wisniewski praises the overthrow of the Hawaiian kingdom.[70]

After traveling the world in the early 1880s, Kalākaua returned home poised to elevate his visible status. Upon his return, he built an elaborate palace furnished with all the niceties one would expect to find in a European palace. The furniture was made from the same company that produced furniture for the White House. The art, champagne, and other decorations were authentic and costly. Although the palace budget was initially $65,000, it ended up costing $350,000. Eventually, after discussing electricity with Thomas Edison himself, Kalākaua installed an electric lighting system that cost nearly as much as the palace did without it. Writing about these expenditures, Wisniewski complains that the only thing Kalākaua gained was an increased love for music and an unquenchable appetite for expensive parties.[71] Gavan Daws also presents Kalākaua as a politician who loved expensive fripperies for no reason other than upsetting haole businessmen in Honolulu. Presenting a variety of quotes from the kingdom's greatest critics, Daws determines that Kalākaua's reforms (building a Hawaiian navy, removing pro-annexationists from his government, restoring his power through various political and cultural means) were concocted by deceitful advisors like Walter Murray Gibson.[72] Like his predecessors, Daws drops Hawaiian kings into the backseat of his historical narrative and has determined that haole advisors were the true brains behind such operations. Rather than consider Kalākaua a conscious actor of appropriating his anti-white haole advisors to his benefit, and fighting an uphill battle of saving Hawaiian sovereignty, these historians once again depict him as gullible, submissive to questionable foreigners, and overindulgent.

When Kalākaua built an elaborate European-style palace in the middle of Honolulu, wore British-style suits, read classic European literature, dined at Buckingham Palace, and insisted on serving French champagne to his guests, he was actively engaged in creative resistance. While he presented himself in this manner, Kalākaua simultaneously frustrated hungry colonial powers who insisted he was an incompetent, savage Hawaiian. Although Americans were ultimately undeterred, Kalākaua successfully convinced many European and Asian nations that he was a capable Hawaiian ruler. For example, in 1881 the Prince of Wales (who later became King Edward VII) defended King Kalākaua's standing at a party in England. Giving precedence to Kalākaua over the German crown prince, he explained, "Either the brute is a king, or he's a common or garden nigger; and if the latter, what's he doing here?"[73] Sally Engle Merry has argued that Kalākaua adopted and mimicked some Western ideals of civility as a way of averting colonial invasion. As evidence, she points to treaties with European nations that guaranteed Hawaiian sovereignty as long as they proved that they were "civilized."[74] For Merry, the idea of civilization was ambiguous, as it was often turned against colonizers, and elite colonial subjects often mimicked "civilized" living for power and control. Drawing from Bhabha, Merry states, "Mimicry is both resemblance and menace. Occupying such an in-between position, the same and yet different, generates deep anxiety."[75] In other words, assimilation was not only a necessary strategy, but also often a front. According to Merry, assimilation was necessary for preserving sovereignty as it debunked the justifying notion that Hawaiians were uncivil. Mimicking European civility was often seen as superficial by local Hawai'i residents, since Kalākaua was also resurrecting previously banned Native cultural arts—those cultural practices, such as the hula, that were seen as licentious, crude, and barbaric. Hence, on the surface he was for all intents and purposes a brown European, but in his own community he was lifted as the father of a Hawaiian cultural restoration.

However, mimicry was not a perfect strategy, because Hawaiian leaders adopted Western laws that were advantageous for both Hawaiian nationalists and advocates of colonization. The Hawaiian adoption of Western-style legal codes and structures were "core institutions of colonial control" that gave capitalists in Hawai'i the free labor and privatized land they desired.[76] For Merry, it was a sovereignty paradox since "in order to produce a government able to deal with the foreign residents and to gain respectability in the eyes of the imperialist foreign community, the leaders adopted the forms of modern government and rule of law, but these forms required foreigners skilled in their practices to run them."[77] Although paradoxical, the strategy of mimicry seemed to work for Hawaiians in the mid-1800s—as Hawai'i was the last of all the Pacific Islands to be colonized and their sovereignty was preserved during a period of heightened assimilation.

Conclusion

Throughout most of the twentieth century, tourist-driven and pro-American haole media venues stereotyped Hawaiian men as overtly compliant Natives. As the tourist industry needed a feminized and safe location for haole visitors to feel welcome, they found a mascot in sexualized Hawaiian women. In the process, island men were pushed behind the tourist promotion stage and rendered nearly invisible. But American movies found a place for them, mainly as backdrops, but occasionally as chiefs and warriors. In playing supporting roles, Native Hawaiian and Pacific Islander men fulfilled their ultimate job of helping American heroes like John Wayne and Burt Lancaster become strong and masculine heroic icons. Native men helped the haole hero climb to new heights on the testosterone ladder by playing their nonmasculine foils. As these portrayals were beamed on to movie screens across America, not only were Native men interpreted as subordinate people desirous of manly assistance, but at the same time, the United States appeared more and more justified in occupying islands in the Pacific, such as Hawai'i. While the significance and impact of Hollywood films can be debated, one would expect academic historical narratives to be more careful in its storytelling. Unfortunately, several of the most-read works on Hawaiian history by American authors followed Hollywood in depicting Hawaiian men. In several of these historical narratives Hawaiian kings were often eclipsed by haole advisors and regularly painted as incompetent in comparison to their haole counterparts.

These deeply embedded stereotypes of the unmanly and incapable Hawaiian male were difficult to reconcile in the 1970s. As Hawaiians became increasingly and visibly vocal in their distaste for haole colonialism during the Hawaiian renaissance, the submissive Hawaiian image appeared more Hollywood than history. As I argue later, resistant men helped dismantle this historic stereotype. But in this moment of cognitive dissonance another historic discourse emerged and was applied to disgruntled Hawaiians. They again became the radical, savage Natives, sometimes called terrorists. However, as I will show in chapter 7, some Hawaiians, as seen through the Hui O He'e Nalu, found ways to navigate an identity within this trope.

CHAPTER 5

The Hawaiian Renaissance and Hawaiian Surfers

Several Hawaiian historians have marked the 1970s as the beginning of a Hawaiian renaissance. While Native pride burgeoned in Hawaiians during this time and their frustrations toward American control over the islands increased, the Hawaiian renaissance reinvigorated Kānaka Maoli (and advocates) to restore and preserve Hawaiian culture and language. This era is not only characterized by projects of preserving culture, but also of political activism and protest.

Although not often recognized, many of the Hawaiian strategies of protests in the 1970s were born out of a 1960s environmental group called Save Our Surf (SOS). Organized by a Marxist-trained local-haole surfer named John Kelly and run by young local surfers, SOS was a grassroots peoples' movement that halted most coastal development and dredging projects proposed in Hawai'i between 1960 and 1990. Although they initially focused on protecting surfing breaks, SOS's agenda had broadened by 1970. Through successful protests, sit-ins, rallies, and political lobbying, SOS inspired local youth activism at the dawn of the Hawaiian renaissance. After expounding on the influence of SOS on the formation of a Hawaiian renaissance, I will analyze two other prominent groups formed in the mid-1970s: the Polynesian Voyaging Society, which built a Hawaiian double-hulled voyaging canoe called *Hōkūle'a,* and the Protect Kaho'olawe 'Ohana, which protested the U.S. military bombings on the island of Kaho'olawe.

In this chapter I not only examine how Hawaiian surfers contributed to, and were shaped by, the Hawaiian renaissance, but also analyze connections between ka poʻina nalu (the surf zone) and Hawaiian resistance in the 1960s and 1970s. Again, Hawaiian and local surfers were accustomed to fighting for the surf and open ocean. Although most Hawaiian surfers in the 1970s were not dancing hula or speaking Hawaiian, they nonetheless helped shape Hawaiian renaissance activism. This has been the case with surfers in SOS and the Hui O He ʻe Nalu, and also with Hawaiian surfers who sailed on board *Hōkūleʻa*. The most memorable surfer on *Hōkūleʻa* was Eddie Aikau. To this day Eddie is revered as a Hawaiian surfing legend who sacrificed his life for his culture and for his people. In this chapter I analyze these connections.

Renaissance, John Kelly, and Save Our Surf

Hawaiian historian and cultural activist George Kanahele was partially responsible for coining the term "Hawaiian renaissance" in a speech he gave to the Hawaiʻi Civic Club in 1977, which was subsequently published in local newspapers. Kanahele explained that although the term "renaissance" could imply that the culture had previously died, he argued that it still accurately emphasized the tremendous growth in Hawaiian culture and activism in the 1970s. For Kanahele, the resurgence among Hawaiians "reversed years of cultural decline; it has created a new kind of Hawaiian consciousness; it has inspired greater pride in being Hawaiian; it has led to bold and imaginative ways of reasserting our identity; it has led to new political awareness; and it has had and will continue to have a positive impact on the economic and social uplifting of the Hawaiian community."[1] For many, the 1970s ushered in exciting movements where Hawaiian cultural awareness and pride burgeoned. Hawaiian music, dance, language, history, activism, and many other things became topics of great interest to many and have been increasingly promoted from the 1970s until today.

Resistance and protest among Hawaiians in the 1970s can also be traced to activism elsewhere in the world, particularly in the United States. In 1977 Kanahele said of the growing Hawaiian activism, "The Blacks, Chicanos, American Indians, and others have reasserted their rights and their roots. No doubt the Hawaiian cultural and political activism is part of that legacy."[2] Although influenced by the age of ethnicity in the United States, Hawaiians also looked to struggles of the Maori of Aotearoa (New Zealand) for inspiration, and thus Hawaiian activist groups modeled many of their objectives on Tangata Maori movements in New Zealand—especially their movement for Native language revitalization.

The 1970s is also characterized as an era of activism, when Hawaiians, "like a dormant volcano coming to life again . . . [were] erupting with all the pent-up energy and frustrations of a people on the move."[3] Part of that coming-to-life process was reasserting pride in Hawaiianness. Shortly after World War II, American narratives insisted that Hawai'i was the great melting pot, a place where "everybody tried to be part of the same homogenized lump."[4] But starting in the 1970s, more people took pride in being Kanaka Maoli, and such pride led to resistance and activism. For some Hawaiians a renewed awareness of their condition as colonized Natives led to frustration. Kanahele explained, "For some, of course, these feelings may turn into belligerency or militancy, but that is a natural part of the price that comes with the revitalization of a people, particularly those who feel that they are strangers in their own land."[5] But more commonly, frustrations led to unity and resistance, as seen in the early 1970s, when Hawaiian groups united to protect Hawaiian rights.

Many historians have pointed to the Kalama Valley protests as the starting point for Hawaiian modern activism. In 1970 some Hawaiian and local residents of the rural Kalama Valley refused to leave their homes after the non-Hawaiian, pro-development Board of Trustees for the Kamehameha Schools Bishop Estate pulled their leases for a community of upscale homes and a golf course. Despite bulldozers reminiscent of *The Grapes of Wrath* just outside their homes, these Kalama families stood their ground in protest. Among them was Moose "Mayor of Kalama" Lui, who was known for lecturing bulldozer operators as they encroached on Kalama homes. At least one resident, Dick King, was arrested for criminal trespassing after he refused to leave. George Santos, a Hawaiian pig farmer, was one of the last to face eviction before his home was finally razed in 1971. Although Kalama Valley residents and supporters—who made human chains around homes and properties—were eventually removed, these protests sent a shockwave through the islands. Activist and professor of Hawaiian studies Haunani-Kay Trask explained, "The beginning of the sovereignty movement is generally taken to be the struggle against Kamehameha Schools at Kalama Valley, when the people were evicted so that the estate could build those fancy houses."[6] Among those who organized and executed these protests at Kalama Valley was a local-haole surfer named John Kelly. With his group of young Hawaiian and local

surfers, who were already accustomed to protesting, Kelly was integral to the
Kalama protests in particular and burgeoning Hawaiian activism generally.

Son of acclaimed artists, Kelly was raised in Hawai'i near Diamond
Head, where he learned to surf, dive, and swim from experienced Hawaiian
watermen and Beachboys in the 1930s.[7] As an experienced waterman and
surfer, Kelly was among those who braved mountainous waves in Mākaha
and the North Shore at a time when most surfed in Waikīkī. He also contributed to the development of modern surfboard designs.[8] A couple of
years after he graduated from Roosevelt High School in 1937, Kelly first
employed his ocean skills while working for the navy as a lifeguard. While
working at Nimitz Beach on December 7, 1941, he watched Pearl Harbor
erupt in a cloud of smoke. Gathering floating bodies in Pearl Harbor had a
profound impact on him; it shaped his early disdain for hegemonic governments who used people as pawns in their power-seeking games.[9] After the war
he earned a degree from the Julliard School and later returned home eager to
make a difference in local Hawai'i communities. For nine years he directed a
youth music school in one of Hawai'i's most impoverished districts, Pālama
Settlement. Working with youth of Native Hawaiian and local immigrant
plantation backgrounds, Kelly was in his element. Though he had expanded
the program from seventeen students to four hundred, he was fired in 1959
because of his involvement in antinuclear protests, having served earlier
that year as a delegate to the Fifth World Conference against Hydrogen and
Atomic Bombs in Hiroshima. Kelly explained that he was fired after partici-
pating in this conference because "some Pālama Settlement board members
were big corporate landowners leasing land to the military."[10] The military-
dependent Territorial government in Hawai'i had no tolerance for an antiwar
activist like Kelly, and he struggled to find work in the early 1960s. During
this time he founded the surfer-activist group Save Our Surf.

Composed primarily of local and Hawaiian high school surfers, both male
and female, Kelly organized SOS to protest rapidly rising development projects that threatened local surf and fishing areas. The complete destruction of
a popular Honolulu surfing break in the mid-1960s particularly fueled SOS's
activity. Kelly explained, "When before our eyes, a crane dumped boulders
into the sea to destroy a favorite Ala Moana surfing site, a new realism came
home. Several of us decided to act."[11] Kelly found it easy to mobilize locals
and Hawaiians to fight for their surf, most likely because they had inherited a
tradition of protecting the ocean. Thus SOS was intensely adamant about preserving their threatened space. When developers proposed to widen Waikīkī

Beach, dredge reefs, and build roads or hotels over surf breaks, SOS rallied to stop them. Operating under the motto "Educate, Organize, and Confront," they were well-informed and successful activists.[12] Although SOS was managed with a "hang loose" policy, having no constitution, bylaws, or elected leaders, and meeting only twice a week—usually on the carpeted floor of a local school library—by 1971 they were called "undoubtedly the swingingest and surely one of the most effective local environmental groups in the whole country" by nationally syndicated columnist Stewart Udall.[13] Astoundingly, Kelly and his teenage friends won a majority of their battles against Hawai'i's most formidable giants, such as the Dillingham Corporation, the U.S. Army Corps of Engineers, the Department of Land and Natural Resources, and the Hawai'i Tourism Bureau. In their thirty years of existence, SOS "won thirty-four major environmental victories totaling over $2 billion dollars in taxpayers' money saved from destructive dredging and coastal interventions."[14]

After only ten years of existence, SOS had already become an accomplished antidevelopment environmental group. Perhaps the most memorable among many victories occurred in 1969, when SOS exposed Dillingham Corporation's semi-secret plans to dredge and fill all the reefs around the

SOS flyer for a public hearing on Wai'anae development projects. (Courtesy of Colleen Kelly)

eastern third of O'ahu to make room for a new highway. The master plan involved connecting Diamond Head and Koko Head with a freeway built atop the reef several yards offshore. After they "finagled" these plans from the Department of Transportation, SOS publicized, protested, and, by 1970, ultimately stopped the $56 million project.[15] Developers came up with a flurry of extravagant project proposals in the late 1960s and early 1970s, and many of these plans aimed to reshape Hawai'i's coastlines. In addition to the reef highway, Dilco (Dillingham Corporation's development company) proposed building high-rise condominiums atop Ala Moana reefs after filling the area between Magic Island and Kewalo Harbor with cement in phase III of the Magic Island plan—otherwise called Dillingham's land grab. The state supported Dilco by putting half a million dollars into building a large retaining wall for the landfill project. The initial phase, scheduled to begin in June 1970, involved building a six-hundred-foot jetty through the Kewalo channel. Since this would have destroyed the surf areas called Sharks Hole and Harbors, SOS rallied the public and eventually stopped the project.[16] In the same year, on the Waikīkī side of Magic Island, another project proposed extending Ala Moana Harbor's parking lot out onto the reef, destroying the premier surfing breaks of Ala Moana Bowls and Rockpiles. After Kelly gave his slideshow presentation to thousands of students at nearby McKinley High School, SOS members mobilized to stop yet another coastline project. Perhaps the most difficult coastline development endeavor to stop was the Waikīkī Beach widening project. After investing time and money into the proposal, the state was adamant about importing one hundred feet of new beach in the Kūhiō area. Since this widening project would have buried several surfing breaks in sand, SOS worked hard to stop it. Although SOS was eventually successful, tourist industry advocates and Honolulu politicians made this battle particularly challenging. Perhaps fed up with SOS protests, Mayor Frank Fasi told Kelly, "You tell your surfers to go ride the north shore. With four million tourists coming here every year, there just aren't going to be any surfing areas left on the south shore."[17] Fortunately for surfers, SOS's efforts over the years proved Mayor Fasi wrong.

SOS regularly took their protests to legislators at Hawai'i's State Capitol building. Perhaps most memorable was their "Unite to Save Hawaii" rally on March 31, 1971. Advertising the event with flyers printed in Kelly's basement and posted at surf breaks, schools, and community centers around O'ahu, SOS summoned more than two thousand local surfers to the open-air capitol building's rotunda floor. In addition to demanding that the military open

Kailua's North Beach to the public and that development plans for Sandy Beach be halted, SOS had a number of other items to protest. As outlined on their flyers, they were taking a stance against "the plundering and cementing of Hawaii. Land-poor Hawaiians and local farmers evicted by the greedies. Threatened families at Kalama, Kahana, Halawa, Waimanalo, Waianae, Kona, and elsewhere [predominantly Native Hawaiian communities]. Scores of surfing sites in danger. State giveaway land deals to giant corporations at Sand Island, Waikiki and other places. Farms, reefs, historic sites, and wilderness areas chewed up by bulldoser$. Poverty wages. Worst housing crisis and highest cost of living in the U.$."[18] While occupying the entire floor of the expansive capitol rotunda, which resembles the belly of a volcano, young local surfers listened to powerful speeches while nine SOS surfers

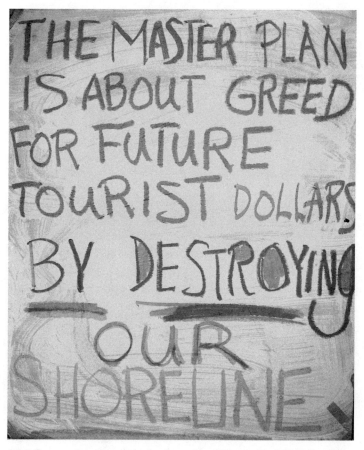

SOS flyer against shoreline development. (Courtesy of Colleen Kelly)

SOS flyer for rally at the Hawai'i State Capitol, 1971. (Courtesy of Colleen Kelly)

Rally at the capitol building in 1971. (Courtesy of Colleen Kelly)

delivered an urgent message to legislators upstairs. They demanded "1) Stop the destruction of surfing areas! 2) Stop the pollution of our coastal waters! And 3) Preserve public access to the coastlines!"[19] To their chagrin, legislators slammed their doors on these surfing "troublemakers." In response, the two thousand surfers began jumping up and down in unison. As the entire building shook, nervous legislators fled to the balcony in fright. Six armed police officers yelled to Kelly, "Eh, Kelly, tell 'em to stop! The cement's cracking! It's falling on us downstairs!" Kelly paused for a moment, then placed his hand on the shoulder of one of the police officers and, with a Pidgin-English accent, said, "You know what, bradda. You go see the governor up there and give him this message: when he stops pouring cement into our surf, we'll stop cracking cement here at the state capitol."[20]

Although SOS focused much of its attention on coastal development, it was also on the front lines of Native Hawaiian protests and issues. In addition to helping organize and man the protests at Kalama Valley, Kelly and SOS protested other communities where Native Hawaiians were being evicted. In 1972 the state tried to evict Hawaiian families living in the traditional Hawaiian fishing village of Mokauea. Only ten acres in size, Mokauea Island in Ke'ehi Lagoon was still home to fourteen Hawaiian families at this time. Despite eviction notices, the families stayed on their island until 1975, when Governor George Ariyoshi ordered that the remaining people be arrested for trespassing and their homes burned to the ground. After five of the fourteen homes went up in flames, SOS quickly intervened. After helping the fishermen organize into the Mokauea Fishermen Association (MFA), SOS got the State Historic Preservation Office involved. Shortly thereafter the island was declared a protected historic site, and SOS helped restore the tattered island community.[21] Likewise, Kelly protested the military conquest of Native Hawaiian communities on O'ahu's west side. In the early 1900s Mākua Valley, near the northwest tip of O'ahu, was a village owned by Hawaiian families (kuleana land) and the Crown (Crown land). In 1942 the U.S. Army took control of the area, evicted Hawaiian families, and used it for target practice. By 1982 forty families had made their way back to Mākua, only to face eviction again by the state of Hawai'i in 1983. While Kelly and fifty supporters attended the trial of those arrested for trespassing, they refused to stand after the bailiff said, "All rise." Although the judge threatened to charge them with contempt of court, they remained seated. They were protesting not just the evictions, but were also calling into question the Waianae District Court judge's authority over Hawaiians in general. In essence, they were challenging the overthrow and annexation of Hawai'i. Mākua Valley helped spur a growing movement toward Hawaiian political autonomy, self-determination, or sovereignty. Sovereignty movements, more common at the turn of the millennium, were bolstered not only by these early protests, but with the development of university courses that began teaching the complex political history of Hawaiian colonialism.

While working in the Department of Ethnic Studies at the University of Hawai'i at Mānoa, Kelly taught some of the first courses to ever critically analyze the history and politics of colonialism in Hawai'i. Founded in 1970 with the slogan "Our History, Our Way," the Department of Ethnic Studies was born out of local disdain for colonial education, a perspective that had dominated the university since its inception in 1907.[22] Invested from the beginning, the Kelly family and SOS were integral to the formation and success of the department at UH Mānoa. While Kelly's wife, Marion, was among the department's first faculty members, Kelly also taught courses in the mid-1970s. Like SOS, the ethnic studies department had to battle politicians and administrators for its survival. Shortly after its creation, the university tried to shut it down. Working in conjunction with SOS, students and faculty rallied and protested to keep ethnic studies alive. Kelly then advertised and promoted the department with flyers and forums, where students were enticed to join something that "combines theory with practice, and attempts to develop an understanding of our local peoples' culture and history and their needs in the changing conditions in Hawaii today."[23] While ethnic studies faculty covered the local history of labor and migration in the early 1970s (e.g., Ethnic Studies 201: Chinese in Hawai'i, and Ethnic Studies 202: Filipinos in Hawai'i), topics in Hawaiian history were most often emphasized by 1973 (e.g., Ethnic Studies 221: The Hawaiians, Ethnic Studies 320: Hawai'i and the Pacific, Ethnic Studies 397: Land Tenure Change in Hawai'i, and Ethnic Studies 398: Social Movements in Hawai'i). Marion Kelly and Myron "Pinky" Thompson (Nainoa Thompson's father) taught Hawaiian history courses in the early 1970s; John Kelly joined them after 1974. Influenced by German scholar Dr. Karl Niebyl, Kelly applied a Marxist approach to analyzing the corporate conquest of the islands under American and business-driven colonial powers. This radical brand of Hawaiian history worked to expose the immoral, illegal, and exploitive nature of the Mahele, the overthrow, annexation, Territory politics, the U.S. military in Hawai'i, and more. While dredging up archival files on developers and local business elites (like Dillingham Corporation) with SOS, Kelly meanwhile uncovered a long history of abuse against Hawaiians at the hands of the military and business elites in Hawai'i. He emphasized these findings to his students in his ethnic studies courses. But in the 1960s, prior to teaching in the ethnic studies department, Kelly gave impromptu lectures on Hawaiian history to young local surfers. One of his most attentive students was a young Hawaiian named Edward Ryan Aikau.

Eddie Aikau and *Hōkūle'a*

Born on May 4, 1946, on the island of Maui, Eddie Aikau was the third of six children born to Sol and Henrietta Aikau. A tight-knit, hard-working Hawaiian family, the Aikaus moved to Honolulu when Eddie was just entering his teen years. While his father worked on the docks unloading cargo from mainland ships, the Aikau family found creative ways to make ends meet. For example, in exchange for maintaining a Chinese cemetery in Honolulu, the family was allowed to live on the cemetery grounds for free. After the children completed their daily chores around the house and cemetery, they usually went surfing. In their early teens, Eddie and his younger brother, Clyde, became the most accomplished surfers in nearby Waikīkī and Ala Moana. While their surfing skills improved, Eddie's attention in school wavered. After much deliberation with his father, "Pops," sixteen-year-old Eddie dropped out of high school and began working at the Dole Cannery. While most of his paycheck went to his family, he still managed to save enough money for a new big-wave surfboard. Although Eddie desperately wanted to ride big waves, especially after watching footage of Kealoha Kaio at Waimea, the North Shore was far from Honolulu. Recognizing Eddie's plight, Pops asked his friend John Kelly for help. Pops knew Kelly and respected his efforts to preserve Hawaiian rights and beaches. Thus when he discovered that Kelly made regular trips to the North Shore, Pops asked him to take Eddie along. Kelly willingly made the detour to pick up the young Hawaiian surfer. During these long car rides over bumpy plantation roads, Kelly taught Eddie the complex colonial history of Hawai'i, a stark contrast from the pro-American lessons he had learned in school. Sammy Lee, another young local passenger, recounted to author Stuart Coleman how they learned lessons about Pearl Harbor, the Mahele, plantations, politics, and colonialism. Coleman summarizes, "As they bounced through endless pineapple fields, stirring up clouds of red dust in their wake, he would tell them about how the Hawaiians lost their land; how a few rich haole families had divided it into plantations, housing developments and tourist resorts. In this way he taught them about land, politics and power, lessons Eddie would remember later in his life."[24]

Surprisingly, the young Waikīkī surfer instantly took to the giant waves like a veteran. By 1969 Eddie had already earned a reputation as one of the world's top big-wave surfers. While his regular placing in the Duke Invitational heightened his popularity, he earned more respect when free surfing the massive Waimea waves. His reputation as a big-wave expert not only brought him fame, but also opened the door to a career change—from canning pineapples to being a North Shore lifeguard. After receiving awards by

Eddie Aikau after winning the 1977 Duke Invitational. (Photo by Parry Medeiros)

the City and County of Honolulu for rescuing hundreds of people in dangerous North Shore conditions, Eddie was revered as a quiet giant. But his confidence in the ocean was rooted in his rising pride in being Hawaiian, in a kind of symbiotic balance. Thus when foreign surfers touted their dominance in Hawaiian waves and Hawaiians formed the Hui O He'e Nalu to offset them, Eddie and his family became involved. Eddie's family was integral to the formation of this hui (especially his father, brother Clyde, and sister Myra). Although Bryan Amona and Billy Ho'ola'e Blankenfeld disagree, a 1987 *Honolulu Advertiser* article states that Pops Aikau founded the Hui O He'e Nalu.[25] Regardless who founded it, Eddie's family was an essential part of the Hui's early history. In 1976 Eddie served as a mediator between haole professional surfers and the Hui—on one particular occasion at Kuilima, Eddie helped a few Australian surfers make peace with the Hawaiian locals.[26] Although Eddie contributed to a rising Hawaiian pride among North Shore surfers, he set his sights on a deeper ocean project, sailing the newly built *Hōkūle'a* traditional voyaging canoe.

In 1973 Hawaiian artists Herb Kane, University of Hawai'i anthropology professor Ben Finney, and a young local-haole Hawai'i Beachboy named Tommy Holmes formed the Polynesian Voyaging Society (PVS). Earlier in the year Kane and Holmes had asked Finney to help build a replica model of an ancient Hawaiian or Polynesian long-distance voyaging canoe. Finney was a good candidate since he had built a smaller, similar craft while living in Santa Barbara nearly a decade earlier. As an artist and a Hawaiian interested in rediscovering his ancestors' culture, Kane had researched and drawn sketches of various Polynesian voyaging canoes with a determination to one day sail one. Kane shared with Finney his dream of sailing such a craft roundtrip to Tahiti. He also told Finney he would like it to be crewed primarily by Hawaiians, Tahitians, and other Polynesians. Finney replied, "Sounds good to me."[27]

Finney also saw this as a great research opportunity. The idea of reconstructing a long-distance traditional voyaging canoe was alluring because he believed it would settle a particular academic dispute, one in which he was actively engaged at the time. Finney's academic adversaries, made up primarily of armchair academics like Andrew Sharp, had proposed a new theory that Polynesians settled the Pacific Islands by accident. For Finney, this theory was troubling because it hinged on a racist notion that Polynesians were not smart enough to traverse the vast Pacific Ocean by design. While his published articles defended the ingenuity of Polynesian voyagers, they did not resolve the dispute. Finney believed a replicated voyage would quiet his opponents.[28]

After successful fund raising in the early part of 1974, the PVS built *Hōkūleʻa*. Kane had designed the ship with a series of detailed drawings based on historical sources. Over the next year the PVS, with the help of both paid and volunteer workers, completed their canoe. In 1975 the *Hōkūleʻa* celebrated its first launch into Hawaiian waters off Kualoa Bay on the east side of Oʻahu. Over the next few months PVS founders and a variety of local Hawaiian crew members sailed *Hōkūleʻa* throughout the Hawaiian Island chain. During these trips Kane recruited more Hawaiian crew members, primarily expert swimmers and surfers from Oʻahu and Molokaʻi, to train and work on the canoe. As they did, the canoe quickly became a symbol of the Hawaiian renaissance. It was as if it carried the revival of Hawaiian culture and pride on its deck. Finney explained how for many Hawaiians, including Kane, the project became a mission. *"Hōkūleʻa's* sacred mission, Kane began to preach, was to uplift the Hawaiian people, to be the catalyst for the Hawaiian renaissance. Culture is nothing without its artifacts, he reasoned. The restoration of the voyaging canoe, once the central artifact of Polynesian culture, would reawaken in young Hawaiians an ethnic pride worn down by the Americanization of Hawaii and all the developments that have transformed the Hawaiians into an underprivileged group."[29]

Hōkūleʻa launch, 1975. (Photo by Parry Medeiros)

Eddie was among a constituency of Hawaiians who trained on *Hōkūleʻa* in 1975 as part of their preparation to sail from Hawaiʻi to Tahiti. As it did for the other crew members involved in this training, the canoe became a symbol of Eddie's Hawaiian identity. This was especially true for most of the Hawaiian surfers involved in this project, as they already had a cultural connection with the ocean. But cultural pride provoked high emotions, and this took its toll on some of the crew. As racial tensions slowly mounted during the canoe project, some Hawaiian crew members saw the PVS leadership as top-heavy and too haole. Discouraged by these tensions, some crew members, Eddie Aikau included, pulled out of the crew who would sail on the first voyage to Tahiti. However, Eddie anticipated joining them on their planned second voyage.

Perhaps to prevent strife on the canoe, Kane even asked Finney to sit out during their interisland training voyages. Since Finney was mostly interested in the main trip, their upcoming voyage to Tahiti, he reluctantly complied. As crew members spent more time celebrating the canoe on the outer islands instead of carrying out the rigorous and necessary training, near tragedy struck and the canoe was swamped. It was towed to nearby Kauaʻi, from which they had disembarked hours earlier, and a council was brought together. Here, the PVS decided to restructure the leadership on the canoe and make needed renovations. Kane was replaced as captain and later opted out of the voyage to Tahiti. However, he was replaced by another Hawaiian, Elia "Kawika" Kapahulehua—a Native of Niʻihau, fluent Hawaiian-language speaker, and experienced sailing captain. The ship was also now guided by the navigational genius of a Micronesian named Mau Piailug.

Under its new structure, *Hōkūleʻa* sailed successfully to Tahiti in the spring of 1976. Relying on traditional methods of reading waves, stars, and wind, Mau accurately guided *Hōkūleʻa* across nearly three thousand miles of open ocean. Although Mau's navigation went smoothly, tensions on deck made social conditions quite rough. Frustrations climaxed in violence the day before the canoe sailed into Papeete, Tahiti, on June 3, 1976. The majority of the Hawaiian crewmen—Mākaha surfer Buffalo Keaulana and five of his friends in particular—resented the haole leadership. However, of the seventeen people on board, only five were haole, and two of those were National Geographic cameramen. To make things more complicated, the captain, whom many crew members resented, was a full-blooded Hawaiian. To six of the Hawaiians (whom Finney called "the gang") Kawika was a puppet of Finney. But their animosity toward Finney stemmed from a core, unarticulated debate over who was in charge of the voyage and why. For "the gang,"

Finney had coopted a Hawaiian mission in the name of haole research and at the expense of the Native sailors. These Hawaiian crew members felt that their leaders were unsympathetic to the Hawaiian struggle.

Authenticity and authority were at the heart of this conflict. For all the Hawaiians on board the ship, Kawika included, ritual was crucial to their success. Whether it was prayer, making offerings to the Hawaiian god Kanaloa, ensuring that Hawaiian religious ki'i (carved statues) were treated properly, or following the council of Hawaiian kahuna (priests), ritual was not only essential, but also that which authenticated the trip for Hawaiians. Finney often saw ritual as nonessential, and he considered much of the kahuna work sorcery.[30] However, Finney was a stickler for authenticity, and, often to the chagrin of Hawaiian crew members, he insisted that they sustain themselves throughout the voyage with only traditional items. For example, only traditional foods were allowed—dried fish, poi, fresh fish they caught en route, and dried bananas. Modern devices and amenities were also taboo—watches, radios, maps, jibs (smaller triangular sails), and the like. Finney became quite upset when he found out that some Hawaiians had smuggled unauthorized items on board—a candy bar, a miniature radio, a miniature stove, and pakalolo (marijuana). Tensions over what validated the authenticity of the voyage were reflective of and intertwined with struggles over authority. For the Hawaiians, the renaissance empowered them to reassert their authority in a society that had historically marginalized them. Whereas many saw Hawaiians of earlier decades as submissive to haole dominance and colonization, these younger Hawaiians were activists who were determined to reclaim that which had been taken from them. Since the *Hōkūle'a* was symbolically the vessel that ushered in this period of change, resistance, and renaissance for Hawaiians, crew members were angry at the thought of haole overseeing that voyage. Although Finney often criticized the Americanization and colonization of Hawai'i, he was unable to submit his authority to Hawaiians on the first voyage—even though he made several concessions. While the Hawaiians saw the renaissance as a tool for claiming authority over the voyage, Finney used his research to legitimize his authority.

Power struggles between Finney and Buffalo Keaulana on board *Hōkūle'a* revealed deeper issues. Several displaced battles over authority were played out on the ship. Most notable was one fought over the addition of a jib sail. Nine days into their thirty-three day voyage, and while Finney slept, some crew members attached a makeshift jib to the forestay of the canoe. Irate over the thought of jeopardizing his research project—a jib is not a Polynesian device—Finney convinced Kawika to make them lower it at once. Keaulana replied, "Tahiti is a long way and we're having a hard time getting there. We need all the help we can get." According to Keaulana, Finney had "no right to tell them that their ancestors did not have a jib."[31] While Keaulana's defense of the jib was most likely an attack on Finney's claim to authority (his research), he did make his point: he told Finney he was angry over "haoles telling Hawaiians what to do!"[32] The exchange that followed is telling. Finney responded, "But it's my job as president of the Voyaging Society to see that we stick to our plans!"[33] Here, Finney backed up his authority with emblems of his class. Using what many locals would classify as "typical haole behavior," Finney reminded Keaulana of his position and status—he spoke not only of his "job," but his "presidency" over an official "Voyaging Society" organization.[34] While historically it has often been difficult for Hawaiians to counter such status claims, since modern society often validated Western status symbols—especially in an American-run Hawai'i that ranks Natives low on the social scale—Keaulana confidently rejected Finney's comment and validated his authority by linking himself to the ocean and the waves.[35] He said, "When it gets rough, when the big waves start coming over the canoe, we're [Hawaiian crew of surfers] going to be standing here steering the canoe and you're going to be down inside hiding."[36] Here, Buffalo made it clear that his confidence and expertise in raging surf trumped Finney, and it made him feel better. After making this all clear to Finney, Buffalo found his resolve, tension dissipated, and the meeting ended.

Although some of the Hawaiian crew members crossed a line by the end of the voyage, the tensions reveal the particular kinds of issues and frustrations that plagued many Hawaiians of this era, and surfers in particular. After the six Hawaiians who made up this "gang" aimed their frustrations about slow sailing at the leadership of the canoe, they separated themselves from the others, stopped performing some of their duties on the ship, and eventually attacked three other crew members (Finney and Kawika included). The gang was composed mostly of accomplished watermen and surfers. Some of them, most notably Keaulana, were also instrumental in starting the Hui O He'e Nalu shortly after their return from Tahiti. And like Keaulana, North Shore Hawaiian surfers shared a similar concern about haole authority and claims to authenticity. They also found, as did Keaulana, self-validation when connecting themselves to the ocean and the surf and defining themselves as Hawaiian watermen.

The return trip to Hawai'i was calm, peaceful, and quick. With the tension of the first trip left in *Hōkūle'a*'s wake, the PVS began planning for a second trip. Most likely because of his reputation as an ocean lifesaver and skilled surfer, Eddie Aikau was selected (from a long list of qualified candidates) to sail *Hōkūle'a* to Tahiti on its 1978 voyage. As throngs of Hawai'i residents bade farewell, the crew found itself reluctant to sail into the gale-force winds and rough seas. Bowing to spectator pressure, the captain, David Lyman, opened the sails and the canoe rocketed into the raging seas. While still only a few miles out from Lāna'i, one of the hulls took on water and the canoe capsized. Without an escort boat or radio, they sat, drifting in the current. Afraid that they would not be found, Eddie finally convinced the captain to let him paddle his surfboard to Lāna'i and get help. Eventually an airplane spotted *Hōkūle'a* and the crew was rescued. Eddie was never found.

Though Eddie's death caused grief among many Hawaiian surfers, his passing inspired an increase in Hawaiian cultural identity and pride, which Eddie died preserving. Master navigator Nainoa Thompson explained this sacrifice. "At a deeper level, Eddie tried to rescue not only the crew of the *Hōkūle'a* but the symbolism and dignity of the canoe because he knew it carried the pride of his people."[37] In honor of Eddie's memory, the Hui O He'e Nalu worked together with other forces to create the world's most respected big-wave professional surfing competition, the Quiksilver Eddie Aikau Memorial. This invitational meet is held only when the waves are larger than twenty feet and the conditions are perfect. Over the years, the Hui O He'e Nalu has helped organize opening ceremonies for the event and still assists with water safety, security, and the like.

Kaho'olawe Protests

Moments before *Hōkūle'a* embarked on its first voyage to Tahiti in April 1976, a group of Hawaiian protesters from Maui and Moloka'i asked if the crew would take them to the island of Kaho'olawe, used by the U.S. Navy for target practice. After the U.S. Coast Guard warned Captain Kapahulehua that they would confiscate *Hōkūle'a* and pull his license if he did, Kapahulehua flatly told the Kaho'olawe protesters no. But for the crew, Finney included, the thought of sailing these Hawaiians to the forbidden, sacred island was appealing. If the *Hōkūle'a* stirred pride in Hawaiian ingenuity, Kaho'olawe protesters fueled Hawaiian resistance. The combination of the two groups would kindle exciting publicity.

On December 8, 1941, the U.S. government leased all twenty-eight thousand acres of Kaho'olawe and began using it as a military bombing target. Although the government said they would return it to the state at the end of World War II, President Dwight Eisenhower instead signed an executive order in 1953 that gave jurisdiction of the island to the U.S. Navy. The navy continued to shell and bomb Kahoʻolawe, catastrophically damaging the island ecology. For example, after the military detonated a five-hundred-ton bomb—created to simulate an atomic blast—at Sailor's Hat in 1965, the island's groundwater supply was depleted. Also, the deadly litter accumulated from military tests overwhelmed Kahoʻolawe's landscape and threatened the safety of would-be visitors to the island. In the mid-1970s several Hawaiians organized a hui on the nearby island of Maui and began planning strategies for stopping the bombs and reclaiming the island for the people of Hawaiʻi.

Modeling themselves after a Native American cohort that had occupied the island of Alcatraz months prior, on January 4, 1976, nine Hawaiian protesters boated onto Kahoʻolawe in an attempt to occupy the island.[38] Called the "Kahoʻolawe 9," the group docked, planted a coconut tree, gathered ʻopihi (Native shellfish) and crabs, and explored the battered island. By the end of the day seven of the nine were taken off the island and returned to Maui. The remaining protesters, Walter Ritte and Dr. Emmet Aluli, held out for two days—playing hide-and-seek with a U.S. Marine helicopter for most of that time. The occupation did not go as planned. The group initially had arranged for twenty members to come to the island, and they had hoped to stay for much longer. But when a U.S. Coast Guard helicopter threatened to confiscate their boats, some went back to Maui. Charles Maxwell, one of the Hawaiian organizers of the occupation, said that they were not discouraged by the results of the first attempt. He said, "This will happen again and again and again" in order to "prove to the government . . . that this island is owned by the aboriginal Hawaiian people and we will not stop until we accomplish this."[39]

Maxwell proved true to his word. After the first occupation, the group gathered more support and organized another attempt. On January 12, 1976, and after telegramming U.S. president Gerald Ford, asking him to return the island to the Hawaiians, Emmet Aluli, Walter Ritte, his wife, Loretta Ritte, and his sister, Scarlett Ritte, returned to Kahoʻolawe. Five days later they were removed; Walter Ritte was arrested for trespassing on a military reservation and jailed by the FBI. On January 19 he was released on a five-hundred-dollar bail. As group support and opposition grew, the protesters organized a hui called the Protect Kahoʻolawe Ohana (PKO). Founded by Kanaka Maoli activists like Walter Ritte, Emmet Aluli, and George Helm, the PKO returned to the island on several different occasions. They also filed a civil suit against the U.S. Navy in federal court. In 1976 the PKO sued the navy for violating historical site laws, environmental protection laws, and the Native American Freedom of Religion Act. At some point thereafter, the most charismatic Hawaiian leader in the PKO, George Helm, mysteriously disappeared with Kimo Mitchell. The two were last seen paddling on a surfboard near Molokini, a smaller island between Maui and Kahoʻolawe. Some speculated that their disappearance was no accident, and that foul play was a factor. Aluli called Helm a smart, gifted leader who had become a kind of prophet for the PKO group and the Hawaiian people in general.[40] The disappearances of Helm and Mitchell fueled the steadfastness of Hawaiian activists.

In 1981 the PKO settled with the navy outside the courtroom. They signed a consent decree stating that the navy would not bomb the island for ten days out of every month, would bomb only the middle third of the island, would eradicate island goats, protect archaeological sites, and conduct soil conservation projects. The PKO could visit the island each month during the ten-day no-bombing period. Although the bombing subsided over the next few years, it was not until 1990 that they it was officially stopped. In November of that year a measure was drafted by Hawaiʻi U.S. senators Daniel Inouye and Daniel Akaka and signed into law, stating that the military would no longer bomb the island. In 2003 the island was turned over to the state of Hawaiʻi. Today, the PKO organizes regular cleanup projects on Kahoʻolawe, supported by volunteers who share the desire to rid the island of an overwhelming amount of military debris.

Kahoʻolawe has been described by many Hawaiians as a place where one can find one's identity as a Native Hawaiian and simultaneously find a renewed resolve to resist imperialism. Emmet Aluli said of the Kahoʻolawe protests, "It was a very beautiful island, an island that was being destroyed, an island that was actually calling us deeper to a commitment to stop whatever destruction was happening. We decided then that we had to follow our naʻau, as we put it those days, our guts, and to fight to end the bombing of Kahoʻolawe."[41] Sam Amalu said of the protests in 1976, "From the day that James Cook set foot on Hawaiian soil, the Native people of Hawaiʻi have suffered endless hardships, and these hardships still continue to this very day. A little flame has been lit at Kahoolawe. Pray God it will become a torch and a beacon."[42] I believe Amalu's prayer was answered. The protests did light a fire of resistance in Hawaiʻi that burned bright in the late 1970s. Along with the PVS and SOS, the PKO's protests were critical fuel for the growing fire of resistance in the era called the Hawaiian renaissance.

Masculinity, Surfers, and the Hawaiian Renaissance

Although North Shore surfing pride correlated with a cultural and political renaissance that grew in the islands in the late 1970s, surfing did not need a rebirth. While Hawaiian cultural restoration projects were undertaken in which more people learned to speak the Hawaiian language and dance the hula, the Hawaiian practice of surfing remained continuous, and Hawaiian men had a place there. A crucial problem for the cultural renaissance was that several Hawaiian men saw cultural restoration art forms like the hula as soft and unmanly expressions of their identity. In 1977 Hawaiian historian and cultural advocate George Kanahele noted that although more Hawaiian men were dancing hula in 1977, in earlier years "no local boy would be caught dead dancing the hula for fear of being called a sissy."[43] In his work on the Hale Mua O Maui, Ty Tengan explains that starting in the early 1990s Hawaiian male groups, originally called Nā Koa (courageous ones, the warriors) and often based around traditional Hawaiian martial arts training, were formed in direct reaction to the perceived feminization of Hawaiian culture.[44] While many expressions of Hawaiian culture were seen as unmasculine to a number of Hawaiian men, groups like Nā Koa sought to create a space for men in a modern and cultural context. While even Hawaiians now defined some modern notions of manhood along Western gender lines, Hawaiian men often found cultural continuity in the surf.

Poʻina nalu was a place where Hawaiian men forged masculine identities prior to, during, and since the twentieth century. In that century, surfing was perceived as an inherently Hawaiian sport and a clearly masculine activity.[45] Perhaps because colonial and missionary influence generally stopped at the shoreline, the ocean was one of few places where Kanaka men could participate in an expressive cultural form and remain masculine. Thus not only were Hawaiian surfers inspired by the spirit of cultural pride in the 1970s, but more importantly, they were motivated to preserve a Native space where Hawaiians could be both masculine and cultural.

Surfers helped shape the Hawaiian renaissance in more profound ways than others have previously considered. While most historians point to the 1970s as the dawn of Hawaiian renaissance activism, the SOS protests of the

1960s foreshadowed and set the stage for others. Since the early 1900s surfers had become accustomed to fighting for their surf zone; thus SOS was one of the most successful environmental groups of its time. Though they stopped many coastal development projects, they also supported Native Hawaiian struggles against evictions and other civil rights violations. With the establishment of the Department of Ethnic Studies, the Kelly family and SOS educated Hawai'i's peoples about Native Hawaiian perspectives in history. In addition to SOS, the *Hōkūle'a* voyages and Kaho'olawe protests contributed to a spirit of pride and resistance throughout Hawai'i in 1976, which is the same year Hawaiian surfers on the North Shore began organizing the Hui O He'e Nalu. As the *Hōkūle'a* delivered the spirit of Hawaiian cultural pride to Kānaka Maoli, the Hui had direct access to that sentiment through some of its founding members. The frustrations some Hawaiian watermen had on the first voyage to Tahiti reflected the feelings many Hawaiians had toward haole claims to authority and authenticity during these years of revival and resistance. These conflicts also revealed that Hawaiians found validity in the ocean and surf. Through such influences, and the involvement of Hui surfers like Eddie Aikau and Buffalo Keaulana, the Hui both participated in and benefited from the vibrant 1970s movement. But as the Hui molded and defined itself through such cultural influences, Hollywood and the Honolulu newspapers increasingly defined them not as cultural activists, but as terrorists.

CHAPTER 6

The Hui O Heʻe Nalu

The predominantly Native Hawaiian North Shore organization, Hui O Heʻe Nalu, was formed in reaction to a burgeoning, predominantly haole professional surfing industry that started on the North Shore in 1976. For Hui members, this industry threatened a Hawaiian pastime, social sanctuary, and cultural identity. The Hui O Heʻe Nalu was first created by a group of North Shore Hawaiian surfers at a home near Sunset Beach. As their membership grew in the late 1970s and early 1980s, their purpose remained the same: to resist the exploitation of the North Shore by haole surfers and the surfing industry. They challenged this professional industry first through protest, then through compromise. The Hui helped reduce the number of competitions held on the North Shore, gained access to profits from these events, and provided activities and services for the North Shore community. The club, still in existence today, has evolved over the years. Despite such fluidity, heʻe nalu (surfing) has remained the glue that holds the membership together. For Hui members, heʻe nalu is a cultural and indigenous pastime, something they have strongly identified with as Hawaiians. Considering the context of Hawaiʻi in 1976—a period of intense Native activism and cultural rejuvenation—as well as the history of Hawaiian resistance against foreign conquest in the surf zone since the overthrow of the Hawaiian kingdom, Hawaiian members of the Hui O Heʻe Nalu were products of both their past and their present. Thus they engaged with waves of resistance to protect their identity, culture, and space from further conquest. While Hui aggressiveness in preserving their space in the surf has often been seen as excessive, one cannot divorce the Hui from the colonial history that gave birth to them. While acts of violence, even by Hawaiians, at the time are deplorable, critics of Hawaiian aggressiveness conveniently ignore the violence inflicted on Hawaiians for centuries and refuse to recognize how these abuses have shaped the Hui.

Because a history of the Hui O Heʻe Nalu has not been previously written, my first objective here is to record a cohesive historical narrative. Since I am primarily constructing this narrative from oral history interviews, this chapter emphasizes individual perspectives and issues of identity from a predominantly Hawaiian constituency. Also, while this chapter establishes the narrative and amplifies Native voices, chapter 7 will analyze deeper issues on the politics of identity, representation, and media stereotyping.

Professional Surf History on the North Shore

In 1976 the North Shore of Oʻahu was the birthplace of a professional surfing tour now called the Association of Surfing Professionals (ASP) World Tour. Although professional surfing existed a decade prior, it was far less energetic and ambitious. Starting in 1965, the Duke Kahanamoku Surfing Classic was the sole competition on the North Shore, and it was not technically a professional meet until it offered a cash prize of one thousand dollars to its winner in 1968. Later, the 1970 Smirnoff Pro and the 1971 Pipeline Masters joined the Duke Kahanamoku Surfing Classic. Although these earlier contests began attracting an international surfing contingency, they were still isolated events in the sense that they were not affiliated with a surf circuit, or series of surfing events. Also, the only way to get into these events was through invitation, and such invitations were limited, determined by contest officials, and based on a person's reputation in the surf on the North Shore. Although these three events made up the bulk of professional surfing competitions on the North Shore in the early 1970s, by 1977 there were twenty-four annually run surf meets (at various competitive levels) held on the North Shore.[1] It was amid this excitement that a professional surfing series was formed.

In 1976 two mainland-born and Honolulu-raised haole surfers, Fred Hemmings and Randy Rarick, started International Professional Surfers (IPS).[2] The first of its kind, the IPS was a circuit of professional surfing events that, through accumulated points, crowned an annual world surfing champion.[3] Among other things, the purpose of the IPS, according to Hemmings, was to "qualify surfing as a legitimate sport."[4] But they also made money with these events—primarily from contest sponsors and television stations. Though considered jewels of the IPS crown, the North Shore events (e.g., the Pipeline Masters, the Duke Kahanamoku Classic, the Smirnoff Pro, and others) became part of a series of professional surfing contests that incorporated others from New Zealand, Australia, Florida, South Africa, and Brazil. As these events generated greater hype for surfing and the North Shore events were broadcast on American national television networks (such as ABC and NBC), the IPS opened millions of eyes to the O'ahu countryside.

The events on the North Shore, held at popular breaks like Sunset, Hale'iwa, Pipeline, and Laniakea, invited spectators and enticed would-be champion surfers from around the world to this pristine, seven-mile shoreline. In this way the events encouraged a large-scale migration—or for some surfers, pilgrimages—to the legendary North Shore surf. But for Native Hawaiians from the North Shore and adjacent communities, their far-from-Waikīkī neighborhoods were "being inundated with surfers from around the world, and" as one North Shore resident explained, "no one at the time knew how to deal with it."[5] While frustration in many local Hawaiians increased, for other Hawaiian surfers the competitions were opportunities to win accolades.

Chuck Waipā Andrus drops into a wave at Pipeline in the early 1980s, North Shore, O'ahu. (Courtesy of Chuck Andrus)

Like their ancestors of old, many Hawaiian surfers reveled and excelled in competitive surfing. In fact, Hawaiian surfers frequently outperformed other competitors in the North Shore contests during the late 1960s and 1970s. Among the more prominent surfers were Barry Kanaiaupuni, Reno Abellira, Clyde Aikau, Eddie Aikau, Larry Bertlemann, Buttons Kaluhiokalani, Michael Ho, and Dane Kealoha. Although Hawai'i surfers were known to dominate in the large Hawaiian waves, a young cohort of Australian surfers challenged these top Hawaiian surfers in the mid-1970s.

Young Australians and the Bronzed Aussies

Although Hawaiian surfers have "always led the way in progressive oceanic innovations," young Australian surfers began pushing competitive surfing performances.[6] In 1976 three of Australia's brightest surfers organized a team called the Bronzed Aussies. Consisting of Mark Warren, Peter Townend, and Ian Cairns, they were also among the top competitors in the new IPS series—one of them, Townend, won the first IPS world title. Inspired by an Australian trio that dominated professional tennis in the 1960s, the Bronzed Aussies felt they could grab more media attention and a stronger competitive edge as a unit. Through their "radical" approach to wave riding and their flamboyant fashion style on the beach—they often wore unusual jumpsuits to the surf contests—they found the attention they were looking for.[7] Though other Australian surfing professionals, like Wayne "Rabbit" Bartholomew, were not officially part of the team, the Bronzed Aussies' spirit characterized most Australian surfers on the North Shore at this time. First and foremost, they marketed themselves as aggressive and extremely competitive. After they claimed three of the seven IPS events on the North Shore in 1976, they started flaunting their success.

The young Australians strutted and ruffled a few feathers on the North Shore in 1975 and 1976. Although Hawaiian surfers won four of the seven IPS events in 1976, the Australian surfers boasted to the media how they had toppled a thousand-year Hawaiian surfing reign. Australian surfers gained a reputation for trash-talking, in and out of the water. In a 1977 surfer magazine article a fellow Australian surfer claimed that the Bronzed Aussies and Rabbit Bartholomew in particular were "absolute monster[s] in the water, [who] would continually cut people off."[8] Not only were they notoriously aggressive in the water, but the spirited Australians also paraded themselves as the world's greatest surfers in surfing media and claimed dominance over Hawaiian waves and Hawaiian surfers in newspaper articles and surfing magazines.[9] In a letter, Rabbit Bartholomew boasted to Peter Townend (this letter eventually got into the hands of local surfers), saying, "We're as hot as shit over here, Australians are the biggest thing in surfing, they [Hawaiians] are looking to us for inspiration."[10] Even IPS contest director Fred Hemmings called them "provocative characters . . . with an aggressive style that did not endear them to the North Shore regulars." "In the short run," Hemmings continued, "they made business difficult."[11] Though some Australians, like Rabbit, later learned cultural sensitivity, in 1976 they enjoyed tooting their horns in true Bronzed Aussie–sportsman fashion.

During this time, local Hawai'i and Native Hawaiian surfers became less tolerant of Aussie attitudes and antics.[12] Several Hawaiian surfers were upset by Australian aggressiveness in the water and their claims of dominating the North Shore. Local Hawaiian surfers took to calling the Australians the "Bronzed A-holes."[13] Terry Ahue, a legendary Hawaiian surfer and lifeguard, characterized these surfers as "real arrogant kinds of people. They were called those days the Bronzed Aussies. . . . They were over here just like walking all over us. You know, with our kind heart and everything we give, and let them come here. But they started trying to take over everything. 'Oh we're this, we're that.' "[14] Another Hawaiian surfer said, "They came off as real arrogant and egotistical; they weren't well liked. It's one thing doing this in your own country, but to come do this in someone else's country is basically having no respect."[15]

Many Hawaiians also saw the Australians as racist. Ahue explained, "The problem was, they came over here and [were] like, 'Hawaiians get out of the way' . . . because the way they are brought up over there, they are real competitors. That's just their nature. But we were considered aborigines, I guess, when they came over here. So we were like a second race to them. So they thought they could just, White man rule, and take over. And we said screw this, this is not going to happen."[16] Many Hawaiian surfers learned firsthand about such racism while traveling on the IPS surf tour. Bryan Amona learned the reality of racism and segregation while in South Africa and related this treatment to the way Australians treated Hawaiians on the North Shore.

> In South Africa we weren't treated well at all. I mean, it depended on the color of your skin; if you were dark skinned you weren't treated well at all. They had the apartheid thing going on back then and they were very preju- diced. And all the lower-class people were the ones doing all the menial work, the servants, the waiters, and all that. These were all black people

or Indian people who were in these jobs. And you go to a restaurant and they wouldn't serve us. They would look at us like, "What are you doing here?" You know, "You're just like me; I am not going to serve you. You don't belong here. You should be in another restaurant, or someplace else with your own kind." And coming from Hawai'i, we didn't understand that. Especially Dane [Kealoha] and I, we were like, "What's up?" We'd go into the restaurant and we'd be the first guys in the restaurant, but we'd be the last guys to get served. And the only way we'd get served is we'd ask our haole friends, like Buzzy Kerbox, "Hey could you order food for us, 'cause they're not serving us." They wouldn't serve us. And it was a big cultural shock going to use the restroom and there would be signs saying "Colored" and "Non-coloreds." I wouldn't know which one to use; I'd just walk into any one. And I'd get stink eye, like, "Hey, what are you doing here? You don't belong here." It was real different back then.[17]

Although Amona noted that South Africa was on the extreme end of racial prejudice, he still noted that "the Australians, they brought a lot of that

Bryan Amona, key founder of the Hui O He'e Nalu, at 'Ehukai Beach Park, 2008. (Photo by Mark Holladay Lee)

[racism] over [to Hawai'i]," but "Hawai'i is such a diverse bunch of people, there's no room for it. There's no room for prejudice; it just doesn't work over here. And they may want to try it, but it doesn't work."[18]

As frustration mounted in Hawaiians, the Australian surfers found themselves in a difficult position with a handful of Native Hawaiian surfers of the north and east sides of O'ahu.[19] Hawaiian North Shore surfers were not only offended by Australian aggressiveness and racist attitudes, but also threatened

"Rabbit" Bartholomew strutting his stuff in Everlast boxing robes. (Courtesy of Merkel/A-frame Photo)

by the exploitative nature of the surfing world in general. Many haole surfers were introduced to a community of Native Hawaiians who were more intent on preserving their community from foreign encroachment than impressing judges at professional surf contests. Unfortunately, most haole still perceived Native Hawaiians as happy-go-lucky, passive Natives. Amona explained, "Since the Hawaiians were laid back and real low key they [Australians] thought, 'Oh, these guys are nothing. We're going to walk all over them.' Basically that's how the Hawaiians were, low key, lots of aloha. Then they just said they had enough, no more aloha, the aloha ran out. These guys [Australians] ended up getting lickings. Push came to shove, they just pushed, pushed, pushed, and pretty soon the guys just snapped, and they found out, hey, these Hawaiians can get pretty angry if you mess with them."[20]

One of the first violent incidents occurred at Sunset Beach on October 3, 1976. While in the surf lineup at Sunset Point, Rabbit Bartholomew was confronted by a couple of North Shore Hawaiian surfers. According to Bartholomew, he had been warned by surfer "Owl" Chapman (whom Rabbit dismissed as "tripping out"), given the cold shoulder by surfer Ken Bradshaw, and ignored by Barry Kanaiaupuni before three Hawaiian surfers paddled up to him, asked if his name was Rabbit, then punched him. Then they held him under water, brought him back up, and punched him again. Teetering on the edge of consciousness, Rabbit barely managed to get to the shore. As tourists took photos of a bleeding Bartholomew surrounded by a crowd of Hawaiian surfers on the beach, Bartholomew thought of Captain Cook and the melee that had taken his life in Kealakekua. "It was like a ritual of manhood, a full public display of anger. I had no idea of the history and heritage of Hawai'i and how everyone—from the early traders, to the missionaries, to the modern-day real estate developers—had always come and taken from them. But I must have appeared the absolute enemy trying to steal the last vestige of their heritage—surfing. I didn't know any of this at the time—I was just a naïve kid."[21]

After this incident, Rabbit first hid in a nearby bush, then later in a North Shore Kuilima Hotel room (now called Turtle Bay).[22] While in the room, Bartholomew was joined by the captain of the Bronzed Aussies, Ian Cairns, who had also earned a bad reputation. According to Bartholomew and Cairns, they were afraid for their lives, "doing shifts with tennis rackets, standing guard in case they came for us during the night, huddled in this little condominium."[23] One Hui surfer remembered, "Those guys started to be real uneasy about things, because you know they are in Hawai'i, surrounded by local boys, and let's be honest man . . . you see some of the local braddahs that are walking around, they are not small people. Plus you're in somebody else's homeland. They were starting to feel real small and insignificant."[24]

However, several Hawaiians later said that Australians' fears of Hawaiians attacking them with guns and knives were greatly exaggerated. In a 1977 *Surfer* magazine article, Hawaiian professional surfer Reno Abellira explained, "I knew that under the surface tension, there was a possibility of it going further into more violent acts. But I doubted very much if someone's house was going to get burned, or someone was going to get knifed in the middle of the night. I really doubted that. It was kind of funny . . . really bizarre."[25]

After Bartholomew and Cairns had spent several weeks hiding and surfing only at breaks near the Kuilima Hotel, Eddie Aikau brought Hawaiian and Australian surfers together in one of the hotel's conference rooms to resolve tensions and misunderstandings. Though Eddie confessed to the Australians, "I don't dig what you've done; I'm a proud Hawaiian," he also wanted the conflict to end.[26] Australian surfer Mark Richards remembered the meeting as a great success and claimed that tensions disappeared right afterward.[27]

Hawaiian surfers saw the October 3 incident as less random than the Aussies did. One Hui surfer remembered Hawaiians getting upset over comments made in the media. He said, "We didn't appreciate what they had written and we let 'em know about it. . . . Rabbit was real aggressive; he was acting like a real fool, because of his aggressive nature and competitive nature."[28] But according to some Hawaiians, the final straw was when Bartholomew harassed Hawaiian surfer Barry Kanaiaupuni one day in the water at Sunset Beach. Abellira described the situation in an article and then explained why Hawaiians were so offended by Australians' brash attitudes. "I don't think they fully grasped the situation here; how deeply the Aikaus feel about their surfing. It's a pride trip. I knew some of those guys were going to take Ian and Rabbit the wrong way. . . . It's really a different psyche in Australia. . . . The sportsman/hero type of situation. You're almost expected to be like that. Over here, it's kind of if you've done the job well, you really don't have to go shouting it from one end of the place to the other."[29] Even fellow Bronzed Aussie Mark Warren felt his mates were out of line, telling *Surfer* magazine in 1977, "I kind of felt like they deserved it. . . . He [Ian Cairns] tends to be a little obnoxious . . . but I think it was unfair the way it happened."[30]

According to several Hawaiians, Australian surfers continued to trash-talk Hawaiians in their media after the 1976 surf season. Billy Blankenfeld explained,

> In '78, Fred gave us an article and it was an article that he got from some Australian newspaper. . . . To sum it up real short, Peter Townend said that the Hawaiians had organized a club called the Black Shorts and they were created to intimidate the Australians, or Bronzed Aussies, because that's the only way we knew how to handle them because we were intimidated by their surfing ability. They were better than us so we were going to resort to using guns and knives to threaten them to stay out of the islands and out of the island surfing circuit. And when we read that we were like, that's some profound stuff. Not only was it profound, it wasn't true.[31]

Blankenfeld described his conversation with Townend the following year in Hawai'i. "I let Peter know about it; I told Peter that I felt being a visitor in our home here in Hawai'i, he was mistreating his host by speaking that way. And we let him know about it. I never put a hand on the guy, but I let him know about it."[32]

A few Hawaiians felt that some haole learned to respect Hawaiians as a result of the tensions in 1976. While not all agreed that the problems were solved, many felt it "brought some enlightenment to those who were not from the islands."[33] In a 1977 *Surfer* magazine article, John Witzig historicized events of the previous year on the North Shore and highlighted the accomplishments of many Hawaiian surfers and included more from the Hawaiian view of the 1976 Australian versus Hawaiian story. Four issues later, Rabbit wrote an article that summarized the North Shore events of 1977. In it he complimented Hawaiian surfers such as Dane Kealoha, Michael Ho, Reno Abellira, and Eddie Aikau for their victories and strong performances on the North Shore. Perhaps this was his way of saying, "I can respect the Hawaiians."[34]

Although some problems were resolved, discontent among North Shore Native Hawaiians continued to swell. The 1977 surf season brought with it more surfers, more surfing events, and often renewed frustrations for North Shore Hawaiian locals. By the end of the 1977 surfing season, many Hawaiians realized that disrespectful individual haole were not at the core of their problems. Rather, Hawaiians saw the professional surfing industry itself as an exploitative enterprise that marginalized Hawaiians and colonized their remote countryside. Thus at this time some Hawaiian North Shore residents created a hui to offset the growing professional surfing industry in Hawai'i.

Hui O He'e Nalu Is Formed

Shortly after the Bronzed Aussie incident and the formation of the IPS, local surfers from the north and east sides of O'ahu met at a friend's Sunset Beach house to organize themselves. Billy Blankenfeld remembered their first official meeting. "The guys were like, 'Hey we are going to start a club. We'll go meet up at Cappy's house. So it was me, Bryan, Eddie, Imua, Cappy, Terry, Jim Soutar, Derrick Doerner, all the guys we used to surf with. I think Steve Colbert was there. I can't remember all the names, but we had a bunch of guys. There must have been about thirty guys up there."[35] The first meeting brought people together for a Hawaiian cause, something Bryan Amona still defines as memorable. "It was pretty low key. We met at a [friend's] house in the North Shore, we barbecued, we all got together, rallied around and talked about what we want to do in our club. It was a pretty big thing back then, 'cause we weren't too organized. So for us to get organized, meeting, and being together, with camaraderie, that's what was really big for us back then."[36] After enjoying the company, they defined their group objectives. Primary among them was preserving the waves of the North Shore for generations of Native Hawaiians.

Most of these surfers saw the professional surfing industry on the North Shore as the entity that was responsible for taking a cultural space away from them. Terry Ahue explained, "The club was formed to perpetuate our surfing history here in Hawai'i. At that time the surfing world was moving into Hawai'i. They were here with all the Australians, and all the foreigners were coming here then. . . . So a whole bunch of the local braddahs said, 'Hey wait a minute, you know this is our 'āina [land].' . . . So we formed a club, to control the surfing world, which was run . . . at that time by Fred Hemmings."[37] Tom Pohaku Stone said about the formation of the club, "The Hui was formed . . . to resist that corporate control of our space."[38] So the idea was, according to Blankenfeld, "to start a club . . . so we can have a firm, rooted foothold in our birthright to be surfing here, when we want to be surfing here. And we needed to organize something, put our heads together, and see what good we [could] get out of it."[39]

Several members of the local community felt threatened and marginalized when the IPS claimed to own legal and exclusive rights to North Shore beaches during times of competition, due to city and county–issued permits. "They [contest promoters] felt that the permits gave them the right to chase guys out of the water. But permits don't allow that," explained Seth "Moot" Ah Quin. Hawaiian surfer Daryl Stant also said, "Once the contests started coming here and . . . started getting bigger, they started telling people, the local kids, and the local people from here, that on the best days when Pipe is breaking, Sunset is breaking, and Waimea is breaking, that you cannot surf. And they would kick them out, they would run their contests, and they would leave and not give anything back to the community."[40] The IPS was the primary motivation for the Hui O He'e Nalu's development between 1976 and 1978. The exclusive use of North Shore waves by the IPS competitions was particularly upsetting to many Hawaiians. Chuck Waipā Andrus said, "Of course, when you have more and more contests and all the prime venues and the waves are taken, the local people start to get frustrated. At first it's kind of a novelty, but then the novelty wears off. If you come to surf, and you come from Kahalu'u and there's a contest going on, and they say, 'Oh, you cannot surf here because we have a permit,' you know it kind of gets you frustrated." [41]

Some Hui surfers pose at Waimea Bay in the late 1970s. (Courtesy of Mahina Chillingworth)

After the initial Hui meeting at Cappy's house, the club held monthly meetings in a portable classroom at the old community center near Pūpūkea. The Hui was led by an elected body made up of a president, vice president, treasurer, and secretary. There were also club officers and a variety of other leadership roles. Bryan Amona, vice president at the time, said about these meetings, "We'd talk about surf contests . . . who we were going to try and get into the contests, giving back to the community, having beach cleanups." Amona also helped determine the official name of the club.

> I talked to my Aunty Nalani Kalama. She is no longer with us now, but I asked her, what could we name our club? And she said, "Well what are you guys about, what kind of club?" and I said we're just a bunch of surfers, you know, that's what we were. She told me to go research at the Bishop Museum. And the club of wave riders or wave sliders was the He'e Nalu . . . and being in an association is a hui or club. So we named it Hui O He'e Nalu, you know, Club of Wave Sliders.[42]

After further archival research, the club selected an ancient Hawaiian petroglyph of a surfer as its logo. Circled around this image are the words "Hui O He 'e Nalu, North Shore Hawai'i, est. 1976."[43] The club also selected red, yellow, and black as their club colors, traditionally associated with Hawaiian royalty. Although there were a few non–Native Hawaiian members in the Hui, it was strongly defined as "a Native Hawaiian group . . . centered around the efforts of Native Hawaiians and local people, those whose lifestyle is based on the Hawaiian lifestyle."[44]

After the club worked out its formal structure, it became a legal nonprofit organization. The reasoning behind this, they claimed, was that if they created a legal and legitimate organization, the IPS would be more likely to listen to their concerns.[45] As the Hui's membership rapidly grew, more locals found a place to voice concerns about their endangered Native Hawaiian space. While on the 'Iolani Palace grounds at a Hawaiian rally in September 2002, club founder Eddie Rothman relayed these concerns. "A bunch of people got tired of the way that the land and the people were being treated in Hawai'i, from the foreign surfers, so we formed a club, to make it different. All the foreign surfers . . . were just kind of taking over, doing their usual [crap] that everyone else does when they come to Hawai'i. So the place wasn't respected. . . . That's why we're here at this function [today], for the illegal taking of the lands again. They're still doing it."[46]

By the late 1970s more haole surfers poured into the North Shore. Hawaiian and local Hawai'i surfers feared being marginalized from the North Shore waves. In 1977 one local surfer complained that because of the crowds, "I surf Sunset now and then. . . . I never surf Pipe . . . it's too packed. . . . Usually if I drive up the coast, I'll find something in between here and Sunset."[47] Even when competitions were not being held, more and more haole surfers crowded the lineups. During our conversations, Hawaiian surfers waxed nostalgic about the early 1970s, a time when the North Shore surf was populated primarily by Native Hawaiian surfers. Chuck Waipā Andrus explained,

> In the late sixties early seventies, as I remember, the Windward local guys from this side La'ie, Kahalu'u, all these guys controlled a lot of the spots on the North Shore. In particular at Velzyland, where I surfed a lot, there was a group of guys from Castle High School; they lived in Kahalu'u, they lived in Waiāhole, and they lived out here [Hau'ula], and La'ie people. The Mahelonas, the Ho'opi'is, there was the Gents, the Campbells, the Pachecos, all these guys that controlled the spot. So they kind of allowed or disallowed people to come in. They would excuse people from the spot, or they would let them surf there. And that was more or less how I grew up. So I would just sit on the side and if one of them would say, "Hey boy, go boy" [for the wave], I would go [catch the wave]. But these guys were naturally good surfers; they would come out in cut off jeans, but they didn't care what shorts they wore.[48]

Most Hui members came to see the IPS as a corporate, exploitative money machine that did not have the interests of the local people at heart. One club founder said, "Back then, the surfing contests, yep, they were monopolizing on the waves, they were making money. Fred Hemmings had his sponsors, and they were giving him money; he was organizing, he had the pros come in. I mean, he put everything together, you know. And there is nothing wrong with that; Fred has been business-minded his whole life."[49] But Hui members were not merely upset with the IPS making money from the surf meets; it was also that they felt excluded and exploited by business-minded surfing entrepreneurs.

> The bottom line was, the sponsors and Fred Hemmings in particular, were making all the money, and we would just have to just sit on the side and

we would get nothing; it was just like, "You guys behave yourselves and just sit on the side and let us do our thing," and when they are gone everybody cashes in and they make their money and there's nothing left behind for us. At that time they didn't even think about [it], it was inconceivable in their mind, to even give anything back to the community. They were taking. That's where we were coming from. Okay, if you don't want to give anything back, we are going to ask.[50]

Several Hui members felt that the IPS did not value surfing as a Hawaiian cultural practice and were completely uninterested in preserving the North Shore as a Native Hawaiian space. Terry Ahue said, "Fred Hemmings was a big promoter. And everything [surfing events] was just money for his pocket. That's what he wanted. He didn't care about perpetuating our Hawaiian sport or trying to keep the culture together."[51] In his book, *The Soul of Surfing,* Hemmings took pride in promoting the sport of surfing through professional competitions.[52] As a haole who was raised in Hawai'i, Hemmings held Hawaiian surfing legends like Duke Kahanamoku in high esteem and found meaning in adopting the Hawaiian tradition of wave sliding from legendary surfers in Hawaiian waters. Yet his sentiments toward he'e nalu remained disconnected to Hawaiian Hui members. For him, surfing and the North Shore waves were something to share with the world, rather than preserve for Native Hawaiians. But Hemmings did not see eye to eye with Hui surfers on other things as well—most notably in the way he characterized the club as "thugs" and "terrorists" in the local media (a point I discuss in chapter 7). For example, in a 1987 article he pinpointed "Pops" Aikau as the "frontman" of the Hui and expressed his "disappointment" in Hawaiian "boys" in general and the Aikaus in particular for getting dragged into a club of "crime and corruption."[53]

Although prospective Hui members had to meet specific requirements before they could join, becoming a member of the Hui did not involve money or initiation. You got in through a friend or a sponsor. Blankenfeld further explained, "You had to know somebody in the club, and you were voted in. Like, say, I know you, and I take you to the club and introduce you to the brothers and all the friends of mine and say this is my good friend Isaiah, and he's okay. He surfs, he wants to get involved, and you know I am vouching for him. You know, and everybody says, "Shoots, no problem, you're in," real informal, just like that."[54] The only requirement, other than having a general respect for Native Hawaiians, was "you had to be living on the island for at least ten years. You didn't have to have dark skin. We had a lot of haole braddahs."[55] As club membership soared in the late 1970s and early 1980s, "Pretty much all the local braddahs wanted to get involved. And as the years went by, everyone wanted to wear a pair of Hui O He'e Nalu shorts, everyone wanted to be recognized as a part of the North Shore club."[56]

Beginning in the late 1970s the Hui was nicknamed "the Black Shorts"— after the black surf shorts they all wore. Designed by Hui founders, the shorts had two stripes down the right side—one bright red, the other bright yellow. Also printed on the shorts was the Hui logo. Ironically, the Australian-based clothing company Quiksilver sponsored the Hui and made hundreds of shorts at no cost from 1979 to 1993, when Da Hui, Inc. began manufacturing them. Although the Hui received over two hundred free pairs of shorts annually from companies like Quiksilver and Da Hui, it had a rule that only club members could wear Hui shorts. Although large Hawaiians on the North Shore often sported the black trunks, they were also popular among local kids who surfed on the North Shore and became part of the Hui as well. As Imbert Soren explained, when kids surfed with Hui shorts, nobody harassed them or tried to catch their waves, even when adult Hui members were not around.[57] The shorts became a mark of hierarchy for Hawaiian surfers on the North Shore in the same way that a yellow and red feathered cape marked the chiefs of old Hawai'i.

In addition to bringing people together ideologically, the Hui was also a social network for Native Hawaiian surfers. Amona explained that everyone pulled together in the group to help each other. For example, if someone needed a surfboard, they could go to shapers in the Hui rather than expensive surf shops.[58] Although this kind of community togetherness usually characterized relationships within the club, cordiality was not the norm at every meeting; sometimes members had differences of opinion. Although voting over issues was the most common way Hui members resolved such differences, on at least one occasion things were sorted out "the old fashioned way." Amona explained,

> I was at one time vice president of the club, when it first started. President was Imua, Imua Pa'aina. That's how they voted. I guess the biggest, the baddest Hawaiians they had back then. . . . Eventually we had a big falling out, a big rumble, a big fight, you know, that's what it came down to, you know [*laughs*]. [*Author: Over who was the president?*] No, you know, just about everything. You know, too much partying, too much liquor, too much stuff

going on and [a] lot of just petty stuff. And you know pushing come to shove, you know, I had my group from Kailua, and had the group from North Shore, and all these people, and they cleared the tables and let us beef and that was it, we settled our differences and that was that.[59]

Despite that experience, the early meetings usually united North Shore Hawaiian surfers and provided a forum for voicing Native concerns over threatened cultural space. Perhaps more importantly, meetings were a time to plan effective resistance strategies. Again, most engaged in such planning because of the belief that "outsiders were coming in and taking over things that belonged to the Hawaiians . . . like land, territories, even the beaches, even our surf, and our ocean and things like that. People were coming in and doing their own things and we felt like it was against our culture, so we wanted to make a stand."[60] In the process of defining this threatened cultural space, Hui members found an identity that was linked to their pre-colonial Hawaiian past.

He'e Nalu: A Historic Cultural Identity Marker

Hui members united on the North Shore to preserve a Native tradition and identity. For Hawaiians, surfing was, as Rabbit Bartholomew learned later in his North Shore surfing career, a kind of "last vestige of their heritage."[61] As he'e nalu has historically been an integral part of defining Native Hawaiians, it has also been a cultural identity marker for Native surfers. For many Native Hawaiians in the 1970s, the ocean served as a window to their pre-colonial Hawaiian past. In many ways, the ocean has been a sanctuary for Hawaiians, a place where they could free themselves from their colonized condition on land. Thus, as Kealoha Kaio, Jr., explained, the ocean is a place where Hawaiians can "feel relaxed. . . . You know all the problems that are on land? You can forget about them in the ocean. . . . On the land, there are too much problems."[62] But surfing was more than just a sanctuary for many Native Hawaiians; it also connected them to their ancestors.

As ancient legends of Hawaiian surfers were passed from generation to generation (see chapter 1) and confirmed inner feelings of historic connectivity to the waves, surfing conjured feelings of both pride and preservation. In recent years Hui members have still defined themselves, both individually and collectively, as the direct descendants and inheritors of the ancient Hawaiian tradition called he'e nalu.

Many Hui surfers have felt a connection to their ancient Hawaiian past through encounters with Hawaiian waves in the present. During our interview, North Shore surfer and surfboard shaper Chuck Waipā Andrus took great pride in his Hawaiian ancestry and the fact that surfing is a component of that ancestry. "Surfing has been a part of our history for thousands of years," he said, "and when you surf you have that connection, you connect spiritually and physically to all the elements around you; this is a part of you, it's a Hawaiian thing."[63] His connection was based partially on his heritage as a Native Hawaiian and on his upbringing as a waterman in Hawai'i's surf.

> We spent a lot of time in the water, crabbing, sand sliding, fishing and stuff, and as I got a little older I wanted to start surfing. My grandpa had an eight-foot redwood-plank surfboard that he had made, the Olo style. It was just sitting under the house. So I asked my dad if we could go surfing and he took us to Kahana Bay. I think I was either ten, or something, I don't exactly remember, but I remember the first time I caught a wave on that board, it didn't have a fin on it. And I just caught it after the wave broke and the whitewash was just rushing to the beach. But standing up on that and feeling that rush, I was hooked.[64]

Billy Blankenfeld also expressed a sense of pride in his inherited ocean traditions. "I grew up on the ocean. My dad is an ocean person, my dad is a full-on waterman. My dad taught me how to fish, he taught me to skin dive, taught me how to scuba dive, taught me how to lay net, taught me how to go deep sea fishing, taught me how to sail, taught me how to surf, taught me how to swim. Everything you can think of that has to do with the ocean, my dad taught me how to do."[65] For Blankenfeld, his ocean education was more than priceless; it was also tradition. This was particularly true with regards to surfing. He explained, "As a Native Hawaiian, surfing [*pauses*], gosh, has so much meaning to me. For one thing it's a part of my culture; it was created by the Hawaiian culture, you know, my past ancestors. It's absolutely fun. It was something that instinctively I bonded to, immediately."[66]

Likewise, Tom Pohaku Stone expressed great pride in his heritage as a Hawaiian and a surfer. Today, Stone teaches Hawaiian culture classes in the University of Hawai'i's community college system, runs his own nonprofit educational program, and is a leading expert on making kahiko-style surfboards (ancient-style boards made from wood) as well as holua sleds. For Stone, Hawaiian history and he'e nalu are synonymous. He said, "It's our way of life. It's who we are. We lived to surf. To everybody else today who embraces surfing it's more like a means for them to become wealthy. . . . We were wealthy already because of surfing."[67] While we spoke, it was apparent that when he said, "I get a lot of pride out of who I am as a Native," he meant it.[68] In addition, surfing was somehow a conduit of that pride. This is something that Reno Abellira also saw in the Aikau family. "Theirs is a real intense family structure which may in part reflect how they identify with surfing. . . . They're carrying a banner, sort of. It's like a heavy cultural tie that they've kept intact. They're full-on Hawaiian people, and it's not even something that I can grasp all of the time."[69]

While we sat on the nicely kept lawn of Moot Ah Quin's family house in Lā'ie, Ah Quin's five-year-old daughter hid quietly and playfully behind him. Ah Quin then explained, "Surfing is a passion of mine; it's my passion, I love the water, I love the feeling of riding waves. It doesn't matter if it's a body board, a surfboard, a knee board, or a canoe, just that exhilaration of riding waves. . . . And when it comes to surfing, I can say, I am proud to be Hawaiian."[70] Nearly every Hui surfer interviewed for this study expressed

Tom Pohaku Stone in Hui shorts at 'Ehukai Beach Park, 2008. (Photo by Mark Holladay Lee)

strong and thoughtful feelings about the importance of surfing in their lives as Hawaiians.

As a group, the Hui fostered an identity that was inextricably linked to Hawai'i's past. This is seen not only through declarations like Stone's—that "the Hui is just representing the Native people and their way of life and it just happens to be an aspect of it, and that aspect is surfing"— but also through symbols chosen to represent the club.[71] Describing the selection of club colors, Bryan Amona reiterated, "You know, red and yellow, that's the colors of the ali'i; and the black for the color of our skin, the color of the people, and the color of our ali'i."[72] Such physical symbols, worn regularly by Hui surfers, were again metaphoric reminders of a nostalgic and precolonial past, one in which Hawaiians ruled both in the water and on land.

The Hui's affiliation with a precolonial past not only promoted pride, but also heightened Hawaiian frustrations and fears over losing that space. Throughout the twentieth century surfing remained one of the few prevailing Hawaiian traditions among Native Hawaiians, and for many surfers it became a portal to an ancient and nostalgic Hawaiian world during a time of great turmoil and change in the islands. As he'e nalu took place in an uncontrolled, unowned, and public space (the ocean), many Hawaiians adopted that realm as cultural, pristine, and absent of colonialism. Hence when the IPS claimed rights to North Shore waves, Hui members insisted, "They can't tell us we can't be there, because it's our tradition, our culture; they have no choice, our culture comes first, and our cultural practices."[73] With such convictions, it was easy to rally Hawaiian surfers to protest IPS surf meets on the North Shore.

Protests and Compromise

The Hui protested the IPS contests and their dominance over North Shore surf breaks in the late 1970s. Hawaiian Hui members Bryan Amona, Tom Pohaku Stone, Imbert Soren, and Moot Ah Quin each explained their frustrations toward the IPS's exclusive use of their local surfing beaches. Their most common method of protest was for groups of Hui surfers to paddle into the contest area while the IPS events were going on. Surfing waves in the competition zone made it nearly impossible for the contests to continue. As they did this, tensions between Hui surfers and haole competitors ensued, and fistfights sometimes resulted. Ah Quin explained that the IPS felt "the permits gave them the right to chase guys out of the water. But permits don't allow that. . . . Technically, you cannot ask them to leave." He continued, "When they started to do that, the braddahs would paddle out. They would paddle out and sit in the lineup. And there is nothing you can do . . . but they are not only going to paddle out and sit down. Brah, they are going to start cracking [punching] guys if you tell [them] to move, you know. And they did."[74]

Honolulu city and county police officers were often called to the scene and occasionally confiscated surfboards from Hui surfers. Bryan Amona said that a police officer once tried to confiscate his surfboard, and he refused. The officer let him go—perhaps because Amona was well built and stood well over six feet tall, or perhaps because he was unequivocally opposed to arresting Hawaiian surfers for surfing in their backyards. Contest and local officials quickly realized that Hui members were willing to stand their ground and go to jail over their North Shore surf. Stone explained, "We took it to another level. Yeah, there were a lot of fights and stuff like that. Basically resistance fights. Some of us went to jail over being in the water when a contest was going on, our boards taken away, and stuff like that."[75] As the police became less interested in jailing Hawaiian surfers, on at least one occasion the IPS hired professional wrestlers as security guards to ward off and intimidate Hui surfers. It just made matters worse, explained Imbert Soren, as confrontations between the wrestlers and Hawaiian protesters devolved into physical fighting.[76] Hui members also retaliated against sponsors and television companies supporting these events. Ah Quin said, "The boys, without giving out any names, threw cameras in the water, kicked guys off the beach. It wasn't a very good time for surfing, for the boys, and for TV. It was a very tense time on the North Shore back then."[77]

Though some Hui protests resulted in minor physical injuries, most Hui members suggested that their resistance was centered on preservation, not intimidation. Billy Blankenfeld made clear that "we were never organized to intimidate anybody. If people are intimidated, oh, well, like I tell a lot of people, we cannot help the way we look. I can tell you this much, if you do get to know us, [you will learn that] we are a lot of good, sweet guys, down-to-earth guys, with good hearts. Real decent, logical-thinking human beings."[78]

The Hui also protested the business of professional surfing on the North Shore, particularly the way North Shore Hawaiians were marginalized in this economy. Many were frustrated by the economic exploitation of the North Shore by IPS sponsors and the television companies in particular. Some members had the same sentiments as Blankenfeld, who felt that "everybody cashes in and they make their money and there's nothing left behind for us."[79] But Hui surfers also saw an opportunity and partial solution. "With these events came television. There were companies like ABC Wide World of Sports, and NBC Sports. . . . When they came, they came with their full entourage of people, and the politics here was, the boys wanted work. To me, if you look at it, I think it was only fair. If there are companies from the mainland coming here making money off of surfing, they should give the opportunity for work to the local guys."[80]

After vigorous protests by the club members in the late 1970s, both the Hui and the IPS came to a compromise. The Hui worked to limit the annual events held on the North Shore and agreed to let them continue if the IPS hired the Hui as water patrolmen, security, and lifeguards. The IPS agreed to pay anywhere from seven hundred fifty to one thousand dollars a day to the Hui—which often translated to fifty dollars for each Hui worker per day. The club retained this contract for eight years, but in 1987 Hemmings backed out. However, the Hawaiian Water Patrol, founded by longtime North Shore lifeguard and former Hui president Terry Ahue, has since provided water patrol for the professional meets on the North Shore. His patrol is made up predominantly of Hui members. The Hawaiian Water Patrol is also regarded as one of the most skilled water safety crews in the world. It is responsible

Billy Blankenfeld surfing at Pipeline in the late 1970s. (Courtesy of Billy Blankenfeld)

for introducing and perfecting the use of watercraft in life guarding and has trained various water safety teams in its methods.

Although the club provided beach and water security at a negotiated price, the Hui and IPS directors did not always see eye to eye. When Hemmings broke with the Hui in 1987, he explained in a Hawai'i newspaper that Hui members were extortionists. In a more recent book, Hemmings has said that the Hui intimidated their way into the IPS and demanded seven thousand dollars a day for the contests. He states,

> I ended up with an appointment to meet with Black Shorts representatives at the Kuilima hotel to negotiate a lifeguard contract. Randy Rarick conveniently could not make it. I took his aide, Beth Martin. We walked into the lobby of the hotel. One of the representatives of the group we were to negotiate with looked fearsome. It appeared like they hired him from central casting in an attempt to intimidate me. Beth Martin was visibly scared. We sat down. The demand was that I pay $7,000 a day for "security." My mind was a clenched fist of anger. I forced a smile on my face as I walked out. It was apparent what was happening.[81]

Hui members took offense to these accusations.

> In the beginning it was real controversial; Fred went as far as saying we were trying to extort money, and that is not true. Extorting is when you say, "You are going to pay us or else. You are going to have to pay us for protection or you are going to have to keep looking over your shoulder," and that's not what we did. . . . We just told Fred, we want to do the water patrol. We are going to organize. We'll keep everything safe. We'll get involved, get paid for services rendered.[82]

Club members also said they never sought seven thousand dollars a day and were not in it for the money to begin with. In fact, most, like Blankenfeld, suggested that individual Hui surfers did not make money off of the surf meets because it went back into the North Shore community via Hui events. After questioning Hemmings' motives for calling the Hui extortionists ten years after the fact, Jim Soutar explained that out of a thousand dollars from the contests, five hundred was budgeted for the lifeguards, five hundred for the extra community services provided by the Hui. Blankenfeld also explained, "I got personally, myself and all the guys who did the water patrol, we got paid fifty dollars for the day, each guy, that's all, and we stayed in the water, made sure nobody got hurt, made sure guys stayed out of the water, and you know what, the local people got to be involved."[83]

Events and Evolution

Starting in the late 1970s, the Hui used the money received from the IPS to benefit their community in one form or another. The Hui hosted parties and celebrations of all sorts, and at these events members often handed out gifts and prizes to North Shore community members. Blankenfeld recalled one of their first parties. "I remember our first party we had, it was a club party. . . . It was a huge party . . . all the local surfers were invited. We had it up at Waimea Falls Park."[84] He recalled great food, fun, and a variety of prizes for the local people. "It was a good thing," he said, "because the local people got to be involved." Essentially, "We gave back. Whatever we got we put right back into the community."[85] Some of the most desired prizes were free surfboards. Amona said that since surfboards were so expensive, and local kids could not afford them, the Hui would often sponsor these kids by giving them boards. [86] Hence it was not uncommon for a surfboard or two to be handed out at these Hui events. In addition to parties and other gatherings, the Hui organized regular cleanup projects at various beaches around the island.

The Hui also started competitions of their own. In 1978 they established the Hui O Heʻe Nalu Annual 4th of July Day Paddleboard Race, in which contestants paddle surfboards from Sunset Beach to Waimea Bay. The Hui also created surfing contests for local surfers. The first was an amateur meet held at Ala Moana Bowls, a surf break off of Magic Island, in 1978. Hui surfers were advised by an experienced contest organizer, Myra Aikau (Eddie Aikau's sister), on how to structure and run the event. Starting in 1986 the Hui founded professional meets on the North Shore as well—for example, they helped establish the Quiksilver In Memory of Eddie Aikau Big Wave Invitational, and they created Da Hui's Backdoor Shootout. The founder of the Backdoor Shootout, Eddie Rothman, boasted that this contest gave out a bigger winning purse than any other professional event, and "it's the only contest in Hawaiʻi where 60 percent of the people are local people, in a professional contest. They go and buy houses with that money, and this and that."[87]

When Terry Ahue and Imbert Soren were elected president and vice president, respectively, of the Hui in 1986, they added new community events to the club's calendar. Ahue said, "When I took over I made it more like a family-oriented club."[88] For example, the Hui had an annual Easter egg hunt on the

North Shore (in Pūpūkea), and all the children got eggs and candy; the child who found the golden egg also received a surfboard. The club later hosted Halloween and Christmas parties. Since the North Shore was a community of somewhat limited resources, these events were welcomed by local families there. One community member explained, "I bring my family as often as I can to those functions because it's good for the kids, and it's a safe environment."[89] These events appealed to a more family-oriented crowd, and this family emphasis may have been influenced by Ahue's and Soren's upbringing in the family-centered Church of Jesus Christ of Latter-Day Saints.[90]

Hui from 1993 to Present

In 1993 a rift occurred in the club when Da Hui, the clothing company, splintered from the Hui O He'e Nalu. Although a handful of Hui founders became primary shareholders of Da Hui, several club members felt money from the clothing company was distributed unfairly among a few. One Hui founder explained, "I was very, very upset. . . . I thought the club would have a share, all the officers of the club would have a share, and it ended up not being that way. Because of that I kind of faded out. I kind of left."[91] Many other club members became less active after this company was formed. But according to Henry Soren, people who ran the clothing line did not receive large profits from Da Hui, since, as Soren explained, they sponsored amateur and professional local surfers and gave free clothing to Hui members.[92] Nevertheless, club membership and leadership ultimately changed with the creation of Da Hui.

In 1993, after the split, Norman Thompson, a Hawaiian-Samoan surfer from Lā'ie, became president of the Hui. Norm continued with many of Ahue's objectives by maintaining his Hui-run community events on the North Shore. During this time the Hui also held their own surfing competitions on the North Shore. The Hui Expression Session was unlike any other surf meet in that it did not eliminate or rank surfers in numerical order. The object was to give local surfers an opportunity to express their surfing soul in uncrowded, perfect North Shore surf. Essentially, it was about having fun. Whereas on a good day at Sunset Beach up to seventy people might be in the water fighting over waves, during the Hui's Expression Sessions only six to ten surfers were allowed in the water at a time. These sessions were usually opened with a traditional Hawaiian ceremony, like the Hawaiian 'awa ceremony led by Bula Logan at Sunset Beach in 1993. Unfortunately, and to the chagrin of many, like Tom Pohaku Stone, the Expression Sessions ended almost as soon as they began.

From 1995 till 2003 other Hawaiian presidents led the Hui in new directions. For example, when Moot Ah Quin became president, he continued with community events like beach cleanups and paddleboard races, but he also tried to get the club involved in more political activities. For example, Ah Quin would volunteer Hui services at Native Hawaiian rallies, marches, and demonstrations. In September 2002 Ah Quin stood at the front gate of 'Iolani Palace and allowed hundreds of Native Hawaiian protesters onto the palace grounds. The march around downtown Honolulu commemorated the anniversary of the birth of Hawai'i's Queen Lili'uokalani and protested both the annexation of Hawai'i and the treatment of the queen in the late 1890s. At this particular event, the Hui rallied alongside other Hawaiians who chanted songs of colonial resistance. Ah Quin also tried to promote legislation that would allow surfing to be considered a real sport in Hawai'i public schools. He said, "We're trying to get involved with scholastic surfing and doing things for our kids, because on the North Shore there isn't anything to keep kids involved with good things."[93] More recently, the club has reached out to communities outside the North Shore. A newer member to the Hui explained, "We try and help out not only on the North Shore, but other parts of the island as well."[94] While most Hui members are proud to be involved in general Hawaiian political activism and activities outside the North Shore area, many, like Daryl Stant, conveyed that the North Shore ocean was still their central focus. "In a way," he explained, "it's good for the club; I mean, now they are getting involved in other stuff, instead of just the ocean. . . . As for me, I just love the ocean. You leave the ocean alone, I'll be all right."[95]

The Hui O He'e Nalu was created to preserve North Shore waves for a Hawaiian surfing community. Club members were also protecting an indigenous identity, one based on the historical and cultural practice of he'e nalu. These surfers actively resisted the influx of haole surfers and the IPS because surfing was a treasured tradition to them; it was Hawaiian. For Hui members, being a surfer and being a Hawaiian are inseparable. Thus the Hui has articulated itself as a Hawaiian group that is entitled not only to surfing their local surfing breaks, but to the Hawaiian tradition of surfing itself.

CHAPTER 7

Hui in American Media

"Terrorists" on the North Shore

As the Hui's popularity spread, they became a subject of interest in American media. Hui surfers had been covered in newspapers and magazines, shown in Hollywood movies, and represented in syndicated American reality television since the late 1970s. The stereotype is clear in all of these. In movies and on television they are tough guys who beat up haole surfers for no reason, but more seriously, various newspapers often, and outright, deemed them "terrorists." For example, in July 1987 Honolulu newspapers ran stories like "'Reign of Terror' on the North Shore told," and "Threats forced him to hire 'terrorists,' Hemmings says." Over the years this image has prevailed in the media, even in reputable newspapers more recently. For example, in 2009 the *New York Times* ran a story titled "Surfing's Darker Side on the North Shore."[1] In this chapter I trace the history of media representations that labeled Hui surfers "thugs" and "terrorists," and I then argue that such stereotyping served a distinct function and revealed motives.

Labeling Hawaiian activist groups like the Hui as savage, radical Natives (or even terrorists) in the 1970s and 1980s undermined burgeoning voices of resistance during an era of Hawaiian empowerment. While Hui members were defined as aggressive terrorists, they were simultaneously cast as aberrant and savage Natives. Their disillusionment was thus reduced to hatred, their resistance to barbarism. This process has provided a means to undermine

Native resistance and preserve the status quo—one in which the haole dominates and the Hawaiian is marginal. However, by appropriating the hypermasculine trope when advantageous, Hui surfers often liberated themselves from previous stereotypes—those historic and emasculating representations that previously cast Hawaiian men as submissive, unmanly, and transparent.

Hui in the News and Media

Although surf magazines and Australian newspapers wrote about the Hui in the late 1970s, the club gained its greatest infamy in the late 1980s with *Honolulu Advertiser* and *Honolulu Star-Bulletin* stories that followed the court hearing and trial of two Hui members charged with conspiracy to distribute cocaine.[2] Defense attorney David Bettencourt ultimately proved that the Honolulu Police Department's key informants' claims against the two Hui members were unfounded, and neither surfer was convicted. Covering the trial in July and August 1987, Honolulu newspapers ran regular front-page stories frequently repeating accusations that Hui members were extortionists and narrating the Hui's history as Native troublemakers. The haole-owned Honolulu papers also spread the prosecution's allegations that the Hui O He'e Nalu was a gang of "strong-arm collectors and dealers."[3] In one dramatic courtroom moment, deputy prosecutor Gary Modafferi turned to members of the Hui O He'e Nalu and said that "Black Shorts is the state's largest cocaine ring."[4] He also said that over the years the Hui had "unleashed a 'reign of terror' that has held O'ahu's North Shore in a state of near feudalism."[5]

Modafferi brought Ian Cairns and Fred Hemmings to the witness stand to help paint the Hui as terrorists. Cairns, an Australian professional surfer turned professional surfing promoter, claimed that the Hui had "terrified," "harassed," and "intimidated" him for years.[6] However, it was Hemmings who was more comfortable calling the Hui terrorists than anyone else. On July 30, 1987, Hemmings, founder of International Professional Surfing (IPS) and director of the Triple Crown of Surfing (three events held annually on the North Shore), testified that the Hui were "vigilantes" who "held the North Shore in a reign of terror." Claiming that the Hui had coerced promoters to hire Hui members to work in these contests, he called club members "domestic terrorists."[7] He said that he found it "disturbing that 'many fine local boys' have found themselves involved in crime and corruption" because of the Hui.[8] But Hemmings' oration was interrupted when defense attorney Bettencourt demanded, "Stop making campaign speeches."[9]

Bettencourt had a point. In 1984 Hemmings had been elected to Hawai'i's House of Representatives as a Republican. During his campaign he advocated tightening Hawai'i's criminal justice system by enforcing stricter sentencing and promoting prison industries. Responding to a letter published in a newspaper by a political opponent who criticized his remarks on the North Shore terrorists, Hemmings stated, "I did not claim that I was being extorted." He went on, however, saying, "It is unfortunate that we live in a society where sometimes our justice system protects the alleged rights of criminals over the safety and welfare of victims and society. . . . As a citizen and legislator, I will continue to push for criminal justice reform. We need meaningful victims' rights legislation, prison industries, and mandatory sentencing for heinous crimes."[10] While Hemmings used the Hui to promote his criminal justice reform platform, Hui members questioned his unpredictable friendship with the club.[11] Jim Soutar, a lifeguard and secretary/treasurer of the Hui at the time, commented, "He's worked with us for ten years. . . . We provided a service he asked us to provide." Why, he continued, did it take him "ten years to say that a surf club was extorting him?"[12]

While Hemmings and Modafferi denounced the Hui as a group of Hawaiian surfing "terrorists" in the courtroom, Honolulu newspapers ran stories on the Hui that were printed concurrently with news of terrorism in the Middle East. For example, on July 28, 1987, the *Honolulu Advertiser* ran two headline stories on terrorism. The first, "Terrorists threaten U.S.," emphasized potential attacks by "Moslem fundamentalists" on Americans.[13] The second followed up an earlier cover story, "'Reign of Terror' on North Shore told," and spoke of a Native Hawaiian "terrorist" group called the Hui O He'e Nalu.[14]

As newspapers characterized the club in this light, members of the Hui O He'e Nalu publicly protested the accusations and assured Hawai'i residents that they were not drug dealers or terrorists. On August 9, 1987, sixty Hui members gathered at Sunset Beach Elementary School, where club leader "Pops" Aikau (Eddie Aikau's father) announced, "We are not terrorists." After explaining that he could not keep track of all the activities of every Hui member, he said, "What I see is good, honest surfing people, or else I wouldn't have wasted my time coming out here."[15] Although some members of the Hui were, sadly, involved in crime and drug use, Hui surfers insisted that they did not represent the general membership of the club. During our interviews Hui surfers often admitted that some club members had a history of drug use. However, they often followed this up with a counter-narrative about drug-free Hui surfers. For example, Bryan Amona celebrated the fact that other club members never touched drugs or alcohol throughout their lives.[16] Amona also described his experiences in Hawai'i as a drug counselor; over the years, he said, he helped many Hawaiians become and remain drug free. Billy Blankenfeld has also been active in a variety of antidrug community projects—having worked in various rehab facilities, he also helped local residents break debilitating drug addictions. The overall sentiment of these interviews on the topic of drug use was that it had crippled many local "braddahs," but the media overstepped boundaries by assuming that drugs were central to the general membership of the Hui.

Like Hemmings and local media labeling Hui members as terrorists, Randal Klieser's Hollywood movie, *North Shore,* depicted them in a similar fashion. As the trial continued in the summer of 1987, *North Shore* opened in movie theaters across the United States.[17] This film introduced many non–North Shore residents to a group of Natives who wore black shorts and intimidated haole. The main character, Rick Kane, an Arizona wave-pool haole surfer, finds a Hawaiian girlfriend, along with a bit of trouble from local Hui members, while visiting O'ahu's North Shore. Within hours of his arrival on the island, Kane is chased by Hawaiian men with cane knives, robbed by a Hawaiian Hui member, and told by Hui leader Vince Moaloka, played by Hawai'i's professional surfer Gerry Lopez, to "go home, haole."[18] After falling in love with Moaloka's cousin, Kiana, Kane gets into a fistfight with a "dirty-fighting" Hui member.[19] In the end, American viewers learn that some aberrant and anomalous Hawaiians could be very uncivil to haole on the North Shore.

While another Hollywood movie, *Blue Crush* (2002), could be considered the sequel to *North Shore,* it does so through the eyes of young female surfers. Here, Anne-Marie, a local-haole surfer from the North Shore, jeopardizes her professional surfing career after falling in love with a haole NFL quarterback who is on the island to play in the NFL's Pro Bowl. The Hui O He'e Nalu does not play as prominent a role in this film, but they are still represented through local thuggish characters played by Chris Taloa and Kalā Alexander. In one scene, Anne-Marie takes her new boyfriend to a secluded, "for locals only" beach to teach him how to surf. Upon their arrival, Taloa and Alexander beat him up for no apparent reason other than territorialism. Though the Hui is not mentioned specifically, Alexander, a real-life member, sports a tattoo with the club insignia on his shoulder, and the two men are clearly situated as North Shore local Hawaiians.[20]

Boarding House: North Shore was a reality television show that aired on Warner Brothers' The WB in the summer of 2003. The show followed the lives of six professional surfers, three men and three women, who competed in the North Shore's most prestigious surfing events, the Triple Crown of Surfing. Although surfing was a component of the show, the program centered almost exclusively on the drama that unfolded in and around the home they all occupied. As evidenced by the comments made by viewers on the *Boarding House* Web site, the star of this show was undoubtedly Hawaiian surfer Sunny Garcia. Sponsored by Da Hui Inc. (thus sporting their petroglyph insignia on his surfboard and everyday clothing), Garcia was its representative on the show. Although popular, Garcia was clearly the villain of the bunch. The *Boarding House* online cast biographies described him as "Intimidating, Dangerous, Aggressive, and Legendary."[21] His success as a five-time Triple Crown winner and former Association of Surfing Professionals (ASP) world surfing champion was attributed to his aggressive approach to competitive surfing. He was also depicted as aggressive toward and violent with haole. For example, in one episode Garcia slapped a haole surfer on the beach because he had stared at Garcia's new wife, who lay in a bikini nearby. One local surfer involved in a different conflict with Garcia explained that this show misrepresented the North Shore through their editing of Sunny. "Yeah, he later ended up apologizing. But the show doesn't show that. . . . These reality shows basically film everything and then edit it so it's going to be totally different. It was another lame Hollywood deal. . . . I think it misrepresents what the whole North Shore is about."[22]

Such movies and television shows used Hui surfers to produce a dramatic and desired effect: selling tickets and boosting ratings. For example, hundreds of viewers were appalled enough by Garcia's actions to write complaints about him on the *Boarding House* Web site. One viewer said, "Sunny is a suckerpuncher. Zero respect. I would love to see him get punched in the face. That would make great tv. He is a coward. . . . Get another day job, maybe ultimate fighting, then we will see how tough you really are. When the boys hit back."[23] Such animosity makes for good television ratings, and this often take precedence over honest representation.

Conversely, the 2007 Fuel TV reality show *The 808* broke from the usual format and conveyed an insider's perspective of Hawaiian North Shore surfers. As each of its seven episodes were coproduced and narrated by North Shore locals and Hui surfers, the show contextualized tensions, highlighted the daily lives of several locals on the North Shore, and conveyed the history of the Hui O He'e Nalu as told by Hui founders themselves. In this show, North Shore Hawaiian surfers, rather than being defined by violence, emphasized an identity based on a strong sense of local pride and respect. But fighting was not omitted from their show, either. For example, in episode two, titled "Warrior Spirit," Makua Rothman is filmed fighting with another surfer—after Rothman was cut off by a body boarder on a large wave at Backdoor, Pipeline, which caused him to wipe out. While the violence in this situation is reckless and ultimately unjustifiable, the show at least provided context to the incident, thereby humanizing the encounter. For these surfers, control over the lineup at Pipeline is more than just localism, but also about establishing order for safety's sake. Show narrator Kalā Alexander explained,

> Pipeline and Backdoor are perfect barrels, but you have to put yourself in exactly the right spot to make the wave. If you don't, there is a good chance you are going to take the worst beating of your life and probably hit the coral reef below. . . . People get seriously hurt out there all the time; some even die. . . . Add a hundred guys out on a big day, and let me tell you, the intensity level multiplies quickly. Not only do you have to worry about being in the right spot and making the drop, now you have to worry about twenty guys on the inside, guys paddling up the face, guys bailing their boards, and even sometimes guys dropping in on you. That's why rules were created and that's why there has always been a hierarchy in the lineup.[24]

While Alexander is a member of the Hui O He'e Nalu, he is more well known as the leader of a band of surfers called the Wolfpak. Made up mostly of Kaua'i-born surfers now living on the North Shore, the Wolfpak's primary mission is to police the surfing lineup at Pipeline and to ensure that they get their share of waves. Since 2002 Alexander has been a media magnet and budding celebrity. In addition to starring in *The 808,* Alexander had roles in films like *Blue Crush* and *Forgetting Sarah Marshall,* and he has modeled in several magazines. He has also been popularized on YouTube. In one video, filmed several years ago, he is shown fighting with a confrontational haole surfer who disrupted a Pipeline surfing competition. According to Alexander, however, fights are not as common as portrayed. He continued, "Fighting is never the answer, but it happens. People have to realize there have to be rules out in the water. Respecting the rules and each other is everything."[25] Comparing a Hawaiian hierarchy in the surf to an inner-city basketball court, he explained, "You wouldn't go to a court in Brooklyn or Queens and start shooting baskets in the middle of a game in progress. It's just something you wouldn't do. But if you introduce yourself, and wait your turn, you might get into the next game. The same goes for Pipeline. Pipe is our home court."[26]

On January 22, 2009, the *New York Times* ran a story on Kalā Alexander and the Hui O Heʻe Nalu with a headline article, "Rough Waves, Tougher Beaches," by Matt Higgins, with an accompanying six-minute online video clip, "Surfing's Dark Side on the North Shore," by Erik Olsen and Matt Higgins.[27] While the initial project, at least as described to me, was to contextualize and historicize Hawaiian surfers in light of the professional surfing scene on the North Shore, the final story instead emphasized, almost exclusively and often erroneously, decontextualized violence inflicted on haole surfers by Hawaiians—as represented solely by Kalā Alexander. I had spent over two hours with the *New York Times* reporters, providing ample historical background to Hawaiian surfing and the North Shore so clearly that they had the information needed for a balanced, contextualized story. Although I reiterated to them a central message, that Hawaiian sentiments toward the surfing industry on the North Shore must be explained in the context of Hawaiʻi's colonial experience, in the end they simply reported hype and reinforced the tired senseless-savage narrative. After reading the article and watching the attached video, I e-mailed the reporters and explained,

> The key problem was your emphasis (and brutal video footage) on Kalā Alexander inflicting rage on "innocent white victims." The Hui is made up of hundreds of surfers, and yet you emphasized merely one at his worst— and often out of context. In the articles that you read, and the interview we did together, I explained the historical context of the violence. What readers and viewers did not get is an understanding of how centuries of colonial violence has been inflicted on Hawaiians, or an explanation of how the surf zone became an historical frontier for contesting that violence. Thus, in your story haole surfers are seen as innocent victims, guilty only of the arbitrary crime of disrespect.[28]

Higgins' response was disheartening to me as a Hawaiian historian. He wrote, "In reorganizing the story, the history of colonial conflict in Hawaiʻi and its relevance to surfing became a subordinate matter. Nevertheless, I included a fair amount of your comments that I thought explained the historical context of battles over surf. Yet they were cut by editors concerned about length. That was wrong. And for that I apologize."[29]

In addition to making the story more attractive than accurate, the reorganized story aimed to teach Kalā Alexander a lesson. After our video interview in Lāʻie, the reporters returned to Alexander's home to prod him further. It was during this second interview that Alexander realized their all-too-familiar agenda—to defame the Hui as senseless aggressors. Once Alexander recognized this, he shut the door on them. Higgins explained Alexander's response in an e-mail. "He objected to some of my questions, became enraged, made threats, and attempted to intimidate me, insisting that he be removed from the story."[30] Instead, they made Alexander, and his two YouTube fights, the very center of it. Through this *New York Times* experience, I learned personally how American media omit historical context to implicate Native characters seen as threatening. Also, although often disguised as fair journalism, discourses like these are in essence aggressive forms of literary violence, imposed on people whom they deem their opponents. For example, after Alexander disapproved of the article, asked to be removed, and "attempted to intimidate," the authors instead embarked on an offensive and aggressive agenda to expose Alexander and teach him a lesson. Higgins explained, "For awhile my editors and I considered dropping the matter and moving on. Eventually a new line of thought emerged: Kala, in particular, has attempted to rehabilitate his image and that of the Wolfpak through a television series and good public works. Meanwhile, he has continued to assault surfers and threaten and intimidate people. All of which is newsworthy. With that dissonance as a guide, the focus of the story shifted to Kala."[31] Unfortunately, such media representations are more than jabs at Alexander; these portrayals, intentionally or not, characterize the entire community that he supposedly represented—the Hawaiian surfing community. Thus the media also have a bad history of violence.

Counter-narratives: Honoli'i Pāka Crew

The media could have highlighted other fascinating stories of other Hui members. Through my research and personal experiences I have recorded many such stories. For example, Keith "Skibs" Nehls is a Hawaiian surfer and member of the Hui who has made newsworthy accomplishments. A resident of Hilo, Skibs became tired of the family unfriendly environment at Hilo's premier surfing spot, Honoli'i. A place where King Kamehameha had once enjoyed surfing, by the 1980s Honoli'i was a rundown park, overgrown and neglected by the City and County of Hawai'i. The park had also become a hub for unlawful alcohol and drug consumption, often among underaged Hilo youth. By 2003 Skibs, Ethan Butts, Skippa Butts, and others of the Honoli'i Pāka crew had started cleaning the park. Although it took several months to clear acres of overgrown hillsides sloping down onto the rocky shoreline—where all sorts of garbage lay (from beer cans to abandoned auto-mobiles)—they transformed Honoli'i into a tropical garden of native plants, grassy fields, and rock-art sculptures. The culture of the park, like the changing landscape, also experienced a facelift. As more local families frequented the new Honoli'i, local surfing youth also began caring for it. Under the tutelage of Skibs, these kids regularly mowed, weeded, and cleaned the park before surfing on Saturday mornings. Consequently, Skibs began sponsoring many of them—helping to pay entry fees for surfing tournaments and for expensive surfing equipment. In 2003 Skibs and the Honoli'i Pāka crew organized the Honoli'i Pāka Aloha 'Āina Surfing Classic. This meet, held annually, is marked by food, fun, and many free prizes for all contestants—including several brand-new surfboards. But as revealed in the meet's title, Aloha 'Āina, this event is centered on loving, caring for, and respecting the 'āina (land). While the phrase "aloha 'aina" has many meanings, it essentially underlines the historic, reciprocal, and familial relationship that the people have with the 'āina. Although 'āina technically means "land," it also encompasses the sea as an extension of the land. At the Honoli'i Pāka Aloha 'Āina Surfing Classic people are reminded and encouraged to reconnect with the earth, sea, culture, family, and God through prayers, cultural performance, and surfing. This message has paid off. Not only have others on the island of Hawai'i followed Skib's lead by "adopting" neglected beach parks around the island, but the owners of the surrounding Honoli'i park area even handed their 'āina to Skibs. Although Kamehameha Schools contemplated leasing the land overlooking the beautiful bay to developers of high-end homes, once they discovered what Skibs was doing, they instead offered to lease it to him. Skibs and the Honoli'i Pāka Crew have since reached out to other beaches, including Hakalau Mill, Honomu, Pohoiki, and elsewhere. As with Honoli'i, the land leases to these parks have been offered to Skibs and his crew. Despite the fact that Hui surfers like Skibs and the Honoli'i Pāka Crew have accomplished amazing things, the media continue to depict only the darker side of Hawaiian surfers.

Undermining Hawaiian Resistance with Discourse and Boundaries

American representations of Hawaiian men as radical, savage-like Natives or terrorists has helped to produce parameters or boundaries on Hawaiian masculinity and disparaged anticolonial Native groups, the Hui in particular, during an era of heightened indigenous activism in Hawai'i. As Hawaiians

became increasingly disillusioned with the American occupation of Hawai'i
and increasingly recognized the corrosive effects of this in their communities,
they have, in the latter decades of the twentieth century, made their voices
heard. As some Hawaiians insisted on being heard and as their voices prevailed,
media venues tried to quiet them with debasing labels. For example, as the
Kaho'olawe 9 occupied the military target called Kaho'olawe and demanded
that bombing on the island stop, these Hawaiians were denigrated as radicals
and law breakers.[32] Many Hui members recognized the media stereotyping as
problematic. Tom Pohaku Stone mourned that the "media creates this stigma
of us being hit men and crap like that; that's all crap." He continued, "The
Blacks, Samoans, Hawaiians, we're always portrayed as these savages, and we
never think, we are always the slow-moving, dumb-looking characters. Or
we end up playing the heavy gangsters."[33] Such labels worked to undermine
Hawaiian activism and simultaneously defined resistant Hawaiian men as
aberrant and irrational. Hui members regularly clarified to me what club
members are really like. Erwin Au said, "People used to say, 'Oh the Hui
braddahs are out here, you better watch out.' But most of us weren't like that;
we were just the easiest guys to get along with."[34]

When predominantly haole-operated media venues label Hawaiian activist groups radical or terroristic during such a time of cultural resurgence and
political awareness, historians should ask themselves why. To answer, we must
take into consideration the motives of and benefits to those producing such
discourses. As Michel Foucault has argued, discourse is wedded to power
relations.[35] Thus since those who are in power labor to maintain that power
and control both the production and dissemination of knowledge, they construct discourses that preserve and justify their dominance in that society.
In colonial societies, or societies where foreign governments rule over conquered Natives, as with Hawai'i, the empowered or hegemonic group has
to regularly justify and explain its occupation. Colonial discourses—media
stereotyping of Natives being part of them—are commonly deployed by
those dominant groups in an attempt to justify colonization. When voices
of resistance contradict colonial discourses, the foreign occupation appears
unjust. Consequently, such governments generally find ways to dismiss and
disclaim them. This is precisely what has happened in Hawai'i since the birth
of modern Hawaiian activism in the 1970s.

Several scholars, most notably postcolonial studies critics, have contended
that hegemonic media commonly disparage colonial resistance by labeling
them savage extremists, or sometimes terrorists. Edward Said elaborated

on this point in 1978 when he criticized both historical and contemporary Western representations of the Arab world and the discipline of Orientalism. In *Orientalism,* Said drew from Foucault's notion of a discourse to criticize more than simply an academic discipline that had disseminated false and problematic myths about the Arab world. He argued that "Orientalism can be discussed and analyzed as the corporate institution for dealing with the Orient—dealing with it by making statements about it, authorizing views of it, describing it, by teaching it, settling it, ruling over it: in short, Orientalism, as a Western style for dominating, restructuring, and having authority over the Orient."[36] For Said and the many academics who have applied his ideas elsewhere, this looming method of dealing with, dominating, and defining the Muslim world not only led to the oversimplification and misrepresentation of those who lived in this vast geographic area, but also became a tool for justifying conquest. In later works Said argued that the proliferation of American representations of Arabs (and Muslims in general) as terrorists in movies and television supports a misconceived notion that people from the Middle East are a monolithic race of irrational peoples who need to be "stamped out."[37] From Hollywood shoot-'em-up movies to national news programming, the American media's rendering of the Middle East as a place occupied solely by terrorists caused concern for Said. For him, such misrepresentations were not only rooted in ignorance, but were also created in light of U.S. support for the Israeli occupation of the West Bank, Gaza Strip, and East Jerusalem.[38] Because Americans saw all Palestinians as extremists or terrorists, the Israeli occupation seemed justified.

The fact that news coverage of the Hui as terrorists ran alongside news of terrorism in the Middle East is telling. It not only points to the validity of Said's claims, but also shows that Orientalist discourses functioned even in Hawai'i. Second, it also shows that when news media aligned local "dissidents" with Middle Eastern terrorism, they could produce a more dramatic effect, which essentially makes the "bad guys" appear even worse. Thus Orientalist discourses are flexible and have been used on others outside the Arab world to produce similar effects, even on Hawaiian surfers on the North Shore. The comments from one American viewer of *Boarding House* showed how this concept plays out to viewers, even in the Hawaiian context. Using the nickname "Wichita," this viewer said, "Sunny shares the same basic character flaw with the other bullies of this world—including Saddam Hussein. They all believe they have [the] right to exercise force and inflict injury at will over all other human beings."[39]

Other academics have shown that Orientalist-like discourses helped justify conquest outside the Middle East. Influenced by Said, postcolonial media and film critics Ella Shoat and Robert Stam explain that debasing media labels have been used to undermine and justify exploits on ethnic minority groups, including communities in the United States. They argue that "Native Americans were called 'beasts' and 'savages' because White Europeans were expropriating their land; Mexicans were derided as 'banditos' and 'greasers' because Anglos were seizing Mexican territory." They contend that through such means conquest is justified and Native resistance is deemed senseless.[40] Robert Eskildsen has shown that Japan ironically borrowed Orientalist-like discourses to justify their conquests over Taiwan in 1874. Sorting through Japanese commercial papers Eskildsen found several examples where Japanese media exaggerated the "savage" nature of its Taiwanese subjects. Portraying the Taiwanese as cannibals, the Japanese did this not necessarily to excuse their presence to the Taiwanese, but to validate Japan as a modernized nation that could, like Western nations, civilize its subjugated savages.[41] As a result, Eskildsen argues, this "mimetic imperialism helped shape [Japan's] national identity and the new political order in the Meiji period."[42]

Ania Loomba argues that colonial discourses have been used to control indigenous peoples throughout the world and often served specific colonial functions. Arguing that different stereotypes were "tailored to different colonial policies," she says that in colonial societies in Africa and India certain races were cast as useful in particular occupations.[43] For example, in Bulawayo, Zimbabwe, Africans were forced to perform the lowest and most strenuous wage-labor jobs, and Europeans there represented them as naturally equipped to accomplish such work. Drawing from Abdul JanMohammad, Loomba states that there was a "profoundly symbiotic relationship between the discursive and the material practices of imperialism. . . . English violence in colonial Virginia, for example, was justified by representing the Native Americans as a violent and rebellious people."[44]

Maori scholar Brendan Hokowhitu has shown that Pakeha (haole) stereotypes of Maori men as savage warriors capable only of physical labor constituted a discourse that served a particular colonial need: to keep Maori men in labor, military, and less-intellectual professions. He argues that this encouraged and justified British colonialism as a "taming" mission. Descending from this notion, twentieth-century discourse found a productive place for "physical" and "less intelligent" Maori men as laborers. Throughout the last century, sports have served other specific functions for the dominant Pakeha group. For example, rugby, he argues, became a space where Maori men could "gain public recognition without challenging the dominant discourse," and it "evidenced that New Zealand's colonial system had enlightened and assimilated its savages."[45] Hokowhitu's research has a very personal flair to it. As a Maori student Hokowhitu was, like the majority of his Maori peers, discouraged by teachers from pursuing an intellectual career and instead was encouraged to excel in physical realms like sports. Although he won accolades as a college and university rugby player, he nevertheless disregarded the advice of many Pakeha and went on to complete a Ph.D. Through his research he found that the success of Maori men in sport was related to and aided these historic colonial discourses. Among other things, sports aided the colonial project by perpetuating the notion that Maori physicality, and not intelligence, was their specialty.[46] However, this problem was compounded by the fact that many Maori men "swallowed these constructs" and identify themselves through such definitions.[47]

The boundaries created by colonial stereotyping in particular, and discourse more generally, have proved problematic for Hawaiians and other Pacific Islanders. However, they were not incontestable. Boundary making is quite problematic, even in academic circles. Recently, Fredrik Barth, an anthropologist who initiated theoretical discussions of boundaries in 1969, has criticized scholars' misuse of "boundaries." In "Boundaries and Connections," he states that the term has become a projection apparatus of "Western folk models of thought" and has been made to "serve our own analytical purposes."[48] Most notably, structural anthropologists have consistently imposed their own structures on Pacific Island peoples through their assessments of culture. Ultimately, such anthropology ends up reflecting and laying bare the anthropologist at the expense of Native people.[49] Expounding on George Lakoff's perspectives, Barth refutes structuralist agendas and states that "people are not merely playing out structure, they are each a locus of reason and construction, using complex embodied imagery that they are trying to fit to what they perceive as experience."[50] Barth closes by calling on anthropologists to more carefully and creatively discover new and better ways to "grasp the Native's point of view, his relation to life, to realize his vision of his world."[51]

Appropriating and Countering Stereotypes

The Hui's hypermasculine image consequently countered the stereotype of the emasculated Hawaiian man. By the late 1970s Hawaiian men of the Hui O He'e Nalu were no longer seen as submissive, content Natives. The change, however, meant two things. First, in an effort to resist the perceived notion that Hawaiian men were unmanly, some Hawaiian surfers turned to more aggressive methods of resistance. While their assertive resistance was often misrepresented as terrorism, the Hui faced a new set of problems with this label. In many ways it undermined Hawaiian resistance because such labels cast Hui surfers as barbaric and irrational.

However, the new label also had its advantages. The imagery, as problematic as it was, helped make a previously quieted and invisible people very vocal and visible. Ironically, these new renderings freed Hawaiian men from the early twentieth-century's emasculating stereotypes. Several Hui members felt that popular awareness of their existence as Native men was a positive thing—perhaps because this visible existence was precisely what the ideal, submissive Native trope had formerly extinguished. Bryan Amona explained, "Sure, people would call us terrorists, or the surfing mafia of the world; we were called all kinds of stuff . . . but those kinds of labels didn't really bother me back then because I thought that bad press was better than no press."[52] Although problematic, the label provided a means to voice their concerns and navigate their public identity.

Some scholars, like Ty Kawika Tengan, have argued that colonized men of the Pacific often adopt precolonial, hypermasculine identities "to resist the perceived feminization and emasculation that accompanied colonization in Hawai'i."[53] Perhaps several Hui members were redefining themselves under such terms, but more importantly, the Hui often appropriated these hypermasculine labels to accomplish anticolonial, and sometimes personal, objectives.

In a 2002 *Surfer* magazine interview, Kalā Alexander explained how he consciously performed the radical Native Hawaiian role while auditioning for a part in the Hollywood movie *Blue Crush*. Interviewer Chris Mauro insisted on uncovering Alexander's supposedly irrational nature with persistent questions like, "So did you have to kick any ass to get a role in *Blue Crush*?" "So you wanted to kick the writer's ass?" "So they got a little North Shore debriefing?" "Damn . . . so no ass kicking at all?" and "Please tell me you kicked their asses." Alexander assured him that he had not. He eventually admitted, however, "Well, I did scare 'em once. After I laughed at the lines they gave me, the guy told me to pretend he'd cut me off at Pipeline, just to see how I'd react. I told him normally I wouldn't say a thing, but for his sake I went nuts, screaming at the top of my lungs, spitting in his face, telling him to go back to the mainland. I must have gone off pretty hard because there were security guys outside and they came running in. . . . The director said, 'Enough, enough, okay, okay. You're in. You got a part. . . . We don't know what it is, but you can calm down now.'"[54] In this instance, one Hui surfer consciously used the director's stereotype to his own benefit, performing savage-like, Native radicalism as a way of getting an acting job.

Since the late 1970s Hui members have frequently appropriated the hypermasculine label as a way of achieving their anticolonial objectives. Gananath Obeyeskere has similarly explained why the Maori of Aotearoa (New Zealand) exaggerated cannibalistic practices to Europeans in the late eighteenth century. While European voyagers obsessed over questions about cannibalism, the Maori, who traditionally practiced cannibalism only on extraordinary occasions, embellished the practice in dealing with Europeans in order to terrify strangers who possessed far more advanced weaponry than the Maori had.[55] Like the Hui, they played off of Pakeha stereotypical expectations as a way of averting colonial invasion—which in both cases posited Natives as extremely barbaric.

By deeming Native Hawaiian complaints against colonialism radical terrorism, the dominant group simultaneously rendered their voices senseless and inconceivable. As Said has shown, this method proved effective for Western imperial nations in the Middle East, or the so-called "Orient." Drawing from Said and other postcolonial scholars, we see that Orientalist discourses proved flexible and were often applied in Hawai'i, even on the North Shore. As Honolulu media aligned "radical" Hawaiian surfers with Middle Eastern terrorists, readers were convinced of the surfers' savagery. Although this kind of stereotyping was exaggerated and demeaning to Hawaiians, in the long run Hui surfers learned to work within the parameters of such discourse and often manipulated it to their advantage. Furthermore, while Hawaiian male voices of resistance were represented as savage-like, at least they were being heard. This is significant because the earlier stereotype that had cast Hawaiian men as submissive and unmasculine—promoted primarily through the tourist industry—silenced voices of resistance throughout much of the twentieth century.

Conclusions

The ocean has always been a life source for the Kānaka Maoli 'Ōiwi (Native Hawaiians). It provided not only food and pleasure, but also refuge and inspiration to them. It has also been a portal connecting the islands to one another, linking people to ancestors and relatives scattered throughout the Pacific. But the ocean has also been a place where Hawaiians have enjoyed he'e nalu, the ancient Hawaiian practice today called surfing. The ocean and he'e nalu have tied Hawaiians to their precolonial past during a time when being Hawaiian was disparaged. It was also unique as Hawaiian surfers maintained their place atop a social hierarchy in a time when many Hawaiians were marginalized on land. Because he'e nalu is a cultural practice that has never died out in Hawai'i, it became an identity marker for many Hawaiians and gave them access to their ancient past. During a period of loss and cultural annihilation for Hawaiians on land, this aquatic zone was a door to a precolonial world and gave them confidence as Natives. The po'ina nalu, or Hawaiian surf zone, also represents a significant and overlooked space where Hawaiians continually resisted colonialism. Interestingly, these Hawaiians often achieved their anticolonial objectives against such forces. Thus he'e nalu connects a history of Hawaiian resistance from the 1890s through the 1980s.

Shortly after the so-called annexation, Hui Nalu surfers of Waikīkī preserved their cultural space from the clutches of racist haole elites in the surf. As a result, the ocean surf zone was often seen as a sanctuary for Hawaiians. But it was also a kind of borderland, a place where both power dynamics and colonialism functioned differently than hegemonic authorities expected them to on land. Amid this jostling for control in the waves, Hawaiian surfers formed identities that stood in contrast to their adversaries. Although the Waikīkī borderland was threatened in the 1940s after the Massie affair and, later, World War II, the surf nevertheless remained a refuge for many Hawaiians—not only in Waikīkī, but at many other surfing breaks around the islands. However, Hawaiian surfers were again challenged in the late 1970s as the professional surf industry moved into the North Shore surf. Although members of the Hui O He'e Nalu saw themselves as cultural protectors of Native space when they resisted this corporate and colonial encroachment, others viewed and portrayed them as extremists. Thus a battle over identification became another conflict for the Hui.

While this book has emphasized stories of Hawaiian surfers riding waves of resistance, it has also aimed to bring Hawaiian history into clearer focus. Through this lens we see that surfing hui were seamlessly woven into Hawai'i's past, often in ways not initially perceived. For example, in the 1890s several political hui fought to protect and preserve Hawaiian autonomy during a time when Hawai'i's kingdom was under siege. While they were different from the surfing hui (like the Hui Nalu and Hui O

He'e Nalu), they nevertheless shared ideals about Native preservation and resistance to colonialism. While the Hui Nalu was formed shortly after the conquest of the Hawaiian kingdom, their story is enmeshed with narratives of protest against annexationists specifically. This becomes clear as we see the same people embroiled in annexation debates also contending with each other in the surf—like the Outrigger and Hui Nalu surfing clubs. The Hui O He'e Nalu, formed in 1976, was also a product of its time. While most Hui surfers formulated identities by looking to their ancestral surfing past, the cultural renaissance of the 1970s also helped shape this North Shore group, albeit indirectly. While some have pointed to the Hōkūle'a canoe voyages and the Protect Kaho'olawe Ohana (PKO) protests against the military on Kaho'olawe island as the genesis of renaissance activism, many have overlooked the influence of John Kelly's Save Our Surf (SOS) organization on the Hawaiian renaissance. Starting a decade before the PKO and the Hōkūle'a voyages, SOS was successful at stopping colonial elites in their attempts to literally extend tourism and real estate development over Hawaiian waves. SOS's successes gave locals and Hawaiians of succeeding generations the tools to combat injustice—including groups who in later decades sought Native Hawaiian political autonomy. Meanwhile, Hawaiian surfers of the Hui O He'e Nalu, which was formed during a time of burgeoning Hawaiian demands for restitution, preservation, and autonomy, began protesting those surfing entities and individuals who staked claim over North Shore waves in the 1970s and 1980s.

In comparison to other political and activist groups, which admittedly have made important strides, surfer resistance has been markedly successful at achieving its goals—as seen with the Hui Nalu, Waikīkī Beachboys, SOS, and even the North Shore Hui O He'e Nalu. Whether it was maintaining a hierarchy in the surf for Hawaiians, stopping major development projects, or exerting control in the surf amid a rising surfing industry in the latter part of the twentieth century, in their primes, these organizations accomplished their objectives.

But the outcomes for these organizations have not all been positive. While resistance and protest have proved useful to maintaining space for Hawaiians, unnecessary violence or unlawful behavior has at times hampered their validity. While violence has indeed been part of much of this story, my goal has been to explain and contextualize it, not to justify it. While several media venues have emphasized Hawaiian violence, colonial violence (in the form of diseases, broken treaties, racist politics, marginalization, or literary violence in the media) has been far more brutal and more regularly overlooked. Thus this book has aimed to contextualize tensions in Hawaiian waves by observing colonial relationships in ka poʻina nalu (the surf zone). While most haole surfers did not see themselves as colonizers, to many Hawaiians they were. Less than simply a case of misplaced identity, this is a story about clashing identities.

In addition to a history of colonial conquest in the islands, clashing surfer identities were also central to tensions in twentieth-century Hawaiian waves. For example, the identities of Outrigger haole surfers collided with Native Waikīkī surfers in the early 1900s. While Outrigger haole defined themselves through a white superiority complex, Hui Nalu surfers identified with Hawaiian culture, Native pride, and a strong sense of preserving Hawaiian autonomy. Also, North Shore surfers in later generations clashed with haole surfers who held invented claims to Hawaiian waves. As American surfers (primarily from California) adopted a beach and surfing culture reminiscent of imagined views of Hawaiʻi, a new identity immerged. The appeal of their made-up version of a lackadaisical Hawaiian culture was the polar opposite of conservative American society in the 1950s and 1960s, thus all sorts of "Kahunas" took up "surfin' in the USA."[56] However, as these surfers drew from invented notions of Hawaiian culture at the expense of living Hawaiian surfers, this identity did not sit well with real Hawaiian surfers in the waves. While haole surfer identity has thrived on the myth that they inherited heʻe nalu from ancient and nearly extinct Hawaiian surfers, twentieth-century Hawaiian surfers were often overlooked as anachronistic. Such lack of recognition fueled rage in Native surfers, who saw themselves as living heirs of heʻe nalu. These competing identities have sparked many confrontations between haole and Hawaiians in the surf over the years.

Since the 1980s, the culture of the surf zone on the North Shore has evolved. The popularity of surfing again skyrocketed in the 1990s, and the waves were inundated with even more surfers. During this time, the Hui struggled with its own internal problems. For example, several Hui surfers were disillusioned when some club leaders founded the clothing line Da Hui. While Hui membership slowly faded, other local and Hawaiian surfers formed new groups to fill this power vacuum—like the Wolfpak. As the demographics on the North Shore have changed in the last two decades—into a predominantly white and upper-income group of residents, speculators, and vacationers—many Hawaiians have been forced out of these highly prized beach neighborhoods. Because of inflated real estate prices in Hawaiʻi, numerous Hawaiian families have relocated farther from Hawaiian beaches, and even away from the islands entirely. Many Hawaiians lament this shift in demographics, as reflected in bumper stickers that say, "North Shore: Haolewood," or "Velzyland, gone but not forgotten." Velzyland has historically been a favorite surf spot for Native Hawaiian surfers, including Hui members. At the turn of the millennium, however, the state bulldozed the low-income homes at Velzyland, ignored local suggestions to convert the area into a public park, and instead sold the newly subdivided lots to multi-million-dollar buyers. Appropriately named the "Sunset Colony," this gated community helped displace many Hawaiians. Although some things have changed, Hawaiians today nevertheless flock to the waves and continue to develop identities as Hawaiians in the surf.

Several dedicated surfers have organized groups and run events that perpetuate heʻe nalu for the keiki (children) of Hawaiʻi. Along with many of the Hui O Heʻe Naluʻs community events that are still operating, such as their paddleboard races and beach cleanups, other long-standing community surfing projects continue to thrive. Perhaps most notable among them is the Rell Sunn Menehune Surfing Championship, held annually at Mākaha. In addition to this event, other competitions at Mākaha run by the Keaulana family and others have thrived over the last few decades. While surfers like Skibs Nehls have worked on the island of Hawaiʻi to encourage and assist Hilo youth with surfing and caring for their beaches, others, like professional surfer Duane Desoto of Mākaha, have formed ocean awareness programs for Hawaiʻiʻs children. His organization, called Nā Kama Kai, recruits some of Hawaiʻiʻs best watermen and women to teach kids around Oʻahu to paddle on surfboards and standup paddleboards, as well as canoe surfing and ocean safety. Nā Kama Kai provides access and inspiration for future surfers of Hawaiʻi who may not have the luxury of proximity to the beach. On the east side of Oʻahu, parents of Ke Kula Kaiapuni o Hauʻula (a Hawaiian-language immersion school in Hauʻula) formed Hālau Nalu, a surfing school with an emphasis on Hawaiian culture and language. Here, young surfers not only learn surfing, history, and language, but are also provided with surfboards that are often beyond the means of many families from this moku (district). Tom Pohaku Stone has also been active in teaching youth to make and ride ancient-style Hawaiian wood surfboards, to appreciate the ocean, and to be safe in Hawaiian waters. Through individuals and groups like these, the ocean has been used as a tool for teaching Hawai'i's future generations the cultural and historical significance of he'e nalu.

He'e nalu has been, and always will be, a practice significant to Native Hawaiians. He'e nalu was important in ancient Hawaiian society, and ka po'ina nalu (the surf zone) has been a place where Hawaiian identities have been shaped, bolstered, and redefined in contemporary times. He'e nalu and ka po'ina nalu have helped Kānaka Maoli connect with their ancient past to find meaning, strength, and purpose in the present. May we continue to look to our past as we ride forward on waves to the future.

Notes

Introduction

1   Abraham Fornander, *Fornander Collection of Hawaiian Antiquities and Folklore,* vol. 6 (Honolulu: 'Ai Pokaku Press, 1999), 206–207. Hawaiians have chanted both for large waves and for success in surfing competitions. While some chants blessed surfboards for optimum performance and others were prayers that opened surfing tournaments, many praised individual surfers. But perhaps the most common surfing chant was this one, the pōhuehue chant. While lashing the ocean water with pōhuehue vine (beach morning-glory, *Ipomoea* sp.), a chanter called forth the great waves from the moana (vast ocean).

2   In this book the term "Hawaiian" refers to indigenous natives of Hawai'i, also called Kanaka (person) Maoli (real, true) or 'Ōiwi (lit., "of the bone"). Although most Native Hawaiians have a mixture of other ethnicities today, they are still considered Hawaiian here.

3   The word "haole" is a Hawaiian term that refers to people who are foreign to Hawai'i—most commonly white Americans or Europeans (local people of Portuguese ancestry excluded). Although it can be used for insult (when expletives are placed in front of it, or if the tone of the speaker's voice connotes negativity), "haole" is not, in and of itself, a racially derogatory slur. Most often, people in Hawai'i, Hawaiians included, use the term to identify Caucasian ancestry in themselves or in others. Some Hawai'i-raised haole who have lived among Hawaiians and have earned respect from them are often called local or local haole. These individuals have a different social status and identity than "haole" and are distinguished by their ability to bond with Hawaiians, reciprocate aloha, and speak pidgin. Thus "haole" is a social construct defined by attitude, not simply by a person's race. In contrast to Hawaiian values of behavior, haole attitudes are defined as self- and individual oriented, as opposed to community centered. Such interpretations of "haole" are reflected in the perspectives of surfers interviewed for this book.

4   For more on Hawaiian Masculinity, see Ty Kawika Tengan, *Native Men Remade: Gender and Nation in Contemporary Hawai'i* (Durham, N.C., and London: Duke University Press, 2008).

5   James Cook and James King, *A Voyage to the Pacific Ocean* (London: Printed by W. and A. Strahan for G. Nicol and T. Cadell, 1784), 146.

6   Chuck Waipā Andrus, videotaped interview with author, Hau'ula, Hawai'i, 25 June 2004.

7   Greg Dening, *Performances* (Chicago: University of Chicago Press, 1996), 34.

8   Lilikalā Kame'eleihiwa, *Native Land and Foreign Desires: Pehea Lā E Pono Ai? How Shall We Live in Harmony?* (Honolulu: Bishop Museum Press, 1992); Jonathan Kay Kamakawiwo'ole Osorio, *Dismembering Lahui: A History of the Hawaiian Nation to 1887* (Honolulu: University of Hawai'i Press, 2002), 7.

9   Eric Hobsbawm and Terence Ranger, eds., *The Invention of Tradition* (Cambridge: Cambridge University Press, 1983).

10 David Malo, *Hawaiian Antiquities Moolelo Hawaii* (Bernice Pauahi Bishop Museum, Honolulu, Special publication; 2. Translated by Nathaniel B. Emerson. Honolulu: Bishop Museum, 1951), 223.

11 Mary Kawena Pukui recorded a story of another great surfing chief, Naihe of Kaʻū. As other Big Island chiefs grew jealous of his surfing abilities, they devised a plot against him at a surfing competition in Hilo. They altered the contest rules so that surfers were forbidden to ride a wave until their personal oli (chant) called them forth. Since Naihe was informed of this rule only after venturing far into the ocean (beyond the breaking waves), he drifted hopelessly in the sea. Fortunately his chanter, who had been napping, awakened in time, got wind of the plot, and quickly shouted his personal chant into the Hilo sea. Mary Kawena Pukui, "Songs (mele) of Old Kaʻū, Hawaiʻi," Journal of American Folklore 62, no. 245 (July–September 1949): 247–258.

12 Many practices survived through recuperation and revival; other practices survived through underground preservation efforts.

13 For specific numbers, see debate between Stannard and Bushnell. David Stannard, *Before the Horror: The Population of Hawaiʻi on the Eve of Western Contact* (Honolulu: University of Hawaiʻi Press, 1989); Andrew Bushnell, "'The Horror' Reconsidered: An Evaluation of the Historical Evidence for Population Decline in Hawaiʻi, 1778–1803," *Pacific Studies* 16, no. 3 (1993): 115–162.

14 See Hiram Bingham, *A Residence of Twenty-One Years in the Sandwich Islands* (Rutland, Vt.: Charles E. Tuttle Co, 1981); Kameʻeleihiwa, *Native Land;* and Patricia Grimshaw, *Paths of Duty: American Missionary Wives in Nineteenth-Century Hawaiʻi* (Honolulu: University of Hawaiʻi Press, 1989).

15 She was the daughter of Princess Miriam Likelike, sister of Liliʻuokalani and Kalākaua. Her father, Archibald Cleghorn, was of Scottish ancestry and was the governor of Oʻahu during Liliʻuokalani's reign.

16 Tom Blake, *Hawaiian Surfboard* (Honolulu: Paradise of the Pacific Press, 1935), 60.

17 "Beach Breezes, Some Scenes a Surf Reporter Saw on Sunday," *Santa Cruz Daily Surf,* first edition (20 July 1885).

18 See Noenoe Silva, *Aloha Betrayed: Native Hawaiian Resistance to American Colonialism* (Durham, N.C.: Duke University Press, 2004); and *Act of War: The Overthrow of the Hawaiian Nation,* directed by Puhipau, Joan Lander (Honolulu: Nā Maka o ka ʻĀina, in association with Center for Hawaiian Studies, University of Hawaiʻi at Mānoa, 1993).

19 Silva, *Aloha Betrayed,* 158–159.

20 As J. Kēhaulani Kauanui made clear, the joint resolution was for domestic policy making only, and according to U.S. law, a treaty was required for such an act. Thus a joint resolution vote in Congress was unconstitutional and illegal. See J. Kēhaulani Kauanui, "Precarious Positions: Native Hawaiian and US Federal Recognition" *The Contemporary Pacific* 17, no. 1 (2005): 3–4.

21   Native Hawaiian surfers George Freeth and Duke Kahanamoku became famous as they traveled outside Hawai'i and showed off their skills to the world. Freeth was hired by Henry E. Huntington to hold a surfing exhibition in Redondo Beach, California, to help promote the Redondo–Los Angeles Railway in 1907. Kahanamoku introduced surfing to a variety of American and Australian beaches while he was en route to the Olympic Games of 1912 and 1916.

22   Ben R. Finney, *Surfing: The Sport of Hawaiian Kings* (Boston: Charles E. Tuttle Co., 1966).

23   Haunani-Kay Trask, *From a Native Daughter: Colonialism and Sovereignty in Hawai'i* (Monroe, Maine: Common Courage Press, 1993), 53. In *Staging Tourism,* Jane Desmond has explained this trend. Postcards and stereoscopes used images of sexualized Hawaiian women to sell Hawaiians as "attractive, unthreatening, generous hosts." Jane Desmond, *Staging Tourism: Bodies on Display from Waikīkī to Sea World* (Chicago: University of Chicago Press, 1999), 48.

24   For more history on the South Seas film genre, see Larry Langman, *Return to Paradise: A Guide to South Sea Island Films* (Lanham, Md.: Scarecrow Press, 1998), 286; for a deeper analysis of the colonial discourse generated in these films, see Houston Wood, *Displacing Natives: The Rhetorical Production of Hawai'i* (Lanham, Md.: Rowman & Littlefield Publishers, Inc., 1999), 103–121.

25   Ty Kawika Tengan, *Native Men Remade: Gender and Nation in Contemporary Hawai'i* (Durham, N.C., and London: Duke University Press, 2008).

26   Most notably Buffalo Keaulana.

27   Billy Ho'ola'e Blankenfeld, videotaped interview with author, Kāne'ohe, Hawai'i, July 26, 2004.

28   Bryan Amona, videotaped interview with author, Kailua, Hawai'i, August 29, 2004.

29   Ken Kobayashi, "Reign of terror on North Shore told," *Honolulu Advertiser,* July 21, 1987, A1. Neither of the two surfers was convicted in this trial. Although the surfers interviewed for this volume admitted that some club members had a history of drug use, most were strong advocates of drug-free living. For example, Bryan Amona and Billy Blankenfeld were very active in a variety of anti-drug community projects. Other Hui members were involved in organizations—like the Mormon Church—that strongly discouraged using drugs.

30   Kobayashi, "Reign of terror on North Shore told," A1.

31   Several postcolonial theorists have contended that hegemonic media commonly disparage colonial resistance with debasing stereotypes. Thus "Native Americans were called 'beasts' and 'savages' because White Europeans were expropriating their land; Mexicans were derided as 'banditos' and 'greasers' because Anglos were seizing Mexican territory." Ella Shoat and Robert Stam have asserted that conquest is justified and Native resistance deemed senseless through such representations. See Ella Shoat and Robert Stam, *Unthinking Eurocentrism: Multiculturalism and the Media* (London: Rutledge, 1994), 18.

32   Susan Lee Johnson, *Roaring Camp: The Social World of the California Gold Rush* (New York: Norton, 2000), 100. Likewise, in the pre-twentieth-century

American Southwest James Brooks found a borderland where American slavery and hegemony were in flux. Unlike the usual story of slavery in America, the Southwest was a place where Indian, Mexican, and Euro-American communities all enslaved each other in a captive exchange economy. James Brooks, *Captives and Cousins: Slavery, Kinship, and Community in the Southwest Borderlands* (Chapel Hill: University of North Carolina Press, 2002).

33 Greg Dening, *Islands and Beaches Discourse on a Silent Land: Marquesas, 1774–1880* (Melbourne, Aus.: Melbourne University Press, 1980), 16.

34 Ibid., 32.

35 Ibid., 11, 18.

36 Wayne "Rabbit" Bartholomew and Tim Baker, *Bustin' Down the Door* (New York: Harper, 1996).

37 See Paul D'Arcy, *The People of the Sea: Environment, Identity, and History in Oceania* (Honolulu: University of Hawai'i Press, 2006); Vicente Diaz, *Sacred Vessels: Navigating Tradition and Identity in Micronesia,* video documentary (Guam: Moving Islands Production, 1997); and Epeli Hau'ofa, "Our Sea of Islands," in *A New Oceania Rediscovering Our Sea of Islands,* edited by Epeli Hau'ofa (Suva, Fiji: University of the South Pacific Press, 1993), 2–16.

38 Hau'ofa, "Our Sea of Islands."

39 Ibid.; see also Margaret Jolly, "From Point Venus to Bali Ha'i: Eroticism and Exoticism in Representations of the Pacific," in *Sites of Desire, Economies of Pleasure: Sexualities in Asia and the Pacific,* edited by Lenore Manderson and Margaret Jolly (Chicago and London: University of Chicago Press, 1997), 99–122.

40 For more on the debate about the authenticity of ethnography, see James Clifford's introduction in James Clifford and George Marcus, eds., *Writing Culture: The Poetics and Politics of Ethnography* (Berkeley and Los Angeles: University of California Press, 1986), 1–26.

41 See Brendan Hokowhitu, "Tackling Māori Masculinity: A Colonial Genealogy of Savagery and Sport," *The Contemporary Pacific* 16, no. 2 (Fall 2004): 259–284; Mirinalini Sinha, *Colonial Masculinity: The "Manly Englishman" and the "Effeminate Bengali"* (Manchester, U.K.: Manchester University Press, 1995); and Ty Kawika Tengan, "Hale Mua: (En)gendering Hawaiian Men," PhD dissertation, University of Hawai'i at Mānoa, 2003.

Chapter 1: He'e Nalu

1 *Riding Giants,* film directed by Stacy Peralta, Sony Pictures Classic, 2004.

2 Ibid.

3 Hawaiian surfers were at the forefront of surfing's evolution in the twentieth century. Hawaiian surfboard shapers and wave riders pushed the envelope of surfing, especially in the 1970s, when the sport made its greatest transition from long to short board. This is commonly overlooked in surf history narratives, and yet none dispute that Barry Kanaiaupuni, Eddie Aikau, Ben Aipa, Gerry

Lopez, Larry Bertlemann, Buttons Kaluhiokalani, Dane Kealoha, Michael Ho, and others led the move to progressive, modern-day surfing.

4   Finney, *Surfing,* 23.

5   Malo, *Hawaiian Antiquities Moolelo Hawaii,* 223.

6   In precolonial Hawaiian society there were particular mele (chants) for calling large surf and na heiau (temples) built specifically for surfing. While some chants blessed surfboards for optimum performance and others were prayers that opened surfing tournaments, many praised individual surfers. Mary Kawena Pukui explained that many surfers had individualized chants praising their surfing abilities. Pukui, "Songs (mele) of Old Ka'u, Hawai'i," 247–258.

7   George Kanahele, *Waikīkī 100BC to 1900AD: An Untold Story* (Honolulu: University of Hawai'i Press, 1996). Prayers were often recited at heiau designed specifically for surfing. At the foot of Diamond Head, in Waikīkī, the Papa'ena'ena heiau was a place where kāhuna offered prayers for increased surfing abilities and larger waves. But Papa'ena'ena was also where surf reports were provided to the local community. When wave heights increased, a priest flew kites high above Papa'ena'ena heiau, which in turn encouraged residents to stop their work, get their surfboards, and head to the ocean. Other surfing heiau, like Ku'emanu on Hawai'i's Kona coast, were equipped with a freshwater pool (carved in stone) for surfers to rinse off after an enjoyable surfing session. See Finney, *Surfing,* 55.

8   However, there were some restrictions for commoners, who generally were not allowed to ride the same wave as a chief or use a board designed specifically for a chief. Also, although few, some surfing breaks were kapu, or off limits, to commoners.

9   Malo, *Hawaiian Antiquities Moolelo Hawaii,* 223.

10 Thomas G. Thrum, *More Hawaiian Folktales: A Collection of Native Legends and Traditions* (Chicago: A. C. McClurg and Co., 1923), 111.

11 "He Moolelo no Hiiakaikapoliopele, Helu 7," *Ka Hoku o ka Pakipika* Feberuari 13, 1862, 4.

12 Ibid., 4.

13 Frederick G. Wichman, "Ka He'e Nalu 'ana ma Wai-lua," in *Pele Mā: Legends of Pele from Kaua'i* (Honolulu: Bamboo Ridge Press, 2001), 70–75.

14 Although territorialism still exists and may sometimes be the reason for surfing tensions, in Hawai'i the issues run deeper along historical, cultural, and colonial lines.

15 Thus when locals in Hawai'i first meet, they inquire, "Where you from?" or "Who is your family?" Then, you would not consider (as an outsider) taking waves from a family from that area, or a surfer with a reputable name like Keaulana, Aikau, or Stant, to name a few.

16 Tevita Ka'ili, "Tauhi vā: Nurturing Tongan Sociospacial Ties in Maui and Beyond," *Contemporary Pacific* 17, no. 1 (2005): 88–89.

17 Ibid., 92.

18 Genealogy (often overlooked), rank, and ability to surf well are still valued in Hawaiian surfing hierarchies. The Keaulana family, for example, is known as

ali'i in the surf lineup at Mākaha. They not only have priority when catching waves, but have kuleana (responsibility or stewardship) to that beach. Thus they are lifeguards at Mākaha, host several community beach service events, care for the shoreline, etc. When surfers respect genealogical ranking in the surf (by recognizing their place in that hierarchy), they also value that family's or community's kuleana. Hence a good way for haole to forge healthy relationships in that community is to first assist with the kuleana. For example, they might help the families in beach clean ups, lu'au, etc.

19 Abraham Fornander, *Selections from Fornander's Hawaiian Antiquities and Lore* (Honolulu: University of Hawai'i Press, 1959).

20 According to some sources, Ka'ili is Mo'ikeha's granddaughter. Mo'ikeha is also often simply referred to as Kealiiokauai (the chief of Kaua'i).

21 "He Moolelo No Kailiokalauokeakoa," Helu 2, *Ka Hoku o ka Pakipika*, Buke I. Honolulu, Okatoba 31, 1861, Helu 6.

22 "He Moolelo No Ka'iliokalauokekoa, Helu 7," *Ka Hoku o ka Pakipika*, Buke I. Honolulu, Dekemaba 26, 1861, Helu 14.

23 It is said that rainbows regularly appeared over ali'i, and thus Lā'ie was nearly discovered by the seer Hulumaniani.

24 H. N. Hale'ole, *Ka Mo'olelo o Laieikawai* (Washington, D.C.: Smithsonian Institution, 1919).

25 Ibid, mokuna III.

26 Ibid., mokuna XXI.

27 Ibid., mokuna XXII.

28 She was the sister of Kawaukaohele, who was the mō'ī, or king, of Maui.

29 Samuel Kamakau, *Na Mo'olelo a Ka Po'e Kahiko, Tales and Traditions of the People of Old* (Honolulu: Bishop Museum Press, 1991), 45–49. David Kalākaua, *The Legends and Myths of Hawaii: The Fables and Folk-Lore of a Strange People,* rev. ed. (Rutland, Vt.: Charles E. Tuttle, 1992).

30 Ancient Hawaiians had specific names for many different surfing breaks on the North Shore. Waimea is the only surfing break that uses its original name today.

31 Clarice B. Taylor, "Faithless Lover Turned to Stone," *Honolulu Star-Bulletin,* Wednesday, November 26, 1958, 20.

32 J. C. Beaglehole, ed., *Voyage of the* Resolution *and* Discovery, *1776–1780* (Cambridge: Cambridge University Press, 1967), excerpt from Samwells' Journal, 1165.

33 James King, *A Voyage to the Pacific Ocean, Volume III, 1779–1780* (London: W. and A. Strahan for G. Nicol and T. Cadell, 1784), 146–147.

34 Karina Kahananui Green, "Colonialism's Daughters: Eighteenth-and Nineteenth-Century Western Perceptions of Hawaiian Women," in *Pacific Diaspora: Island Peoples in the United States and Across the Pacific,* edited by Paul Spickard, Joanne Rondilla, and Debbie Hippolite Wright (Honolulu: University of Hawai'i Press, 2002), 230.

35 Ibid.

36 Stannard, *Before the Horror.*

37   John Heckathorn, "Interview with David Stannard," *Honolulu Magazine,* 1989, http://www2.hawaii.edu/~johnb/micro/m130/readings/stannard.html.

38   See Bingham, *A Residence of Twenty-One Years.*

39   "No Ka Molowa," editorial, *Ke Kumu Hawaii,* vol. 3, no. 18 (January 31, 1838), 70.

40   Henry T. Cheever, *Life in the Hawaiian Islands; or, The Heart of the Pacific as It Was and Is* (New York: A. S. Barnes & Co., 1851), 66–68.

41   Mark Twain, *Mark Twain's Letters from Hawaii* (Honolulu: University of Hawai'i Press, 1975).

42   "Ke Kilohana Pookela no ka Lahui Hawaii," *Ka Nupepa Kuokoa,* Buke 4, Helu 51, Honolulu, Dekemaba 23, 1865.

43   Silva, *Aloha Betrayed,* 55.

44   Ibid.

45   "Beach Breezes, Some Scenes a Surf Reporter Saw on Sunday."

46   Desoto Brown, *Surfing: Historic Images from Bishop Museum Archives* (Honolulu: Bishop Museum Press, 2006), 20, 21. Viewing the picture as a surfer, it is not necessarily the men centered in the shot who stand out to me, but rather the waves breaking behind them. The waves are obviously good—well-shaped, long walling lefts. I am very familiar with this wave; I grew up surfing it in my youth. It breaks only a dozen days out of the year, and when it does much of the Hilo surfing community drops everything to ride it. This picture shows that not much has changed, not only because these two experienced surfers seem excited about the northeast swell, but also because there appear to be others riding the waves in the background— one can faintly make out two other surfers dropping in on the outside wave. Even if those smudges are not actually surfers, it raises an important point. Just because many pictures of surfers at the turn of the century show them as riding on, or standing in front of, waves near the shore, we cannot infer, as others have, that only small waves were ridden by unskilled riders at the time. Instead, it says more about the technology of cameras in the 1890s—cameras that were not waterproof and so were not capable of zooming in on surfers farther out in the surf zone.

47   Desmond, *Staging Tourism,* 40.

48   Whereas surf history films like Peralta's *Riding Giants* state outright that the sport was extinct, scholars like Ben R. Finney considered surfing nearly extinct (see *Surfing,* 57).

49   Although London is mostly referring to one particular Hawaiian, George Freeth, several other Hawaiian surfers frequented the waves in 1907, particularly Hui Nalu surfers. See Jack London, "A Royal Sport," in *The Cruise of the Snark* (New York: Macmillan Co., 1911), 57.

50   Ben Marcus, *From Polynesia with Love: The History of Surfing from Captain Cook to the Present* (http://www.surfingforlife.com/history2.html).

51   Rabbit Kekai, conversation with Randy Rarick, Sunset Beach, Hawai'i, December 1, 2009. Video available on line, http://www.triplecrown.com.

52   Kealoha Kaio Sr., videotaped interview with author, Lā'ie, Hawai'i, August 8, 2004.

53   Kealoha Kaio Jr., videotaped interview with author, Lāʻie, Hawaiʻi, July 5, 2002.

54   See glossary for definition of bottom-turn.

55   Greg Noll, conversation with author, Waikīkī, March 2006.

56   Ben Aipa, videotaped interview with Jared Medeiros, Honolulu, September 17, 2009.

57   Ibid.

58   Stuart Coleman, *Eddie Would Go: The Story of Eddie Aikau, Hawaiian Hero and Pioneer of Big Wave Surfing* (New York: St. Martin's Griffin, 2004), 72.

59   Jared Medeiros, "Duke Invitational," senior paper, History 490, Department of History, BYU–Hawaii, fall 2009.

60   *Bustin' Down the Door,* film directed by Jeremy Gosch, Screen Media, 2008.

61   Bryan Amona, "Ala Moana Bowls: Dropping in at the South Shore's Most Famous Left Tube," *Spot Check,* August 31, 2008, www.surfline.com.

62   See Green, "Colonialism's Daughters"; see also Patricia Grimshaw, "New England Missionary Wives, Hawaiian Women and 'the Cult of True Womanhood,'" in *Family and Gender in the Pacific,* edited by Margaret Jolly and Martha Macintyre (Cambridge: Cambridge University Press, 1989), 19–44.

63   While in graduate school in Santa Barbara, California, I was surprised to see it still thriving. For example, there were several restaurants with names like "Kahuna Grill," where the interior oozed a grass-shack ambiance and old Hawaiian surfboards were bolted to the walls. Places like this serve coconut shakes and hamburgers with pineapples, and display pictures of Hawaiian waves and Californian surfers on their walls.

64   As Robert Berkhofer and others have suggested, many Americans felt this way about Native Americans—they were often rendered invisible by white imagination in contemporary times. With no place in a modern world, they were relegated to museums and history books. See Robert Berkhofer, *The White Man's Native: Images of the American Indian from Columbus to the Present* (New York: Vintage, 1979); and Vine Deloria Jr., *Custer Died For Your Sins: An Indian Manifesto* (Norman: University of Oklahoma Press, 1988).

Chapter 2: Colonial Violence and Hawaiian Resistance

1   Metcalf and his crew aboard the *Fair American* were killed by Hawaiian warriors after he massacred unarmed Hawaiians in waters off Olowalu, Maui. His ship then became the queen ship of Kamehameha's navy and two of his spared crewmen became Kamehameha's military generals—John Young and Isaac Davis.

2   Kamehameha conquered all the islands except Kauaʻi through battle. Kauaʻi was later incorporated through treaty.

3   Osorio, *Dismembering Lāhui,* 9.

4   For instance, ʻaikapu forbade women from eating pig, coconut, banana, and some red fish. Since the forbidden foods were affiliated with men and were offered as sacrifices to the gods, Hawaiians believed that "for women to eat these

foods would not only allow their mana [spiritual life-force] to defile the sacrifice to the male Akua [gods], but would also encourage them to devour male sexual prowess." 'Aikapu also required men to handle food preparation and restricted men from eating with women. See Kame'eleihiwa, *Native Land,* 34.

5   Disease also contributed to the abolition of the kapu system, which was later substituted with Western legal and religious systems brought in by missionaries and advisors. As some historians have argued, since Europeans were not dying at the same alarming rates as Hawaiians, many Hawaiians felt that Christianity would preserve Hawaiians' lives better than the Hawaiian gods and the kapu. Lilikalā Kame'eleihiwa argues that when Ka'ahumanu abandoned the 'aikapu and declared that "we intend to . . . live as the white people do," she meant "we intend to live." Kame'eleihiwa continues, "Since the 'Aikapu seemed to no longer preserve the people, perhaps the 'ainoa (free eating, or European ways) would." See Kame'eleihiwa, *Native Land,* 82.

6   Although Hawaiians eventually began converting to Christianity, they wanted more than just religious experiences from the church. Many Hawaiians were interested in learning the power called palapala, or reading and writing. Hawaiian fascination with reading led to the creation of one of the world's most literate nations in the mid-nineteenth century. But Hawaiians did not want to learn reading and writing just for this status. As Sally Engle Merry has noted, "Writing was clearly a source of spiritual power to the Hawaiian." See Merry, *Colonizing Hawai'i: The Cultural Power of Law* (Princeton, N.J.: Princeton University Press, 2000), 65–66. Many Hawaiians believed that palapala was the voice of God and granted Hawaiians access to a spiritual world. Writing also translated into political power for Hawaiians; it became useful for chiefs to communicate with each other as well as with the maka'āinana, or commoners. Palapala also became a tool of resistance. First, it empowered Hawaiians to challenge foreigners. As Hawaiians became literate, they also became more informed about Western history, and more specifically the parasitic nature of Western colonialism. This caused many to grow increasingly suspicious of missionary efforts. An educated group of Hawaiian scholars, trained in the mission schools, became more critical of Euro-Americans in Hawai'i and the influence of haole in Hawaiian government. First, several Hawaiian scholars like David Malo, John Papa I'i, Samuel Kamakau, and others recorded Hawaiian oral mo'olelo on paper. In the process, these scholars became aware, and very critical, of the increasing influence of haole advisors in Hawaiian political spheres. See Osorio, *Dismembering Lahui.*

7   Bingham, *A Residence of Twenty-One Years,* 14.

8   Missionaries saw surfing as sexual because Hawaiians surfed with little or no clothing. Such casual nudity between men and women was too much for missionaries to bear. Missionaries also saw the hula as hypersexual and sinful.

9   Bingham, *A Residence of Twenty-One Years,* 14.

10   Walter Murray Gibson helped King David Kalākaua advance his "Hawai'i for Hawaiians" campaign. He was despised by the haole business community for his support of the Hawaiian monarchy, among other things.

11 This is one of the key arguments of Jonathan Osorio in *Dismembering Lahui*.

12 Catholics and whalers were often at odds with these American Protestants. By 1837 the missionaries convinced King Kamehameha III to forbid Catholics from teaching Hawaiians the "Pope's religion," and missionary prohibition laws turned a whaler's favorite pastimes of drinking and prostitution into punishable crimes. While such missionary influences have been criticized as destructive to Hawaiians, Sally Engle Merry has argued that Hawaiians cleverly pitted haole groups against each other to their advantage. Thus while whalers and other Christian groups posed threats to Hawaiians, the missionary laws helped curtail the agendas of these other foreigners in Hawai'i. Furthermore, whalers and Catholics often blamed Calvinists, rather than Hawaiians, for such laws. See Merry, *Colonizing Hawai'i*. Whether Hawaiians used one set of haole laws to contain other haole or not, missionaries' involvement in government policy making definitely became more hands-on in the 1840s.

13 Judd became the king's leading advisor with the help of Kinau, a Christian convert whom Judd had formerly promoted as rightful heir to the throne. Michael Dougherty, *To Steal a Kingdom: Probing Hawaiian History* (Waimanalo, Hawai'i: Island Style, 1992), 101–102.

14 See Robert Stauffer, *Kahana: How the Land Was Lost* (Honolulu: University of Hawai'i Press, 2004).

15 Osorio, *Dismembering Lahui*, 44. See also Kame'eleihiwa, *Native Land*.

16 Stauffer, *Kahana*, 43–44.

17 Osorio, *Dismembering Lahui*, 46.

18 More recently, a team of anti-Hawaiian lawyers has challenged Kamehameha Schools' admissions policy, ironically in the name of civil rights.

19 Although others have translated the word ea to mean "life," Noenoe Silva explains that "sovereignty" is a better translation, especially in the context of these treaties. See Silva, *Aloha Betrayed*, 37.

20 See 'Umi Perkins, "Teaching Land and Sovereignty—A Revised View," *Hawaiian Journal of Law and Politics* 2 (Summer 2006): 97–111. Also, Osorio, *Dismembering Lahui*, 47–48.

21 Keanu Sai, "The American Occupation of the Hawaiian Kingdom: Beginning the Transition from Occupied to Restored State," PhD dissertation, University of Hawai'i at Mānoa, 2008, 84–85.

22 Ibid.

23 Stauffer, *Kahana*, 2–7.

24 Lenders often issued loans at "very high interest rates and very short terms that were often of just two or three years." Since the nonjudicial laws operated outside the courtroom, lenders purposefully took advantage of families who could not make payments and confiscated their land. Stauffer, *Kahana*, 92–98.

25 Ronald Takaki, *Pau Hana: Plantation Life and Labor in Hawai'i, 1835–1920* (Honolulu: University of Hawai'i Press, 1983).

26 The Honolulu business community urged King William Lunalilo to sign the Reciprocity Treaty in 1873. However, it was highly unfavorable to Hawaiian legislators at the time.

27 "Treaty of Reciprocity between the United States of America and The Hawaiian Kingdom," ratified 1875, Article IV.

28 *Hawaiian Gazette,* November 14, 1873.

29 Sally Engle Merry argues that although his critics chastised him for spending so much money on European luxuries, the king was actually resisting the West by mimicking it. In other words, since the European rationale for colonialism was that Native peoples were too uncivilized and barbaric to rule over themselves, Kalākaua surrounded himself with the most civilized trappings as a way of countering that discourse and preserving his sovereignty. See Merry, *Colonizing Hawai'i.*

30 Tom Coffman, *History Sunday: Conquest of Hawai'i,* History Channel video, 2003.

31 Osorio, *Dismembering Lahui,* 236.

32 *Hawai'i's Last Queen,* American Experience PBS Video Series, 1997.

33 Quoted in Osorio, *Dismembering Lahui,* 241.

34 Ibid., 240.

35 Silva, *Aloha Betrayed,* 127.

36 Ibid.

37 Ibid., 127–129.

38 Article 13.

39 Article 22.

40 For the Blount Report, see *Executive Documents of the House of Representatives,* 53rd Cong., 3rd session, 1894–1895.

41 Ibid., 929–930.

42 Kauanui, "Precarious Positions," 3–4.

43 Silva, *Aloha Betrayed,* 160, 161.

44 Ibid. See transcripts at http://www.pbs.org/wgbh/amex/hawaii/hawaiitrans .html.

45 See David Stannard, *Honor Killing: Race, Rape, and Clarence Darrow's Spectacular Last Case* (New York: Penguin, 2005).

46 For example, the government used Crown and Hawaiian public lands for their benefit. Water and other natural resources have also been taken and used for sugar business needs (e.g., water from Kahana and Waiāhole to the 'Ewa side of O'ahu).

47 For example, Native Hawaiians still have some of the highest mortality, incarceration, drug abuse, high-risk behavior, and obesity rates, and the lowest socioeconomic status in Hawai'i today. Kekuni Blaisdell, *The Health of Native Hawaiians,* vol. 32 (Honolulu: University of Hawai'i Press, 1989).

48 Sai, "The American Occupation of the Hawaiian Kingdom."

Chapter 3: Hui Nalu, Outrigger, and Waikīkī Beachboys

1 She was the daughter of Princess Miriam Likelike, sister of Lili'uokalani and Kalākaua. Her father, Archibald Cleghorn, was of Scottish ancestry and was the governor of O'ahu during Lili'uokalani's reign.

2   This property was given to Ka'iulani by her godmother, Princess Ruth Ke'elikōlani. Although Ka'iulani traveled back and forth between Europe and Hawai'i, she moved home permanently in 1897.

3   Princess Ka'iulani died in 1899 at the age of twenty-three. Some attribute her death to the trauma of annexation. She ultimately died from a severe cold after she was drenched by a rainstorm on the Big Island.

4   The olo-style surfboards were fifteen to twenty-four feet in length and often made from a light balsa-like wood called wiliwili. Only ali'i were allowed to use olo surfboards.

5   Quoted in Blake, *Hawaiian Surf Riders*, 60.

6   Ibid.

7   Native Hawaiian surfers Duke Kahanamoku and George Freeth became famous as they traveled outside Hawai'i and showed off their surfing skills to the world. Freeth was hired by Henry E. Huntington to hold a surfing exhibition in Redondo Beach to help promote the Redondo–Los Angeles Railway in 1907. Duke introduced surfing to a variety of American and Australian beaches en route to the Olympic Games of 1912 and 1916.

8   Stannard, *Honor Killing*.

9   Although most accounts say he arrived in 1907, Joe Stickney, a former friend of Ford who was living in Waikīkī at the time, said (in an oral history interview) that Ford moved to Hawai'i in 1905. Joe Stickney, interview by William C. Kea Sr., "Eight Old-time Members," oral history interview project of the Historical Committee of the Outrigger Canoe Club, July 8, 1968, OH-001, 9.

10   Ibid.

11   Judge Steiner, interview with William C. Kea Sr. "Eight Old-Time Members," oral history interview project of the Historical Committee of the Outrigger Canoe Club, July 8, 1968, OH-001, 7.

12   Alexander Hume Ford, "Out-Door Allurements," in *Hawaiian Almanac and Annual for 1911* (Honolulu: Thos. G. Thrum Compiler and Publisher, 1910), 143–149. Previously, haole believed they were incapable of learning the Hawaiian sport. This idea was popularized by Mark Twain in the 1860s when he wrote, "I tried surf-bathing once, subsequently, but made a failure of it. I got the board placed right, and at the right moment, too; but missed the connection myself.—The board struck the shore in three quarters of a second, without any cargo, and I struck the bottom about the same time, with a couple of barrels of water in me. None but the Natives ever master the art of surf-bathing thoroughly." Mark Twain, *Roughing It* (New York: Penguin Classics, 1981), 523.

13   London, *The Cruise of the* Snark, 54.

14   Ibid., 57.

15   Ford, "Out-Door Allurements," 146.

16   Ibid., 144.

17   Alexander Hume Ford, "Riding the Surf in Hawaii," *Collier's Outdoor America*, 43, no. 21 (August 14, 1909): 17.

18   Ford, "Out-Door Allurements," 146.

19   Ibid.

20 One observer wrote that in the early 1920s Lorrin P. Thurston was "one of Hawai'i's most enthusiastic surfriders." Blake, *Hawaiian Surf Riders,* 51. Lorrin P. Thurston was the son of leading annexationist Lorrin A. Thurston. Lorrin P. was not only an Outrigger surfer, but was also credited with introducing the balsa-wood surfboard in 1926. Blake, *Hawaiian Surf Riders,* 51. Although he did introduce balsa-wood boards in 1926, Hawaiians had used a similar wood, wiliwili, for their surfboards centuries prior.

21 Houston Wood, *Displacing Natives: The Rhetorical Production of Hawai'i* (Lanham, Md.: Rowman and Littlefield, 1999), 45–52.

22 Ibid., 41.

23 Ibid., 45.

24 Ibid.

25 In 1911 Ford said of canoe races, "Crews were organized, and at the regattas, in which both whites and Hawaiians contested, the Outrigger boys were almost invariably victorious" (Ford, "Out-Door Allurements," 144).

26 At first they called themselves the VLS, for Very Lazy Surfers and Volunteer Life Service.

27 Grady Timmons, *Waikīkī Beach Boy* (Honolulu: Editions Limited, 1989), 26.

28 Oral history interview with Alan "Turkey" Love by J. Ward Russell, oral history interview project of the Historical Committee of the Outrigger Canoe Club, July 18, 1986, OH-028, 24.

29 William A. "Knute" Cottrell, interview with William C. Kea Sr. "Eight Old-Time Members," oral history interview project of the Historical Committee of the Outrigger Canoe Club, July 8, 1968, OH-001, 6–7.

30 Although Leonard Lueras explained that their suits were black and gold, in some of the photos it looks like a third color was also used, perhaps red. Since the photographs are black and white, it is difficult to confirm.

31 Oral history interview with Joe Akana by 'Iwalani Hodges, March 15, 1985. In *Waikīkī, 1900–1985: Oral Histories Vol. 1,* Oral History Project, Social Science Research Institute, University of Hawai'i at Mānoa, 55.

32 The Kahanamoku family were na kahu, or advisors, to the Kamehameha monarchy. Duke's father, Duke Halapu Kahanamoku, was named by Princess Bernice Pauahi Bishop after Queen Victoria's son, Alfred, Duke of Edinburgh. Later, Duke Kahanamoku showed such promise as a surfer and swimmer that he dropped out of high school to pursue his career as a waterman.

33 Duke won a gold medal in the100-meter freestyle event in the 1912 Olympic Games held in Stockholm. He was also indisputably the greatest surfer in the world by this time.

34 Although most of his victories were in the 100-meter freestyle, he also won medals in the 800-meter relay and water polo.

35 Ford, "Out-Door Allurements," 144.

36 Ford, "Riding the Surf in Hawaii," 17.

37 Ford, "Out-Door Allurements," 145.

38 Blake, *Hawaiian Surf Riders,* 66.

39 Ford, "Out-Door Allurements," 145.

40   Tom Blake recorded that "about 1918, a riding contest was held, the winner being judged on form." Blake, *Hawaiian Surf Riders*, 65.

41   Ibid., 66.

42   Fred Hemmings, Ben Finney, and others have called the rivalry friendly. However, most older accounts, like Blake's *Hawaiian Surf Riders*, called it an "intense rivalry" (66).

43   Timmons, *Waikīkī Beach Boy*, 26.

44   Finney, *Surfing*, 71. Oral history interview with Joe Akana by 'Iwalani Hodges, 55.

45   John M. Lind, quoted in Sandra Hall, *Duke: A Great Hawaiian* (Honolulu: Bess Press, 2004), 89.

46   The nickname "Steamboat" had more than one meaning; it was also a direct translation of his Hawaiian last name, Mokuahi.

47   Timmons, *Waikīkī Beach Boy*, 27.

48   Oral history interview with Alan "Turkey" Love by 'Iwalani Hodges, May 14, 1986. In *Waikīkī, 1900–1985: Oral Histories Vol. IV*, Oral History Project, Social Science Research Institute, University of Hawai'i at Mānoa, spring 1988, 1653.

49   Hui Nalu surfers were known for playing Hawaiian music for Lili'uokalani in the early 1900s.

50   A California newspaper did a story on Prince Kūhiō and his brothers, who surfed near Santa Cruz, California, while away at school in the United States. "Beach Breezes, Some Scenes a Surf Reporter Saw on Sunday."

51   Lori Kamae, *The Empty Throne: A Biography of Hawaii's Prince Cupid* (Honolulu: Topgallant, 1980), 80–83.

52   Through the Organic Act, Congress loosened strict voting qualifications established by the Bayonet Constitution and maintained by the Republic of Hawaii. After 1900, Hawaiian men older than twenty-one who could speak, read, and write in English or Hawaiian could vote.

53   Lemon Wond "Rusty" Holt Sr., oral history interview with Michi Kodama-Nishimoto, April 1, 1985. In *Waikīkī, 1900–1985: Oral Histories Vol. II*, Oral History Project, Social Science Research Institute, University of Hawai'i at Mānoa, June 1985, 796.

54   Kamae, *The Empty Throne*, 99.

55   Ibid., 112.

56   Fred Paoa, oral history interview with Warren Nishimoto, March 15, 1985, Foster Village, O'ahu. In *Waikīkī, 1900–1985: Oral Histories Vol. II*, Oral History Project, Social Science Research Institute, University of Hawai'i at Mānoa, June 1985, 555–556.

57   Joseph Y. K. Akana, oral history interview with 'Iwalani Hodges and Michi Kodama-Nishimoto, March 8, 1985, Hawai'i Kai, O'ahu. In *Waikīkī, 1900–1985: Oral Histories Vol. I*, Oral History Project, Social Science Research Institute, University of Hawai'i at Mānoa, June 1985, 17.

58   Paoa, oral history interview with Warren Nishimoto, March 15, 1985, 558.

59 Ibid.

60 Akana, oral history interview with ʻIwalani Hodges and Michi Kodama-Nishimoto, March 8, 1985, 18.

61 Ibid.

62 Louis Kahanamoku, oral history interview with Warren Nishimoto, May 20, 1985, Keauhou, Kona, Hawaiʻi. In *Waikīkī, 1900–1985: Oral Histories Vol. II,* Oral History Project, Social Science Research Institute, University of Hawaiʻi at Mānoa, June 1985, 871.

63 Ibid.

64 Timmons, *Waikīkī Beach Boy,* 16.

65 Kahanamoku, oral history interview with Warren Nishimoto, May 20, 1985, 870.

66 Akana, oral history interview with ʻIwalani Hodges and Michi Kodama-Nishimoto, March 15, 1985, 41.

67 Timmons, *Waikīkī Beach Boy,* 17.

68 Kahanamoku, oral history interview with Warren Nishimoto, May 20, 1985, 863.

69 Akana, oral history interview with ʻIwalani Hodges and Michi Kodama-Nishimoto, March 15, 1985, 46.

70 Paoa, oral history interview with Warren Nishimoto, March 15, 1985, 557.

71 Akana, oral history interview with ʻIwalani Hodges and Michi Kodama-Nishimoto, March 15, 1985, 41.

72 Ibid., 50.

73 *Waikīkī, 1900–1985: Oral Histories Vol. I,* 1985, 52.

74 Akana, oral history interview with ʻIwalani Hodges and Michi Kodama-Nishimoto, March 15, 1985, 52.

75 Akana, oral history interview with ʻIwalani Hodges and Michi Kodama-Nishimoto, March 8, 1985, 20.

76 Timmons, *Waikīkī Beach Boy,* 17.

77 See Peggy Pascoe, "Race, Gender, and the Privileges of Property," in *Over the Edge: Remapping the American West,* edited by Valerie J. Matsumoto and Blake Allmendinger (Berkeley: University of California Press, 1999). Pascoe drew from Derrick Bell to argue that miscegenation laws in the American West allowed white men to confiscate Native American land and essentially turn their whiteness into property at the expense of the Native Americans.

78 After condemning and confiscating an eighty-acre parcel of land in Kālia, Waikīkī, the U.S. Army built a bunker on that property in 1911. Although they justified their actions by claiming they needed to protect the "Waikīkī harbor," it quickly became the army's rest and relaxation center in the Pacific. Called Fort DeRussy, this center was located next to, and on top of, a community of Hawaiian families, most notable among them the Kahanamoku family.

79 Paoa, oral history interview with Warren Nishimoto, March 15, 1985, 532.

80 Akana, oral history interview with ʻIwalani Hodges and Michi Kodama-Nishimoto, March 8, 1985, 11.

81 Although Akana said, "We didn't have much fights with the local boys, but we did used to have fights with the soldiers. Soldiers from Fort DeRussy and from Fort Ruger" (ibid.), Louis Kahanamoku remembered getting into fights against local gangs as well. When the Hui Nalu first started running Beachboy services, the hotels expected Dudie's boys to prevent conflicts between tourists and local Hawaiian youth groups, or gangs. The Stonewall, Kālia, Kakaʻako, and Kalihi gangs, among others, were composed mostly of teenagers who liked to surf, swim, and play music. In existence until the mid-1920s, each gang had about fifty members. Several Hui Nalu surfers at one point or another had belonged to gangs from Stonewall or Kālia. These gangs also competed against each other in land sports like baseball and football. Occasionally at such sporting events, these gangs would get into fistfights. One of Duke's younger brothers, Louis, explained, "We played a little baseball. . . . But us [Kālia] we wanted to play the tough guys. Kalihi and Kakaʻako, guarantee going to be a fight, so we want to get in it. [*Laughs*] Oh, I tell you. Yeah, 'cause those guys always fighting, you know." (Kahanamoku, oral history interview with Warren Nishimoto, May 20, 1985.) Each gang also had a kind of leader, or bull. According to one Hui Nalu surfer, Joe Akana, the bull was the person who "could lick everybody in the gang." But Joe's recollection of Johnny Kahoʻokele, the bull of his Stonewall gang, was that he was a smart Hawaiian kuleana lands expert who went to the University of Hawaiʻi but couldn't finish because he did not have money for tuition. But Johnny was also good at fighting, perhaps against other locals and most likely against haole.

82 Quoted in Timmons, *Waikīkī Beach Boy,* 30.

83 See Trask, *From a Native Daughter;* Elizabeth Buck, *Paradise Remade: The Politics of Culture and History in Hawaiʻi* (Philadelphia: Temple University Press, 1993); Wood, *Displacing Natives.* Others, like Teresia Teaiwa and Margaret Jolly, have also argued against the sexualization of women in places like the Bikini Islands and Tahiti. Both Teaiwa and Jolly cogently conclude that the female body became an effective tool for hiding colonial violence (see Teaiwa, "bikinis and other s/pacific n/oceans," *The Contemporary Pacific* 6, no. 1 (1994): 87–109; and Jolly, "From Point Venus to Bali Haʻi").

84 Trask, *From a Native Daughter,* 53.

85 Desmond, *Staging Tourism,* 47.

86 I am not suggesting that tourism's image of women as passive is realistic. In Hawaiian moʻolelo (histories) there are many examples of women as empowered agents, even in the ocean surf. The story of Kelea, a female surfer who out-surfed everyone in Waikīkī and eventually became Mōʻī Wahine (Queen) of Waikīkī (partially because of her skills on waves), is one of many examples.

87 Tengan, "Hale Mua: (En)gendering Hawaiian Men"; Isaiah Walker, "Terrorism or Native Protest? The Hui O Heʻe Nalu and Hawaiian Resistance to Colonialism," *Pacific Historical Review* 74, no. 4 (2005): 575–601.

88 Desmond, *Staging Tourism,* 124–125.

89 Ibid., 125.

90 Love, oral history interview with ʻIwalani Hodges, May 14, 1986, 1654.

91 Quoted in Timmons, *Waikīkī Beach Boy,* 33.

92 William Justin Mullahey, oral history interview with Kenneth J. Pratt, May 6, 1980, Honolulu, oral history project of the Outrigger Canoe Club Historical Committee, OH-008, 6–7.

93 See Pascoe, "Race, Gender, and the Privileges of Property."

94 In November 1945 Keo Nakama, a friend of a haole Outrigger member, was not allowed into the club because he "looked Japanese." The local community was infuriated, and the International Longshoremen and Warehouse Union protested the Outrigger Canoe Club. See *Honolulu-Star Bulletin,* November 29, 1945, C1. Although the Outrigger's influence in the surf diminished, their presence in the Waikīkī hotel industry increased.

95 See Trask, *From a Native Daughter,* 53; Tengan, "Hale Mua," 7–13; Walker, "Terrorism or Native Protest?"

Chapter 4: Unmanning Hawaiians

1 The contradiction of America tightening its grasp over Hawai'i while preaching decolonization becomes a separate but essential dimension to my argument. This seeming paradox requires an explanation. Hence, the rhetoric concludes that unlike other colonies, these people needed us, wanted us, and obviously couldn't exist without us.

2 In one story, Hawai'i, as a woman, requires a man, played by the U.S. military, to conquer, tame, and administer over her. See Kathy E. Ferguson and Phyllis Turnbull, *Oh, Say, Can You See? The Semiotics of the Military in Hawai'i* (Minneapolis: University of Minnesota Press, 1998). In another story, she is a prostitute controlled by a white male pimp, the tourist industry; see Trask, *From a Native Daughter.*

3 Jolly, "From Point Venus to Bali Ha'i," 100.

4 Ibid.

5 Green, "Colonialism's Daughters," 223.

6 Ibid., 226

7 Ibid.

8 Quoted in Bernard Smith, *Imagining the Pacific in the Wake of the Cook Voyages* (New Haven, Conn., and London: Yale University Press, 1992), 73.

9 Eleanor C. Nordyke, *Pacific Images: Views from Captain Cook's Third Voyage* (Honolulu: Hawaiian Historical Society, 1999), 121.

10 Ibid., 115–126.

11 Smith, *Imagining the Pacific,* 84.

12 Ibid.

13 Green, "Colonialism's Daughters."

14 Coffman, *History Sunday.*

15 In *A Residence of Twenty-One Years in Hawaii,* Bingham called Hawaiian culture "savage." It is possible, too, that the notion of Hawaiians as savage and dangerous was heightened after the death of Captain Cook in 1779.

16   However, as Osorio points out, the Hawaiian people continued to look to the ali'i as their protectors and providers. See Osorio, *Dismembering Lāhui,* chapter 2.

17   In 1865 Mark Twain described Hawai'i's monarchs as invalid rulers simply playing dress-up monarchy. See *Mark Twain's Letters from Hawaii.*

18   Brendan Hokowhitu contends that Maori (indigenous) men of New Zealand were educated to see themselves as physical and unintelligent beings, as a way of funneling them into manual labor jobs. See Hokowhitu, "Tackling Maori Masculinity," 259–284.

19   There was a rumor spread by annexationists in the 1880s that Hawai'i's last king, David Kalākaua, was in reality half black. They used this rumor to further connect his "incompetence" to an American racial prejudice against Hawaiians and Blacks. See Wood, *Displacing Natives.*

20   Desmond, *Staging Tourism,* 48.

21   Ibid.

22   Buck, *Paradise Remade,* 4.

23   Ibid., 138.

24   Ibid., 174. Buck does not use the word "decontemporized," as Desmond does. However, she does make the same point when describing images of topless women in the 1890s. One caption reads, "A studio sitting of exotic Hawaiian girls in hula attire, taken around 1890, long after dancers were prohibited from performing bare breasted." Buck, *Paradise Remade,* 89.

25   Ibid., 138.

26   Trask, *From a Native Daughter,* 136–137.

27   Ibid., 144.

28   Ibid.,143.

29   Ibid., 53.

30   Desmond, *Staging Tourism,* 46.

31   Ibid.

32   Ferguson and Turnbull, *Oh, Say, Can You See?*

33   For more history on the South Seas film genre, see Langman, *Return to Paradise,* 286; for a deeper analysis of the colonial discourse generated in these films, see Wood, *Displacing Natives,* 103–121.

34   Stuart Hall, *Representation: Cultural Representation and Signifying Practices* (London: the Open University Press, 1997), 234–235.

35   *Wake of the Red Witch,* film directed by Edward Ludwig, Republic Studios, 1948, videocassette.

36   Rudyard Kipling, "The White Man's Burden: The United States & the Philippine Islands, 1899." *Rudyard Kipling's Verse: Definitive Edition* (Garden City, N.Y.: Doubleday, 1929).

37   Homi Bhabha, "The Other Question: Difference, Discrimination and the Discourse of Colonialism," in *Out There: Marginalization and Contemporary Culture,* edited by Russell Ferguson, Martha Gever, Trinh Minh-ha, and Cornel West (Cambridge, Mass.: MIT Press, 1990), 71–88.

38   Frantz Fanon, "The Negro and Psychopathology," in *Black Skin, White Masks*, edited by Charles Markmann (New York: Grove Press, 1967), 141–209.

39   *His Majesty O'Keefe*, film directed by Byron Haskin, Warner Brothers Studios, 1954, videocassette.

40   This narrative goes back to early voyage accounts that speak of Natives trading a week's supply of food for a single nail.

41   *His Majesty O'Keefe*.

42   This could include land, money, political control, etc.

43   Coco Fusco, *English Is Broken Here: Notes on Cultural Fusion in the Americas* (New York: The New Press, 1995), 42.

44   Ibid., 44.

45   Ibid.

46   Margaret Jolly, "From Point Venus to Bali Ha'i."

47   The United States detonated nuclear bombs on Bikini between 1946 and 1958. They also tested bombs on Enewetak Atoll and built a military support base on Kwajalein Island.

48   Teaiwa, "bikinis and other s/pacific n/oceans," 87–109.

49   Green, "Colonialism's Daughters," 246.

50   Revathi Krishnaswamy *Effeminism: The Economy of Colonial Desire* (Ann Arbor: University of Michigan Press, 1998), 15.

51   Ibid.

52   Ibid.

53   Ibid.

54   Ashis Nandy, *The Intimate Enemy: Loss and Recovery of Self under Colonialism* (New York: Oxford University Press, 1983), 8.

55   Ty Tengan notes this also and describes how a recent Disney movie played off of these older tropes in the character David Kawena, who is "clumsy, awkward, and generally unimportant to the plot." Tengan, "Hale Mua," 8.

56   Ibid., 5

57   Ibid., 49

58   Ibid.

59   Hokowhitu argues that sport also served other specific functions for the dominant group. It became a space where Maori men could "gain public recognition without challenging the dominant discourse," and it "evidenced that New Zealand's colonial system had enlightened and assimilated its savages." Hokowhitu, "Tackling Maori Masculinity," 270.

60   Ibid., 262.

61   Ty Kawika Tengan, "(En)gendering Colonialism: Masculinities in Hawai'i and Aotearoa," *Cultural Values* 6, no. 3 (2002): 251.

62   Ibid., 251.

63   Hokowhitu, "Tackling Maori Masculinity," 277.

64   Drawing from recently discovered Hawaiian petitions to U.S. annexation, Noenoe Silva cogently argues that Hawaiians actively and strategically resisted colonialism. See Silva, *Aloha Betrayed*. Jonathan Osorio's book also

reveals Hawaiians as active and political, even in the late 1800s. See Osorio, *Dismembering Lāhui.*

65 Ralph Kuykendall, *Hawaiian Kingdom, Vol. 1, 1778*–1854 (Honolulu: University of Hawai'i Press, 1938), 29.

66 Ibid., 66.

67 Ibid., 67.

68 Richard Wisniewski, *The Rise and Fall of the Hawaiian Kingdom* (Honolulu: Pacific Printers, 1979), 72.

69 Ibid., 74.

70 Ibid., 72.

71 Ibid., 75.

72 Gavan Daws, *Shoal of Time: A History of the Hawaiian Islands* (Honolulu: University of Hawai'i Press, 1974), 220.

73 Quoted in David Cannadine, *Ornamentalism: How the British Saw Their Empire* (Oxford: Oxford University Press, 2001), 8.

74 Merry, *Colonizing Hawaii,* 113. Merry's book is one of the few American historical works that portrayed Native Hawaiians as agents in their own history. By recognizing acculturation as a creative form of resistance, she presented the Hawaiian kings as clever and creative, rather than submissive and incapable.

75 Ibid., 13.

76 Ibid., 8.

77 Ibid., 89.

Chapter 5: The Hawaiian Renaissance and Hawaiian Surfers

1 George S. Kanahele, *Hawaiian Renaissance* (Honolulu: Project Waiaha, 1982), 10.

2 Ibid., 6.

3 Ibid., 10.

4 Ibid., 6.

5 Ibid., 11.

6 Quoted in Kevin O'Leary, "The Future of Kamilo Nui," *Honolulu Weekly,* November 13, 2005. http://honoluluweekly.com/cover/2005/11/the-future-of-kamilo-nui/.

7 John Kelly, "John Kelly," in *Autobiography of Protest in Hawai'i,* edited by Robert Mast and Ann Mast (Honolulu: University of Hawai'i Press, 1997), 75–76.

8 As a teenager, Kelly and his close surfer friends surfed on old Hawaiian, square-bottomed boards around Diamond Head. Kelly recalled that his first surfboard was his mother's ironing board. One afternoon, he and two friends returned to Kelly's house from the waves at Black Point.

Johnny got a little red axe from the house (which we still have), and chopped off the edges of his square-bottomed board making it pointed instead. He said he was tired of having to surf in one straight line, and decided to "try something." Indeed it worked, and his other two friends followed suit. At his memorial, some older surfers believed that John and his 2 friends began another early change around surfing, that of the transition to a whole different style of surfing. Although I have a hard time thinking 3 people triggered a change that soon extended all the way to California, it may be true. (E-mail to author from Colleen Kelly, November 4, 2009.)

9   Kelly, "John Kelly," 79.

10   Cathleen Toth, "Hawaii Surf Activist Kelly Dies," *Honolulu Advertiser,* October 5, 2007; also Kelly, "John Kelly," 76.

11   John Kelly, "Save Our Surf," *Turning the Tide: Journal of Anti-Racist Activism, Research and Education* 7, nos. 3 and 4 (Summer 1994). http://www.hawaii -nation.org/turningthetide-7-1.html.

12   Kelly, "John Kelly," 90.

13   Stuart Udall and John Sandsbury, "Hawaii SOS Stirs Ecology Wave," *Our Environment,* September 15, 1971. http://www.ilhawaii.net/~msquared/Udall.html.

14   Kelly, "John Kelly," 90.

15   Kelly, "Save Our Surf," 2.

16   "Save Shark Hole," *SOS News* 1, no.1 (March 1970): 5-6. Available on line at http://digicoll.manoa.hawaii.edu/sos/.

17   "At Kūhiō the People Said No!" *SOS News* 1, no. 1 (March 1970): 4.

18   Save Our Surf, "Unite to Save Hawaii! Capitol Rally!" Poster, 1971. Available on line at http://digicoll.manoa.hawaii.edu/sos/ under "A brief on John Kelly and Save Our Surf."

19   "Listen to the People," flyer. http://digicoll.manoa.hawaii.edu/sos/.

20   Ibid.

21   "Evict Dwellers and Burn Down all 14 Homes of the Traditional Native Hawaiian Mokauea Fishing Village," statement on flyer. http://digicoll.manoa .hawaii.edu/sos/index.php. See also http://www.kaimakana.org/mirp.htm.

22   Ibrahim G. Aoude, "The Ethnic Studies Story: Politics and Social Movements in Hawaiʻi," *Social Processes* 39 (1999): xv–xxv.

23   John Kelly, "Ethnic Studies!" Pamphlet. http://digicoll.manoa.hawaii.edu/sos/ index.php.

24   Coleman, *Eddie Would Go,* 47.

25   Bart Asato, "Getting a bad rap, black shorts insist," *Honolulu Advertiser,* August 12, 1987, A4.

26   Bartholomew and Baker, *Bustin' Down the Door,* 154–155.

27   Ben R. Finney, *Hokuleʻa: The Way to Tahiti* (New York: Dodd, Mead and Company, 1979), 20.

28   Ibid., 7–17.

29   Ibid., 29.

30   Ibid., 33.

31   Ibid., 158.

32   Ibid., 159.

33   Ibid.

34   Interestingly, he leaves out "Polynesian" from the title of the Voyaging Society.

35   Ironically, Finney himself theorized on the dilemma of Hawaiian men while on this very voyage (see Finney, *Hokuleʻa*). He explained that new values of

manhood, based on Western achievements and status, often marginalized Hawaiians and contributed to their struggle for recognition. Yet he deployed these new masculine markers to validate himself over them in this instance.

36 Finney, *Hokuleʻa,* 160.

37 Coleman, *Eddie Would Go,* 10.

38 Native American movements of the 1970s had a direct influence on Hawaiian activism for at least one particular Hawaiian group, the Protect Kahoʻolawe ʻOhana. The ʻOhana originally modeled their occupation of the island of Kahoʻolawe in 1976 on the Native American occupation of Alcatraz in 1969 and 1970. See "'Occupation' of Kahoʻolawe in the works?" *Honolulu Advertiser,* January 4, 1976, A1. See Jay Hartwell, "Hoʻomana," in *Pacific Diaspora: Island Peoples in the United States and Across the Pacific,* edited by Paul Spickard, Joanne Rondilla, and Debbie Hippolite Wright (Honolulu, 2002), 322–330.

39 Jan TenBruggencate, "Kahoolawe 'occupation' short-lived," *Honolulu Advertiser,* January 5, 1976, A1.

40 *Kahoʻolawe Aloha ʻĀina,* video recording directed by Nā Maka o ka ʻĀina, 1992.

41 Ibid.

42 Sammy Amalu, "Kahoʻolawe is Symbolic," editorial, *Honolulu Advertiser,* January 6, 1976, C6.

43 Kanahele, *Hawaiian Renaissance,* 3.

44 Tengan, "Hale Mua," 7–13.

45 It is important to note that surfing has not historically been seen as a man's sport. There are many stories of gifted and gracious Hawaiian women who were both talented surfers and feminine women.

Chapter 6: The Hui O Heʻe Nalu

1 In 1972 only three contests were held on the North Shore annually; by 1977 there were twenty-four. See "North Shore Contest Debate Continues," *Surfer Magazine* 19, no. 3 (1978): 90.

2 Although an International Professional Surfers' Association was proposed in 1968 by Fred Van Dyke and Larry Lindbergh, the IPSA was never fully realized—perhaps because of protests by Hawaiian surfers in 1970. That year, the IPSA organized a surfing competition on the North Shore. Because Native Hawaiian surfers felt that invitations excluded many of them from the contest in favor of California surfers, several protested the event. At the precompetition party, a fight broke out between Hawaiian surfers and haole. See Drew Kampion, "North Shore '70–'71," *Surfer* 12, no. 1 (March 1971): 40–44.

3 Shortly after it was formed, Hemmings and Rarick changed International Professional Surfers to International Professional Surfing after Australian surfers criticized the IPS for its local Hawaiʻi focus and for under-representing Australian surfers in their events.

4 Fred Hemmings, "Professionalism Is White," *Surfer* 10, no. 5 (November 1969): 64–65. Hemmings' motive to "legitimate the sport of surfing" was a concern for many surfers in the late 1960s and early 1970s, mainly because there was

a common belief that surfers were lazy delinquents during this time. In some locations, such opinions were often translated into laws that restricted surfers from certain beaches and even imposed surfing taxes. For more on surf tax, see "The Surf Tax" (editorial), *Surfer* 7, no. 4 (1966): 22. And, as Douglas Booth points out, some felt that professional surfing was the solution to this problem as it would legitimate surfing as a respectable sport. See Douglas Booth, "Ambiguities in Pleasure and Discipline: The Development of Competitive Surfing," *Journal of Sport History* 22, no. 3 (Fall 1995): 189–190.

5   Seth "Moot" Ah Quin, videotaped interview with author, Lāʻie, Hawaiʻi, July 13, 2002.

6   "The Magic of a Hawaiian Summer," *Surfer* 19, no. 6 (October 1978): 30.

7   "Radical" was a term that described an aggressive approach to riding waves—making vigorous and more frequent turns on waves with shorter surfboards—but was synonymous with a new and younger breed of surf style, from one that was more laid back to more extreme and aggressive. The introduction of competitions and radical surfing changed the culture of surfing and led to a great schism between the radical "shredders" and those who saw surfing as a natural art form, known as the soul surfers. Although there is still evidence of these factions today, the debate between the two camps was much more heated in the late 1970s.

8   John Witzig, "Paths of Glory: Hawaiʻi Winter 76–77," *Surfer* 18, no. 1 (1977): 56. "Cutting people off" means to aggressively steal waves from other surfers, usually while that person is either catching the wave or already riding it. This is not only a power trip, but can also cause bodily harm to those being cut off in the dangerous North Shore surf. It is the equivalent of blatantly and violently fouling another player on the basketball court—but imagine that the court is a sharp coral reef.

9   See Witzig, "Paths of Glory," 36–62.

10   Bartholomew and Baker, *Bustin Down the Door*, 154.

11   Fred Hemmings, *The Soul of Surfing* (New York: Thunder's Mouth Press, 1999), 113–114.

12   Bryan Amona, videotaped interview with author, Kailua, Hawaiʻi, August 29, 2004.

13   See Hemmings, *The Soul of Surfing,* and Amona interview, August 29, 2004.

14   Terry Ahue, videotaped interview with author, Sunset Beach, Hawaiʻi, August 13, 2004.

15   Amona interview, August 29, 2004. This lack of respect can also be seen in Australia's history of surfing. In the early 1900s the Surf Life Saving Association of Australia (SLSAA) felt that Hawaiian surfing was disorderly compared to Australia's disciplined lifeguards. Many Australians saw the lack of dress codes in Waikīkī as too "loose" for their tastes. Charles Patterson, president of the SLSAA, called Hawaiian surfers "lazy" and criticized their lack of lifesaving equipment. Ironically, the SLSAA later integrated the Hawaiian surfboard into their lifeguarding program. See Booth, "Ambiguities in Pleasure and Discipline," 190.

16   Ahue interview, August 13, 2004.

17 Amona interview, August 29, 2004.
18 Ibid.
19 A more detailed story of the interaction between Bronzed Aussies and Hawaiian North Shore surfers in this period is available in Phil Jarratt, "Jaw War on the North Shore," *Surfer* 17, no. 6 (1977): 46–48; Witzig, "Paths of Glory," 36–62; Bartholomew and Baker, *Bustin' Down the Door;* Coleman, *Eddie Would Go,* 185–196.
20 Amona interview, August 29, 2004.
21 Bartholomew and Baker, *Bustin' Down the Door,* 151.
22 Ibid., 149–150.
23 Ibid., 153.
24 Blankenfeld interview, July 26, 2004.
25 Jarratt, "Jaw War on the North Shore."
26 Bartholomew and Baker, *Bustin' Down the Door,* 154.
27 Witzig, "Paths of Glory," 42.
28 Kimo (last name not given), videotaped interview with author, July 26, 2004.
29 Ibid., 46.
30 Ibid., 56.
31 Blankenfeld interview, July 26, 2004.
32 Ibid.
33 Tom Pohaku Stone, videotaped interview with author, Waimea Valley, Hawai'i, July 5, 2004.
34 Bartholomew, "No Free Rides," 45.
35 Blankenfeld interview, July 26, 2004.
36 Amona interview, August 29, 2004.
37 Ahue interview, August 13, 2004.
38 Stone interview, July 5, 2004.
39 Blankenfeld interview, July 26, 2004.
40 Daryl Stant, videotaped interview with author, Honolulu, September 2, 2002.
41 Andrus interview, June 25, 2004.
42 Amona interview, August 29, 2004.
43 Although the club was not officially formed until 1977, many had loosely banded together in 1976, when the IPS first started.
44 Stone interview, July 5, 2004.
45 Ibid.
46 Eddie Rothman, videotaped interview with author, Honolulu, September 2, 2002.
47 Witzig, "Paths of Glory," 44.
48 Andrus interview, June 25, 2004.
49 Blankenfeld interview, July 26, 2004.
50 Ibid.
51 Ahue interview, August 13, 2004.
52 Hemmings, *The Soul of Surfing.*
53 Ken Kobayashi, "Threats forced him to hire 'terrorists,' Hemmings says," *Honolulu Advertiser,* July 31, 1987, A3.

54 Blankenfeld interview, July 26, 2004.

55 Ibid.

56 Ibid.

57 Imbert Soren, conversation with author, Lāʻie, Hawaiʻi, May 1997.

58 Amona interview, August 29, 2004.

59 Ibid.

60 Kevin (last name not given), videotaped interview with author, Honolulu, September 2, 2003.

61 Bartholomew and Baker, *Bustin' Down the Door*, 151.

62 Kaio interview, July 5, 2002. Months after our conversation the Kaio family home went into foreclosure and was subsequently purchased by an investor from the continental United States.

63 Andrus interview, June 25, 2004.

64 Ibid.

65 Blankenfeld interview, July 26, 2004.

66 Ibid.

67 Stone interview, July 5, 2004.

68 Ibid.

69 Witzig, "Paths of Glory," 56.

70 Ah Quin interview, July 13, 2002.

71 Stone interview, July 5, 2004.

72 Amona interview, August 29, 2004.

73 Stone interview, July 5, 2004.

74 Ah Quin interview, July 13, 2002.

75 Stone interview, July 5, 2004.

76 Soren conversation with author, May 1997. As seen through this interview, some Hui surfers were known to get aggressive on the North Shore. Fistfights were the result of frustration, and protests sometimes took on physical form. However, such fights certainly did not constitute terrorism. Many, like Tom Stone, contend, "We weren't looking for trouble; trouble came to us." Others explained that the club was not responsible for each and every member.

77 Ah Quin interview, July 13, 2002.

78 Blankenfeld interview, July 26, 2004.

79 Ibid.

80 Ah Quin interview, July 13, 2002.

81 Hemmings, *The Soul of Surfing*, 115.

82 Blankenfeld interview, July 26, 2004.

83 Ibid.

84 Ibid.

85 Ibid.

86 Amona interview, August 29, 2004.

87 Rothman interview, September 2, 2002.

88 Ahue interview, August 13, 2004.

89 Primo (last name withheld), videotaped interview with author, Honolulu, September 5, 2003.

90   The North Shore communities of Lāʻie, Hauʻula, and Kahuku are made up primarily of Native Polynesian Mormons. Several Hui leaders were raised in the LDS church. Also, a local bimonthly North Shore newspaper described how Hui meetings opened with prayer and soda drinking. See Ron Valenciana, "'Black Shorts' Extortion on the High Seas?" *North Shore News,* July 26, 1987, 3.

91   Ahue interview, August 13, 2004.

92   Henry Soren, videotaped interview with author, Lāʻie, Hawaiʻi, July 25, 2003.

93   Ah Quin interview, July 13, 2002.

94   Brian (last name not given), videotaped interview with author, Honolulu, September 5, 2003.

95   Stant interview, September 2, 2002.

Chapter 7: Hui in American Media

1   Erik Olsen and Matt Higgins, "Surfing's Darker Side on the North Shore," video, *New York Times,* Sports section, January 23, 2009. Available online at http://video.nytimes.com/video/2009/01/22/sports/othersports/1231545957469/surfing-s-dark-side-on-the-north-shore.html

2   On July 2, 1987, Honolulu Police Department officers from the Vice/Narcotics Division arrested Edward Rothman and Tony Sanchez on a secret grand jury indictment. Rothman was also charged with first-degree and third-degree promotion of dangerous drugs. Sanchez's bail was set at $2 million and Rothman's at $5 million. Both were held in custody at the Oʻahu Community Correctional Center until August 17. They were released shortly after bail was reduced to $20,000 and $75,000, respectively.

3   Ken Kobayashi, "Threats forced him to hire 'terrorists,'" *Honolulu Advertiser,* July 31, 1987, A3.

4   Lee Catterall, "Court told of plot to rape drug agent," *Honolulu Star-Bulletin,* August 6, 1987, A5.

5   Ken Kobayashi, "Surf champ 'felt threatened,'" *Honolulu Advertiser,* July 23, 1987, A4.

6   Ken Kobayashi, "Witness says surfers 'hassled,'" *Honolulu Advertiser,* July 23, 1987, A1.

7   Kobayashi, "Threats forced him to hire 'terrorists.'"

8   Ibid. Although "boys" is common slang in Hawaiʻi, it is possible that Hemmings was using the word in a pejorative sense, like calling African American men "boys." His other comments toward Hawaiian Hui members during the trial can also be interpreted as paternalistic.

9   Ibid.

10   Fred Hemmings, "Hemmings on surfer threats," *Honolulu Star-Bulletin,* August 12, 1987, A15.

11   Hemmings' sentiments and actions were often contradictory. For example, he criticized North Shore localism in a chapter of *The Soul of Surfing* and rhetorically

asked, "So surfers who call Hawai'i home have a franchise on Hawai'i waves? Is that franchise further extended to select ethnic groups?" However, in an earlier chapter he offered a public apology to California professional surfer Corky Carrol for doing exactly what he criticized the Hui of doing in the 1970s. "I read something in a surfing magazine attributed to Corky Carroll that I interpreted to be a 'dig' about Hawaiian surfers. I must have been having a bad hair day or in down biorhythm cycle, because, when I ran into Corky at Paumalu, I verbally accosted and threatened him. It is close to 35 years late—Corky, I am sorry I hassled you." Hemmings, *The Soul of Surfing*, 79.

12   Bart Asato, "Getting a bad rap, black shorts insist," *Honolulu Advertiser,* August 12, 1987, A4.

13   Ken Kobayashi, "Terrorists warn U.S. over escorts," *Honolulu Advertiser,* July 28, 1987, A1.

14   Ken Kobayashi, "Rothman was feared, witness says," *Honolulu Advertiser,* July 28, 1987, A4; Kobayashi, "Reign of Terror on North Shore told," *Honolulu Advertiser,* July 21, 1987, A1.

15   Bart Asato, "Black Shorts: A bad rap," *Honolulu Advertiser,* August 10, 1987, A1.

16   He mentioned specifically people like Chuck Andrus and others active in the LDS faith.

17   Although *North Shore* made only $3.8 million in theaters, it was a popular film among surfers. Interest was recently revived after its release on DVD. See *North Shore,* film directed by William Phelps, Universal Studios, 1987, videocassette.

18   Ibid.

19   The Hui character unsuccessfully coaxes his friends to jump Kane as a group; he then throws dirt in Kane's eyes before punching him and attacking him with a big stick.

20   *Blue Crush,* film directed by John Stockwell, Universal Pictures, 2002, DVD.

21   Internet source, http://www.thewb.com/Faces/CastBio/0,7939,103643,00.html

22   Matt Walker, "Clearing the Airwaves: Liam McNamara Defends his Performance on the Boarding House," *Surfing* online interview, http://surfingthemag.com/news/surfing-pulse/070803_liam/.

23   Internet source, http://www.thewb.com/Faces/CastBio/0,7939,103643,00.html.

24   "Warrior Spirit," *The 808,* episode 2, Fuel TV, 2007. Available on line at http://video.aol.com/video-detail/the-808-the-808-warrior-spirit/2462621765.

25   Ibid.

26   Ibid.

27   Matt Higgins, "Rough Waves, Tougher Beaches," *New York Times,* Sports section, January 23, 2009. Available online at http://www.nytimes.com/2009/01/23/sports/othersports/23surfing.html.

28   E-mail from author to Matt Higgins and Erik Olsen, January 26, 2009.

29   E-mail from Matt Higgins to author, January 27, 2009.

30   Ibid.

31   Ibid.

32 Newspaper articles from the *Honolulu Advertiser* and *Star-Bulletin* covering the Kahoʻolawe 9 routinely portrayed them as law-breaking radicals. Jay Hartwell has pointed out that many in Hawaiʻi, especially the older generation, "dismissed the ʻOhana as crazy activists"; Hartwell, "Hoʻomana," 325.

33 Stone interview, July 5, 2004.

34 Erwin Au, videotaped interview with author, Kahuku, Hawaiʻi, July 11, 2002.

35 See Michel Foucault, *The Archaeology of Knowledge* (New York: Routledge, 1969), and Foucault, *Discipline and Punish: The Birth of the Prison* (New York: Vintage, 1995).

36 Edward Said, *Orientalism* (New York: Vintage, 1978), 3.

37 *Edward Said: On Orientalism,* video recording directed by Sut Jhally (Massachusetts: MEF, 1998).

38 Ibid.

39 Internet source, http://www.thewb.com/Faces/CastBio/0,7939,103643,00.html.

40 See Shoat and Stam, *Unthinking Eurocentrism,* 18.

41 Robert Eskildsen, "Of Civilization and Savages: The Mimetic Imperialism of Japan's 1874 Expedition to Taiwan," *The American Historical Review* 107, no. 2 (2002): 388–418.

42 Ibid., 403.

43 Ania Loomba, *Colonialism/Postcolonialism: The New Critical Idiom* (New York: Routledge, 1998), 97.

44 Ibid., 99.

45 Hokowhitu, "Tackling Maori Masculinity," 270.

46 Ibid.

47 Ibid., 262.

48 Fredrik Barth, "Boundaries and Connections," *Signifying Identities: Anthropological Perspectives on Boundaries and Contested Values,* edited by Anthony P. Cohen (London: Routledge, 2000), 10, 23.

49 See James Clifford, "Introduction," in *Writing Culture: The Poetics and Politics of Ethnography,* edited by James Clifford and George Marcus (Berkeley: University of California Press, 1986), 1–26, for discussions of laying bare the self in ethnography.

50 Barth, "Boundaries and Connections," 33.

51 Ibid., 34.

52 Amona, interview, August 29, 2004.

53 Tengan, "(En)gendering Colonialism," 251.

54 Chris Mauro, "In the Hot Seat with Kalā Alexander," October 4, 2002, http://www.surfermag.com/magazine/archivedissues/kala/index.html

55 Gananath Obeyesekere, "'British Cannibals,' Contemplation of an Event in the Death and Resurrection of James Cook, Explorer," *Critical Inquiry* 18 (1992): 634.

56 Of course, this is a play on the Beach Boys song, "Surfin' USA," which is representative of this California surf culture. The Beach Boys, "Surfin' USA," Capitol Records, 1963.

Glossary

ali'i — chief, chiefess, ruler, monarch, noble.

backside surfing — surfing with your back facing the wave. Surfers who are regular, or natural, footed (left foot forward on the board) surf backside when going left on a wave.

barrel — the hollow part of the wave that forms under the breaking crest. Riding in the barrel of the wave is one of the most desirable, timeless maneuvers a surfer performs. The North Shore, Pipeline in particular, is known as having the world's most barreling waves.

bottom turn — a turn one makes at the bottom of a wave to return back to the face of it.

break — crest, po'i; the curling of a wave.

deep — to be close to, or behind, the curl or barreling part of the wave. Or, waiting for waves behind the area where the wave is known to break.

floater — riding on the crest or barreling part of a wave; floating on the very curl of the wave.

front-side surfing — surfing with your body facing the wave. Surfers who are regular, or natural, footed (left foot forward on the board) surf front side when going right on a wave.

haole — a Hawaiian term that refers to people who are foreign to Hawai'i; most commonly white Americans or Europeans (local people of Portuguese ancestry excluded). Although it can be used as an insult (when preceded by an expletive, or if the tone of the speaker connotes negativity), "haole" is not, in and of itself, a racially derogatory slur. Most often, people in Hawai'i, Hawaiians included, use the term to identify Caucasian ancestry in themselves or in others. Some Hawai'i-raised haole that have lived among Hawaiians and have earned respect from them are often called local or local-haole. These individuals have a different social status and identity than other haole and are distinguished by their ability to bond with Hawaiians, reciprocate aloha, and speak pidgin. Thus "haole" is a social construct defined by attitude, not merely by a person's race. In contrast to Hawaiian values of behavior, haole attitudes are defined as self- and individual oriented, as opposed to community centered. Such interpretations of haole are reflected in the perspectives of surfers interviewed for this book.

Hawaiian — here refers to indigenous natives of Hawai'i, also called Kānaka Maoli or 'Ōiwi (lit., "of the bone"), as opposed to someone who simply lives in Hawai'i. Although most Native Hawaiians have a mixture of other ethnicities today, they are still considered Hawaiian.

he'e nalu — surfing, surfer; lit., wave sliding.

Hōkūleʻa—Star of Gladness; also the name of a double-hulled Hawaiian voyaging canoe built in 1975.

Hoku o Ka Pakipika—Star of the Pacific; title of Hawaiian-language newspaper of the 1860s.

hoʻokupu—tribute, gift, offering.

hui—club, association, union, group; to congregate.

Hui Aloha ʻĀina—Hawaiian political organization opposed to annexation in the 1890s. Organized and delivered petitions against annexation.

Hui Kalaiʻāina—Hawaiian political organization opposed to annexation. Along with Hui Aloha ʻĀina, helped petition against Hawaiʻi annexation to the United States.

Hui Nalu—surf club. Formed in Waikīkī in 1906 primarily by Hawaiian surfers.

Hui O He ʻe Nalu—club of surfers, club of wave sliders. Surf club formed in the mid-1970s on the North Shore of Oʻahu.

Kanaka Maoli—Native Hawaiian.

keiki—child, youngster.

kūʻē—to oppose, resist, protest; also part of the title for the petitions against annexation.

kuleana land—land parcels claimed by Hawaiian families at the time of the Mahele (1848–1854). Some Hawaiian families still live on their kuleana land today.

lineup—the place where surfers sit and wait to catch waves where they first break or crest.

longboard—surfing on a longer, round-nosed board. Often involves a different repertoire of maneuvers, such as riding on the rounded nose of the board with one or both feet.

Mahele—division, zone, land division, 1848–1854. Process where land ownership in Hawaiʻi shifted to Western notion of ownership.

makaʻāinana—commoner, citizen, people in general.

moana—ocean, open sea.

moku—district or island.

moʻolelo—story, tale, myth, history, tradition, legend, record.

nalu—wave, surf.

nā nūpepa—newspapers, Hawaiian newspapers.

ʻŌiwi — Native, people of the bone.

oli — chant.

papa heʻe nalu — surfboard.

Pau Malū — Sunset Beach.

poʻina nalu — surf zone.

puʻuhonua — place of refuge, sanctuary.

ripper — a surfer who does quicker, more radical surfing, as opposed to going straight or doing long, slow turns.

shortboard — shorter, pointed-nosed surfboard. They are generally about five to seven feet long.

shred — slang for doing quick, dramatic turning maneuvers whereby the surfer throws a lot of spray in the process.

sit — to wait for waves on your surfboard, usually in the lineup.

SUP — stand-up paddle surfing. A form of surfing where the rider stands on a thicker, wider, and longer board while paddling with a long, oar-like paddle.

360 (three-sixty) — a maneuver in which a surfer turns his or her surfboard in a complete 360-degree spin while riding the wave.

waʻa kaulua — double-hulled canoe.

wahine — woman.

Bibliography

Act of War: The Overthrow of the Hawaiian Nation. Film directed by Puhipau, Joan Lander. Honolulu: Na Maka O Ka ʻAina, in association with Center for Hawaiian Studies, University of Hawaiʻi at Mānoa, 1993. Videocassette.

Ah Quin, Seth "Moot." Videotaped interview with author, Lāʻie, Hawaiʻi, July 13, 2002. [This and subsequent interviews will be archived at the Brigham Young University–Hawaii Archives.]

Ahue, Terry. Videotaped interview with author, Sunset Beach, Hawaiʻi, August 13, 2004.

Aipa, Ben. Videotaped interview with Jared Medeiros. Honolulu, September 17, 2009.

Akana, Joe. Oral history interview with ʻIwalani Hodges and Michi Kodama-Nishimoto, March 8 and March 15, 1985. In *Waikīkī, 1900–1985: Oral Histories Vol. 1,* Oral History Project, Social Science Research Institute, University of Hawaiʻi at Mānoa, 1985.

Amona, Bryan. "Ala Moana Bowls: Dropping in at the South Shore's Most Famous Left Tube." *Spot Check,* August 31, 2008. www.surfline.com.

———. Videotaped interview with author, Kaneʻohe, Hawaiʻi, July 26, 2004, and Kailua, Hawaiʻi, August 29, 2004.

Andrus, Chuck Waipā. Videotaped interview with author, Hauʻula, Hawaiʻi, June 25, 2004.

Aoude, Ibrahim G. "The Ethnic Studies Story: Politics and Social Movements in Hawaiʻi." *Social Processes* 39 (1999): xv–xxv.

Au, Erwin. Videotaped interview with author, Kahuku, Hawaiʻi, July 11, 2002.

Barth, Fredrik. "Boundaries and Connections." In *Signifying Identities: Anthropological Perspectives on Boundaries and Contested Values,* edited by Anthony P. Cohen. London: Routledge, 2000, 17–36.

Bartholomew, Wayne "Rabbit." "No Free Rides." *Surfer* 19, no. 1 (1978): 45.

Bartholomew, Wayne "Rabbit," and Tim Baker. *Bustin' Down the Door.* New York: Harper, 1996.

Beaglehole, J. C., ed. *Voyage of the* Resolution *and* Discovery, *1776–1780.* Cambridge: Cambridge University Press, 1967.

Berkhofer, Robert. *The White Man's Native: Images of the American Indian from Columbus to the Present.* New York: Vintage, 1979.

Bhabha, Homi. "The Other Question: Difference, Discrimination and the Discourse of Colonialism." In *Out There: Marginalization and Contemporary Culture,* edited by Russell Ferguson, Martha Gever, Trinh Minh-ha, and Cornel West. Cambridge, Mass.: MIT Press, 1990.

Bingham, Hiram. *A Residence of Twenty-One Years in the Sandwich Islands.* Rutland, Vt.: Charles E. Tuttle Co., 1981. [Original publication: Hartford, Conn: Huntington Press, 1849.]

Blaisdell, Kekuni. *The Health of Native Hawaiians.* Vol. 32. Honolulu: University of Hawaiʻi Press, 1989.

Blake, Tom. *Hawaiian Surf Riders, 1935.* Redondo Beach, Calif.: Mountain and Sea Publishing, 1983. [Original publication: *Hawaiian Surfboard,* Honolulu: Paradise of the Pacific Press, 1935.]

Blankenfeld, Billy Hoʻolaʻe. Videotaped interview with author, Kāneʻohe, Hawaiʻi, July 26, 2004.

Blount Report. *Executive Documents of the House of Representatives,* 53rd Cong., 3rd session, 1894–1895.

Blue Crush. Film directed by John Stockwell. Universal Pictures, 2002. DVD.

Booth, Douglas. "Ambiguities in Pleasure and Discipline: The Development of Competitive Surfing." *Journal of Sport History* 22, no. 3 (Fall 1995): 189–190.

Brian [last name not given]. Videotaped interview with author, Honolulu, September 5, 2003.

Brooks, James. *Captives and Cousins: Slavery, Kinship, and Community in the Southwest Borderlands.* Chapel Hill: University of North Carolina Press, 2002.

Brown, Desoto. *Surfing: Historic Images from Bishop Museum Archives.* Honolulu: Bishop Museum Press, 2006.

Buck, Elizabeth. *Paradise Remade: The Politics of Culture and History in Hawaiʻi.* Philadelphia: Temple University Press, 1993.

Burkhofer, Robert. *The White Man's Native: Images of the American Indian from Columbus to the Present.* New York: Vintage, 1979.

Bushnell, Andrew. "'The Horror' Reconsidered: An Evaluation of the Historical Evidence for Population Decline in Hawaiʻi, 1778–1803," *Pacific Studies* 16, no. 3 (1993): 115–162.

Bustin' Down the Door. Film directed by Jeremy Gosch. Screen Media, 2008.

Cannadine, David. *Ornamentalism: How the British Saw Their Empire.* Oxford: Oxford University Press, 2001.

Cheever, Henry T. *Life in the Hawaiian Islands; or, The Heart of the Pacific as It Was and Is.* New York: A. S. Barnes & Co., 1851.

Clifford, James. "Indigenous Articulations." *Contemporary Pacific* 13, no. 2 (2001).

———. "Introduction." In *Writing Culture: The Poetics and Politics of Ethnography,* edited by James Clifford and George Marcus. Berkeley: University of California Press, 1986, 1–26.

Clifford, James, and George Marcus, eds. *Writing Culture: The Poetics and Politics of Ethnography.* Berkeley and Los Angeles: University of California Press, 1986.

Coffman, Tom. *History Sunday: Conquest of Hawaiʻi.* History Channel video, 2003.

———. *Island Edge of America: A Political History of Hawaiʻi.* Honolulu: University of Hawaiʻi Press, 2003.

———. *Nation Within: The Story of America's Annexation of the Nation of Hawaiʻi.* Kaneohe, Hawaiʻi: Tom Coffman/EPICenter press, 1998.

Coleman, Stuart Holmes. *Eddie Would Go: The Story of Eddie Aikau, Hawaiian Hero and Pioneer of Big Wave Surfing.* New York: St. Martin's Griffin, 2004.

Cook, James, and James King. *A Voyage to the Pacific Ocean.* London: Printed by W. and A. Strahan for G. Nicol and T. Cadell, 1784.

Cottrell, William A. "Knute." Interview with William C. Kea Sr. "Eight Old-Time Members." Oral history interview project of the Historical Committee of the Outrigger Canoe Club, July 8, 1968, OH-001.

D'Arcy, Paul. *The People of the Sea: Environment, Identity, and History in Oceania.* Honolulu: University of Hawai'i Press, 2006.

Daws, Gavan. *Shoal of Time: A History of the Hawaiian Islands.* Honolulu: University of Hawai'i Press, 1974.

Deloria, Vine Jr. *Custer Died for Your Sins: An Indian Manifesto.* Norman: Oklahoma University Press, 1988.

Dening, Greg. *History's Anthropology: The Death of William Gooch.* Melbourne, Aus.: University of Melbourne Press, 1995.

———. *Islands and Beaches Discourse on a Silent Land: Marquesas, 1774–1880.* Melbourne, Aus.: Melbourne University Press, 1980.

———. *Mr Bligh's Bad Language: Passion, Power and Theatre on the Bounty.* New York: Cambridge University Press, 1992.

———. *Performances.* Chicago: University of Chicago Press, 1996.

Denoon, Donald, ed. *The Cambridge History of the Pacific Islanders.* New York: Cambridge University Press, 1997.

Desmond, Jane. *Staging Tourism: Bodies on Display from Waikīkī to Sea World.* Chicago: University of Chicago Press, 1999.

Diaz, Vicente. "Fight Boys, Til the Last . . . Island-style Football and the Remasculinization of Indigeneity in the Militarized American Pacific Islands." In *Pacific Diaspora: Island Peoples in the United States and Across the Pacific,* edited by Paul Spickard, Joanne Rondilla, and Debbie Hippolite Wright. Honolulu: University of Hawai'i Press, 2002, 169–194.

———. *Sacred Vessels: Navigating Tradition and Identity in Micronesia.* Video documentary. Guam: Moving Islands Production, 1997.

Dougherty, Michael. *To Steal a Kingdom: Probing Hawaiian History.* Waimanalo, Hawai'i: Island Style, 1992.

Edward Said: On Orientalism. Video recording directed by Sut Jhally. Massachusetts: MEF, 1998.

Eskildsen, Robert. "Of Civilization and Savages: The Mimetic Imperialism of Japan's 1874 Expedition to Taiwan." *The American Historical Review* 107, no. 2 (2002): 388–418.

Farnon, Frantz. "The Negro and Psychopathology." In *Black Skin, White Masks,* edited by Charles Markmann. New York: Grove Press, 1967, 141–209.

Ferguson, Kathy E., and Phyllis Turnbull. *Oh, Say, Can You See? The Semiotics of the Military in Hawai'i.* Minneapolis: University of Minnesota Press, 1998.

Finney, Ben R. *Hokule'a: The Way to Tahiti.* New York: Dodd, Mead and Company, 1979.

———. *Surfing: The Sport of Hawaiian Kings.* Boston: Charles E. Tuttle Co., 1966.

Ford, Alexander Hume. "Out-Door Allurements." In *Hawaiian Almanac and Annual for 1911.* Honolulu: Thos. G. Thrum Compiler and Publisher, 1910, 143–149.

————. "Riding the Surf in Hawaii." *Collier's Outdoor America* 43, no. 21 (August 14, 1909): 17.

Fornander, Abraham. *Fornander Collection of Hawaiian Antiquities and Folklore,* vol. 6. Honolulu: 'Ai Pokaku Press, 1999. [Originally published as *Memoirs of the Bernice Pauahi Bishop Museum of Polynesian Ethnology and Natural History,* vol. VI. Honolulu: Bishop Museum Press, 1919.]

————. *Selections from Fornander's Hawaiian Antiquities and Lore.* Honolulu: University of Hawai'i Press, 1959.

Foucault, Michel. *The Archaeology of Knowledge.* New York: Routledge, 1969.

————. *Discipline and Punish: The Birth of the Prison.* New York: Vintage, 1995.

Fusco, Coco. *English Is Broken Here: Notes on Cultural Fusion in the Americas.* New York: The New Press, 1995.

Gegeo, David W. "Cultural Rupture and Indigeneity: The Challenge of (Re)visioning 'Place' in the Pacific." *Contemporary Pacific* 13, no. 2 (2001).

Green, Karina Kahananui. "Colonialism's Daughters: Eighteenth- and Nineteenth-Century Western Perceptions of Hawaiian Women." In *Pacific Diaspora: Island Peoples in the United States and Across the Pacific,* edited by Paul Spickard, Joanne Rondilla, and Debbie Hippolite Wright. Honolulu: University of Hawai'i Press, 2002, 221–251.

Grimshaw, Patricia. "New England Missionary Wives, Hawaiian Women and 'the Cult of True Womanhood.'" In *Family and Gender in the Pacific,* edited by Margaret Jolly and Martha Macintyre. Cambridge: Cambridge University Press, 1989, 19–44.

————. *Paths of Duty: American Missionary Wives in Nineteenth-Century Hawai'i.* Honolulu: University of Hawai'i Press, 1989.

Hale'ole, H. N. *Ka Mo'olelo o Laieikawai.* Washington, D.C.: Smithsonian Institution, 1919.

————. *Lā'ieikawai.* Honolulu: Kalamakū Press, 2006.

Hall, Sandra. *Duke: A Great Hawaiian.* Honolulu: Bess Press, 2004.

Hall, Stuart. *Representation: Cultural Representation and Signifying Practices.* London: The Open University Press, 1997.

Harmon, Alexandra. *Indians in the Making: Ethnic Relations and Indian Identities around the Puget Sound.* Berkeley: University of California Press, 1998.

Hartwell, Jay. "Ho'omana." In *Pacific Diaspora: Island Peoples in the United States and Across the Pacific,* edited by Paul Spickard, Joanne Rondilla, and Debbie Hippolite Wright. Honolulu: University of Hawai'i Press, 2002, 322–330.

Hau'ofa, Epeli. "Our Sea of Islands." In *A New Oceania Rediscovering Our Sea of Islands,* edited by Epeli Hau'ofa. Suva, Fiji: University of the South Pacific Press, 1993, 2–16.

Hawai'i's Last Queen. American Experience PBS Video Series, 1997.

Heckathorn, John. "Interview with David Stannard." *Honolulu Magazine,* 1989. http://www2.hawaii.edu/~johnb/micro/m130/readings/stannard.html.

Hemmings, Fred. "Professionalism Is White." *Surfer* 10, no. 5: 64–65.

————. *The Soul of Surfing.* New York: Thunder's Mouth Press, 1999.

Hereniko, Vilsoni, and Rob Wilson, eds. *Inside Out: Literature, Cultural Politics, and Identity in the New Pacific.* Lanham, Md.: Rowman & Littlefield, 2003.

Higgins, Matt. "Rough Waves, Tougher Beaches." *New York Times,* Sports section, January 23, 2009. Available online at http://www.nytimes.com/2009/01/23/sports/othersports/23surfing.html.

His Majesty O'Keefe. Film directed by Byron Haskin. Warner Brothers Studios, 1954. Videocassette.

Hobsbawm, Eric, and Terence Ranger, eds. *The Invention of Tradition.* Cambridge: Cambridge University Press, 1983.

Hokowhitu, Brendan. "Tackling Maori Masculinity: A Colonial Genealogy of Savagery and Sport." *The Contemporary Pacific* 16, no. 2 (2004): 259–284.

Holt, Lemon "Rusty" Wond Sr. Oral history interview with Michi Kodama-Nishimoto, April 1, 1985. In *Waikīkī, 1900–1985: Oral Histories Vol. II,* Oral History Project, Social Science Research Institute, University of Hawai'i at Mānoa, June 1985.

Howell, David. "Ainu Ethnicity and the Boundaries of the Early Modern Japanese State." *Past and Present* 142 (1994).

JanMohamed, Abdul R. "The Economy of Manichean Allegory: The Function of Racial Difference in Colonialist Literature." In *"Race," Writing, and Difference,* edited by Henry Louis Gates. Chicago: University of Chicago Press, 1985.

Jarratt, Phil. "Jaw War on the North Shore." *Surfer* 17, no. 6 (1977): 46–48.

Johnson, Susan Lee. *Roaring Camp: The Social World of the California Gold Rush.* New York: Norton, 2000.

Jolly, Margaret. "From Point Venus to Bali Ha'i: Eroticism and Exoticism in Representations of the Pacific." In *Sites of Desire, Economies of Pleasure: Sexualities in Asia and the Pacific,* edited by Lenore Manderson and Margaret Jolly. Chicago and London: University of Chicago Press, 1997, 99–122.

Kahanamoku, Louis. Oral history interview with Warren Nishimoto, May 20, 1985, Keauhou, Kona, Hawai'i. In *Waikīkī, 1900–1985: Oral Histories Vol. II,* Oral History Project, Social Science Research Institute, University of Hawai'i at Mānoa, June 1985.

Kaho'olawe Aloha 'Āina. Video recording directed by Nā Maka o ka 'Āina, 1992.

Ka'ili, Tevita. "Tauhi vā: Nurturing Tongan Sociospacial Ties in Maui and Beyond." *Contemporary Pacific* 17, no. 1 (2005): 83–114.

Kaio, Kealoha Jr. Videotaped interview with author, La'ie, Hawai'i, July 5, 2002.

Kaio, Kealoha Sr. Videotaped interview with author, Lā'ie, Hawai'i, August 8, 2004.

Kalākaua, David. *The Legends and Myths of Hawaii: The Fables and Folk-Lore of a Strange People.* Rev. ed. Rutland, Vt.: Charles E. Tuttle, 1992. [First edition published in 1888.]

Kamae, Lori. *The Empty Throne: A Biography of Hawaii's Prince Cupid.* Honolulu: Topgallant, 1980.

Kamakau, Samuel. *Na Mo'olelo a Ka Po'e Kahiko, Tales and Traditions of the People of Old.* Honolulu: Bishop Museum Press, 1991.

————. *Ruling Chiefs of Hawai'i*. Honolulu: Kamehameha Schools Press, 1992.

Kame'eleihiwa, Lilikalā. *Native Land and Foreign Desires: Pehea Lā E Pono Ai? How Shall We Live in Harmony?* Honolulu: Bishop Museum Press, 1992.

Kampion, Drew. "North Shore '70–'71." *Surfer* 12, no. 1 (1971): 40–44.

Kanahele, George S. *Hawaiian Renaissance*. Honolulu: Project Waiaha, 1982.

————. *Ku Kanaka, Stand Tall: A Search for Hawaiian Values*. Honolulu: University of Hawai'i Press, 1993.

————. *Waikīkī 100BC to 1900AD: An Untold Story*. Honolulu: University of Hawai'i Press, 1996.

Kauanui, J. Kēhaulani. "Precarious Positions: Native Hawaiian and US Federal Recognition." *The Contemporary Pacific* 17, no. 1 (2005): 3–4.

Kekai, Rabbit. Conversation with Randy Rarick. Sunset Beach, Hawai'i, December 1, 2009. Video available on line, http://www.triplecrown.com.

Kelly, John. "John Kelly." In *Autobiography of Protest in Hawai'i*, edited by Robert Mast and Ann Mast. Honolulu: University of Hawai'i Press, 1997, 75–90.

————. "Save Our Surf." *Turning the Tide: Journal of Anti-Racist Activism, Research and Education* 7, nos. 3 and 4 (Summer 1994). http://www.hawaii-nation.org/turningthetide-7-1.html.

Kevin [last name not given]. Videotaped interview with author, Honolulu, September 2, 2003.

Kimo [last name not given]. Videotaped interview with author, Honolulu, September 2, 2003.

King, James. *A Voyage to the Pacific Ocean, Volume III, 1779–1780*. London: W. and A. Strahan for G. Nicol and T. Cadell, 1784.

Kipling, Rudyard. "The White Man's Burden: The United States & the Philippine Islands, 1899." *Rudyard Kipling's Verse: Definitive Edition*. Garden City, N.Y.: Doubleday, 1929.

Krishnaswamy, Revathi. *Effeminism: The Economy of Colonial Desire*. Ann Arbor: University of Michigan Press, 1998.

Kuykendall, Ralph. *Hawaiian Kingdom, Vol. I, 1778–1854*. Honolulu: University of Hawai'i Press, 1957.

————. *Hawaiian Kingdom, Vol. II, 1854–1874: Twenty Critical Years*. Honolulu: University of Hawai'i Press, 1966.

————. *Hawaiian Kingdom, Vol. III, 1874–1893: The Kalakaua Dynasty*. Honolulu: University of Hawai'i Press, 1968.

Langman, Larry. *Return to Paradise: A Guide to South Sea Island Films*. Lanham, Md.: Scarecrow Press, 1998.

Limerick, Patricia. *The Legacy of Conquest: The Unbroken Past of the American West*. New York: Norton, 1988.

London, Jack. *The Cruise of the* Snark. New York: Macmillan Co., 1911.

Loomba, Ania. *Colonialism/Postcolonialism: The New Critical Idiom*. New York: Routledge, 1998.

Love, Alan "Turkey." Oral history interview with J. Ward Russell. Oral history interview project of the Historical Committee of the Outrigger Canoe Club, July 18, 1986, OH-028.

———. Oral history interview with 'Iwalani Hodges, May 14, 1986. In *Waikīkī, 1900–1985: Oral Histories Vol. IV,* Oral History Project, Social Science Research Institute, University of Hawai'i at Mānoa, spring 1988.

"The Magic of a Hawaiian Summer." *Surfer* 19, no. 6 (October 1978): 30.

Malo, David. *Hawaiian Antiquities Moolelo Hawaii.* Bernice Pauahi Bishop Museum, Honolulu, Special publication; 2. Translated by Nathaniel B. Emerson. Honolulu: Bishop Museum, 1951.

Marcus, Ben. *From Polynesia with Love: The History of Surfing from Captain Cook to the Present.* http://www.surfingforlife.com/history2.html.

Markmann, Charles, ed. *Black Skin, White Masks.* New York: Grove Press, 1967.

Mauro, Chris. "In the Hot Seat with Kalā Alexander." October 4, 2002. http://www .surfermag.com/magazine/archivedissues/kala/index.html.

Mcgregor, Davianna. *Na Kua 'Aina: Living Hawaiian Culture.* Honolulu: University of Hawai'i Press, 2007.

———. "Recognizing Native Hawaiians: A Quest for Sovereignty." In *Pacific Diaspora: Island Peoples in the United States and Across the Pacific,* edited by Paul Spickard, Joanne Rondilla, and Debbie Hippolite Wright. Honolulu: University of Hawai'i Press, 2002, 331–354.

Medeiros, Jared. "Duke Invitational." Senior paper, History 490, Department of History, BYU–Hawaii, fall 2009.

Merry, Sally Engle. *Colonizing Hawai'i: The Cultural Power of Law.* Princeton, N.J.: Princeton University Press, 2000.

Mullahey, William Justin. Oral history interview with Kenneth J. Pratt, May 6, 1980, Honolulu. Oral history project of the Outrigger Canoe Club Historical Committee, OH-008.

Nandy, Ashis. *The Intimate Enemy: Loss and Recovery of Self under Colonialism.* New York: Oxford University Press, 1983.

Noll, Greg. Conversation with author. Waikīkī, March 2006.

Nordyke, Eleanor C. *Pacific Images: Views from Captain Cook's Third Voyage.* Honolulu: Hawaiian Historical Society, 1999.

North Shore. Film directed by William Phelps. Universal Studios. Videocassette.

"North Shore Contest Debate Continues." *Surfer* 19, no. 3 (1978): 90.

Obeyesekere, Gananath. *The Apotheosis of Captain Cook: European Mythmaking in the Pacific.* Princeton, N.J.: Princeton University Press, 1992.

———. "'British Cannibals,' Contemplation of an Event in the Death and Resurrection of James Cook, Explorer." *Critical Inquiry* 18 (1992): 630–654.

O'Leary, Kevin. "The Future of Kamilo Nui." *Honolulu Weekly,* November 13, 2005. http://honoluluweekly.com/cover/2005/11/the-future-of-kamilo-nui/

Olsen, Erik, and Matt Higgins. "Surfing's Darker Side on the North Shore." Video, *New York Times,* Sports section, January 23, 2009. Available on line at http://

video.nytimes.com/video/2009/01/22/sports/othersports/1231545957469/
surfing-s-dark-side-on-the-north-shore.html.

Osorio, Jonathan Kay Kamakawiwoʻole. *Dismembering Lahui: A History of the Hawaiian Nation to 1887.* Honolulu: University of Hawaiʻi Press, 2002.

Paoa, Fred. Oral history interview with Warren Nishimoto, March 15, 1985, Foster Village, Oʻahu. In *Waikīkī, 1900–1985: Oral Histories Vol. II,* Oral History Project, Social Science Research Institute, University of Hawaiʻi at Mānoa, June 1985.

Pascoe, Peggy. "Race, Gender, and the Privileges of Property." In *Over the Edge: Remapping the American West,* edited by Valerie J. Matsumoto and Blake Allmendinger. Berkeley: University of California Press, 1999.

Perkins, ʻUmi. "Teaching Land and Sovereignty—A Revised View." *Hawaiian Journal of Law and Politics* 2 (Summer 2006): 97–111.

Primo [last name not given]. Videotaped interview with author, Honolulu, September 5, 2003.

Pukui, Mary Kawena. "Songs (mele) of Old Kaʻū, Hawaiʻi." *Journal of American Folklore* 62, no. 245 (July–September 1949): 257–258.

Riding Giants. Film directed by Stacy Peralta. Sony Pictures Classic, 2004.

Rothman, Eddie. Videotaped interview with author, Honolulu, September 2, 2002.

Rothman, Makua. Videotaped interview with author, Honolulu, September 2, 2002.

Sai, Keanu. "The American Occupation of the Hawaiian Kingdom: Beginning the Transition from Occupied to Restored State." PhD dissertation, University of Hawaiʻi at Mānoa, 2008.

Said, Edward. *Orientalism.* New York: Vintage, 1978.

Shoat, Ella, and Robert Stam. *Unthinking Eurocentrism: Multiculturalism and the Media.* London: Rutledge, 1994.

Silva, Noenoe. *Aloha Betrayed: Native Hawaiian Resistance to American Colonialism.* Durham, N.C.: Duke University Press, 2004.

Sinha, Mirinalini. *Colonial Masculinity: The "Manly Englishman" and the "Effeminate Bengali."* Manchester, U.K.: Manchester University Press, 1995.

Smith, Bernard. *Imagining the Pacific in the Wake of the Cook Voyages.* New Haven, Conn., and London: Yale University Press, 1992.

Soren, Henry. Videotaped interview with author, Lāʻie, Hawaiʻi, July 25, 2003.

Soren, Imbert. Conversation with author, Lāʻie, Hawaiʻi, May 1997.

Stannard, David. *Before the Horror: The Population of Hawaiʻi on the Eve of Western Contact.* Honolulu: University of Hawaiʻi Press, 1989.

———. *Honor Killing: Race, Rape, and Clarence Darrow's Spectacular Last Case.* New York: Penguin, 2005.

Stant, Daryl. Videotaped interview with author, Honolulu, September 2, 2002.

Stauffer, Robert H. *Kahana: How the Land Was Lost.* Honolulu: University of Hawaiʻi Press, 2004.

Steiner, Judge. Interview with William C. Kea Sr. "Eight Old-Time Members." Oral history interview project of the Historical Committee of the Outrigger Canoe Club, July 8, 1968, OH-001.

Stickney, Joe. Interview with William C. Kea Sr. "Eight Old-Time Members." Oral history interview project of the Historical Committee of the Outrigger Canoe Club, July 8, 1968, OH-001.

Stone, Tom Pohaku. Videotaped interview with author, Waimea Valley, Hawai'i, July 5, 2004.

"The Surf Tax." Editorial. *Surfer* 7, no. 4 (1966): 22.

Takaki, Ronald. *Pau Hana: Plantation Life and Labor in Hawai'i, 1835–1920.* Honolulu: University of Hawai'i Press, 1983.

Teaiwa, Teresia. "bikinis and other s/pacific n/oceans." *The Contemporary Pacific* 6, no. 1 (1994): 87–109.

Tengan, Ty Kawika. "(En)gendering Colonialism: Masculinities in Hawai'i and Aotearoa." *Cultural Values* 6, no. 3 (2002): 229–238.

———. "Hale Mua: (En)gendering Hawaiian Men." PhD dissertation, University of Hawai'i at Mānoa, 2003.

———. *Native Men Remade: Gender and Nation in Contemporary Hawai'i.* Durham, N.C., and London: Duke University Press, 2008.

Thompson, Norm. Conversation with author, Lā'ie, Hawai'i, May 1997.

Thrum, Thomas G. *More Hawaiian Folktales: A Collection of Native Legends and Traditions.* Chicago: A. C. McClurg and Co., 1923, 111.

Timmons, Grady. *Waikīkī Beach Boy.* Honolulu: Editions Limited, 1989.

Trask, Haunani-Kay. *From a Native Daughter: Colonialism and Sovereignty in Hawai'i.* Monroe, Maine: Common Courage Press, 1993.

Tuhiwai-Smith, Linda. *Decolonizing Methodologies: Research and Indigenous Peoples.* London: Zed Books, 1999.

Twain, Mark. *Mark Twain's Letters from Hawaii.* Honolulu: University of Hawai'i Press, 1975.

———. *Roughing It.* New York: Penguin Classics, 1981. [First printed in 1872.]

Udall, Stuart, and John Sandsbury. "Hawaii SOS Stirs Ecology Wave." *Our Environment,* September 15, 1971. http://www.ilhawaii.net/~msquared/Udall.html.

Wake of the Red Witch. Film directed by Edward Ludwig. Republic Studios, 1948. Videocassette.

Walker, Isaiah. "Hui Nalu, Beachboys, and the Surfing Boarder-lands of Hawai'i." *Contemporary Pacific* 20, no. 1 (2008): 89–113.

———. "Terrorism or Native Protest? The Hui O He'e Nalu and Hawaiian Resistance to Colonialism." *Pacific Historical Review* 74, no. 4 (2005): 575–601.

Walker, Matt. "Clearing the Airwaves: Liam McNamara Defends his Performance on the Boarding House." *Surfing* online interview. http://surfingthemag.com/news/surfing-pulse/070803_liam/.

White, Geoffrey, and Lamont Lindstrom, eds. *The Pacific Theatre: Island Representations of World War II.* Pacific Island Monograph Series no 8. Honolulu: University of Hawai'i Press, Center for Pacific Island Studies, 1989.

Wichman, Frederick G. "Ka He'e Nalu 'ana ma Wai-lua." In *Pele Mā: Legends of Pele from Kaua'i.* Honolulu: Bamboo Ridge Press, 2001, 70–75.

Wilson, Rob. *Re-imagining the American Pacific: From South Pacific to Bamboo Ridge and Beyond.* Durham, N.C.: Duke University Press, 2000.

Wisniewski, Richard. *The Rise and Fall of the Hawaiian Kingdom.* Honolulu: Pacific Printers, 1979.

Witzig, John. "Paths of Glory: Hawai'i Winter 76–77." *Surfer* 18, no. 1 (1977): 36–67.

Wood, Houston. *Displacing Natives: The Rhetorical Production of Hawai'i.* Lanham, Md.: Rowman & Littlefield Publishers, Inc., 1999.

Wright, Kenny. Videotaped interview with author, La'ie, Hawai'i, July 26, 2004.

Index

Abellira, Reno, 130, 135–136, 145
activism: ethnic movements, 8;
     Hawaiian, 2–3, 8, 105–115, 125,
     127, 162, 169, 194n. 38; political,
     2, 105–106, 125, 152, 169. *See
     also* Hawaiian renaissance
agency, 3, 12, 24, 42
Ah Quin, Seth "Moot," 138, 145–147,
     152
Ahue, Terry: on Bronzed Aussies, 131;
     and Hawaiian Water Patrol, 148;
     on Hui origins, 137; on IPS, 141;
     as president of the Hui, 150–151
'aikapu, 44, 180n. 4, 181n. 5
Aikau, Clyde, 35, 38, 115, 117
Aikau, Eddie, 3, 8–9, 34–36, 115,
     176n. 3; and Duke Invitational,
     35–36; and Hui O He'e Nalu,
     117, 122, 126, 150; and John
     Kelly, 115; as lifeguard, 116; and
     Rabbit Bartholomew, 135–137;
     surfing with Kealoha Kaio, 34–35
Aikau, Myra, 117, 150
Aikau, "Pops," 115, 117, 141
'Āinahau, 30, 58–59, 62
Aipa, Ben, 35–36, 176n. 3
'Aiwohikupua, 22
Akana, Joe, 71–76, 187n. 81
ali'i, 43–44, 49, 101, 178n. 23, 190n.
     16; colors of, 146; and politics, 49,
     58; in the surf, 5, 16, 58, 67, 146,
     177n. 18, 184n. 4
aloha: ambassadors, 39;
     misappropriated, 90; ran out, 9,
     134
Aluli, Emmet, 123–124
American Board of Commissioners
     for Foreign Missions (ABCFM),
     44–45, 88. *See also* missionaries
American heroes: in Hollywood films,
     92–95, 104

Amona, Bryan: and *Bustin' Down the
     Door,* 37; on community service,
     150, 175n. 29; on Hui image,
     155–156, 166; on Hui origins,
     117, 136, 139, 142, 146; on
     racism, 131–134; on resistance, 9,
     134, 146–147
Anahu, Hiram, 72, 74
Andrus, Chuck Waipā: and drug-free
     surfers, 199n. 16; North Shore in
     1970s and 1980s, 129, 138, 140;
     on surfing as Hawaiian tradition,
     144
annexation of Hawai'i: history, 49–56,
     68–69; protests against, 12, 54–55,
     114, 152, 191n. 64; supporters
     in Outrigger Canoe Club, 59–61,
     65–66, 80, 82, 185n. 20; and
     surfing, 10, 57–59, 64, 65–67,
     168–169
Apology Resolution, 55–56
Au, Erwin, 162
Australian surfers, 14–15, 32–33,
     142, 194n. 3, 195n. 15; Bronzed
     Aussies, 130–137, 154; myths and
     tensions, 37, 117

Barth, Fredrik, 165
Barthes, Roland, 89
Bartholomew, Wayne "Rabbit," 11,
     130–135, 143
Bayonet Constitution, 48, 51–53, 68,
     186n. 52
beach: as boundary, 11; culture, 40–41
Bertlemann, Larry, 37–38, 130,
     177n. 3
Bingham, Hiram, 27, 44–45, 189n. 15
birds of Hawai'i, 20–22
black shorts, 63, 136, 142, 149, 154,
     156, 198n. 90
Blake, Tom, 14, 66

disease, 5, 26, 43, 49, 88, 170, 181n. 5
Doerner, Derrick, 137
Dole, Sanford B., 61, 115
Duke Invitational (Duke Classic), 35–38, 40, 116, 128–129

808, The (TV series), 157–158
emasculation, 99, 166. *See also* stereotypes of Hawaiian men
Emma, Queen, 49, 60–61
empowerment: cultural renaissance, 120, 153; defying colonialism, 3, 58, 78–79; through literacy, 181n. 6; and women, 4, 24, 25, 188n. 86
encounters: sexual, 75, 86; in the surf, 16–17, 144, 158; with the West, 3, 26, 42–44, 86
environmentalism, 2, 105, 109, 124–126, 193n. 13. *See also* Kelly, John; Save Our Surf
Espere, Tiger, 35
exclusive waves, 2, 32, 57, 137–138, 146
expertise in waves, 4, 7, 14, 121
exploitation: of Hawaiian waves, 1, 127, 147; of native resources, 44

Fanon, Frantz, 95
Fasi, Frank, 110
feminization of Hawai'i: effects on men, 166; as prostitute, 90; by tourist industry, 3, 83, 104
Finney, Ben R., 7, 66, 117–122, 179n. 48, 186n. 42, 193n. 35
fistfights: and American heroes in films, 95; on *Boarding House,* 157; explained, 158; on *Fuel TV's The 808,* 157–158; on *Hōkūle'a,* 119–120; in *North Shore,* 156; on North Shore, 2, 142, 194n. 2, 197n. 76; Rabbit punched, 134; in Waikīkī, 67, 76–77, 188n. 81
forbidden waves, 2. *See also* exclusive waves

Ford, Alexander Hume: established Outrigger Canoe Club, 32, 57, 59–61, 184n. 9; revived surfing myth, 14, 15, 31–32; and surf competitions, 65–66, 185n. 25
Fornander, Abraham, 173n. 1
Fort DeRussy, Waikīkī, 76, 187n. 78, 188n. 81
Fortescue, Grace, 79–80. *See also* Massie affair
Foster, Mary, 48
Freeth, George: and debunking myth of extinction, 15, 60, 179n. 49; popularizing surfing, 6, 31, 59, 175n. 21

Garcia, Sunny, 38, 157
gender: categories, 3, 6, 39, 85–87, 98; expectations, 10–12, 64; roles, 25–26; stereotypes, 6, 10–11, 24–25, 39, 83–85
genealogy, 19, 43, 177n. 18
Gibson, Walter Murray, 45, 101–102, 181n. 10
Gidget, 14–15, 40
Gold Rush, 10, 49
Green, Karina Kahananui, 26, 86, 97

Hā'ena, 21
Hālau Nalu, vii, 171
Hale Mua, 98; and masculine identities, 99, 125
Hall, Stuart, 93
haole: definition of, 173n. 3
Hau'ofa, Epeli, 11–12, 176n. 37
Hawaiian Homes Commission Act, 58, 69
Hawaiian kingdom, 50, 52, 100–102; haole influence on, 29, 45, 100–102; and land, 46–49; overthrow of (*see* overthrow of Hawaiian kingdom); restoration attempts, 52, 55, 58, 68

About the Author

Isaiah Helekunihi Walker is an assistant professor of history at Brigham Young University–Hawai'i on the North Shore of O'ahu. He earned his PhD from the University of California at Santa Barbara. He has previously published academic articles on surfing and Hawaiian history in the *Contemporary Pacific* and *Pacific Historical Review*. Born and raised in the Hawaiian ocean-based community of Keaukaha on the island of Hawai'i, Professor Walker has been an avid surfer since his keiki (childhood) days.

Production Notes for Walker | *Waves of Resistance*

Cover design by Julie Matsuo-Chun

Text design and composition by Jansom
    with display type in Cracked
    and text type in Adobe Garamond Pro

Printing and binding by Sheridan Books, Inc.

Printed on 60 lb. House White, 444 ppi